Partheneia Sacra

PARTHENEIA SACRA

By

H.A.

·
·M·
·D·C·
·X·X·X·
·I·I·I·

INTRODUCTION BY
IAIN FLETCHER

MCML
THE HAND AND FLOWER PRESS
ALDINGTON KENT

MADE AND RE-PRINTED IN ENGLAND
FOR THE FIRST TIME BY
THE HAND AND FLOWER PRESS
AT THE DITCHLING PRESS LTD
A 1950 D

INTRODUCTION

AFTER the Council of Trent a greater certitude prevailed in the Catholic world. Catholicism entered a new phase. It was a phase which revealed some of the attributes of early Protestantism. Characteristically the Protestant Reformers had insisted on those elements in religion favourable to their own bias of temperament. For them exuberance was not all, or indeed anything to the point. When the Catholics, therefore, experienced a period of reform, they selected for peculiar celebration whatever had become distinctively their own by reason of its rejection by their opponents.

This Tridentine world possessed a vivacity of spirit which the *post-lude* to the Peace of Augsburg—for example's sake—altogether failed to capture. Exuberance would break in. El Greco flanks Murillo on the Art Gallery wall. But the exuberance was universal. It was also an exuberance of suffering. The religious faces, traditionally associated with the manifold art of that time, have no calm hour to them; no rational self-love directs those acts of piety and anguish. There was a world whose climate reveals a radical fertility of the spirit, yet with a tinge of rigour behind the radiance; something out of Spain to show what lay behind the representation of the *Kartharsis* of the Martyrs; the stigmata of the Mystics; those 'rosiall buds of martyrdom' the Holy Innocents; the infant Christ; and the ardent assumption of God's ever-virgin Mother.

Prime movers in the Catholic Reformation were the Jesuits. It was a Jesuit, Lainez, with his fervours, who swayed the Council of Trent itself. It was the Jesuits who provided for the Church educators at home and matryrs abroad. It was the Jesuits who canalised the many cultural processes of the time and directed them remorselessly towards the greater glory of God. Nothing could more exactly symbolise the double aspect of this time than their books. In those volumes of devotion and exhortation, together with the schematised oratory, appear the figures of the many martyrs, to whose number most of the known countries of that time were adding their intemporate quota. Embalmed by a holy science—*Iconomystics*—their bodies are fixed in urgent and horrifying positions, straining upwards with bitterly triumphant faces, with tortured and triumphant limbs. Humanism was not enough. Behind all the graces of the person is an iron piety.

The *Exercitia Spiritualia* of Ignatius had established a definite devotional pattern: that of applying the senses to the final mysteries of faith. Touch, taste, sight and smell were solicited to engage with abstractions such as The Four Last Things; varying states of soul; the rewards of the life lived in piety. To point the pains of Hell more vehemently the devotee was asked to let his touch riot in the sensation of burning, to linger over the minutiae of eternal torment. The way was clear to the adoption of the Emblem and *tableaux vivants*. Such could externalise what the senses might only evoke with brevity and uncertainty. Nor were Emblems designed purely for use outside the Society. Novices were trained by this means. Doctor Mario Praz has powerfully summed up the effects of education through Emblems: 'Rather than mortifying the senses in order to concentrate all energies in an ineffable tension of the spirit, according to the purgative way of the mystics, the Jesuits wanted every sense to be keyed up to the pitch of its capacity, so as to conspire together to create a psychological state pliant to the command of God.

The fixity of the emblematic picture was infinitely suggestive; the beholder little by little let his imagination be eaten into as a plate is by acid. The picture eventually became animated by an intense, hallucinatory life, independent of the page. The eyes were not alone in perceiving it; the depicted objects were invested with body, scent and sound: the beholder was no longer before them, but in their midst. He was no longer impressed only, but obsessed.'

For the Jesuits, the Emblem was an extremely useful medium for propaganda. As in China they assumed the gown of mathematics, and to other countries sent missionaries apt in those sciences which were most relished, so with extreme agility of technique they adapted their Devotional Books and Emblems to the temperament and experience of the intended reader. The Emblem united what was pleasing to the senses with what was profitable to the soul. The lavish Humanist culture of the Society could metaphrase neo-Classical Emblems of the Renascence into decorous Catholic ones. Pagan rhetoric is displaced by Christian. The victim of Love's soft wound appears as the way-lorn maiden, *Anima*. The infant Cupid lays aside his bow and wings to become the infant Christ, and Venus the Goddess becomes Mary the Virgin *benedicta in mulieribus*. But this new figure—Help of the Helpless; Mother of the Fatherless—is fertile, yet unerotic; human as the Mother of Jesus and heavenly as the Queen of Heaven.

The Catholic minority in England at the close of the 16th century was much larger than it has been customary to estimate. It consisted, however, of many who were 'passive' Catholics. While loyal at heart to the older Faith such Catholics were not prepared to proclaim their fidelity. To proclaim it would have involved not only the stigma of belief in a corrupt form of religion, but also the ambiguities of being viewed as a potential traitor to the State. After the Elizabethan Settlement the severest discrimination was exercised against priests in particular. The intention was to starve Catholics of the Sacraments and to deny them any form of devotional life.

The Catholic reaction comprehended two forms of resistance. Firstly, the establishing on the continent of a number of Colleges and Seminaries where Priests could be trained for missionary activity. Douai (with S. Omer the most notable of these) was founded in 1568. Secondly, the dissemination of English Devotional Books, printed at one or other of the Colleges. From the Anglican viewpoint the devotional book was not a weapon in the theological war. The imprecision of Anglican dogma was largely responsible. To the many 'passive' Catholics the Church of England on its devotional side must have appeared crepuscular indeed. But if the Protestant devotional book could have small effect on Non-Protestants, the converse was untrue.

In Gee's *Foote out of the Snare* (1624) occurs a list of books openly sold in London, whose very titles—floridly sacreligious—must have cast many a Puritan into an ecstasy of protest. *Jesus Psalter; Angelicall Exercises to stirre up ye love of the blessed Virgin; Jesus, Maria, Joseph*, lately come out of the Presse, printed by Simons, a *Carmelite*, now in London; *The Mysterie of the Rosary; The Virginall Vow*. Even *Molina of Mental Prayer* had the smell of the beast all over it.

Literature in this kind was smuggled through continuously and, although a sporadically severe watch was kept, much of it must have been distributed among active Catholics. Those which were seized by the authorities were used as ammunition by Anti-Roman controversialists. A letter of William Crashaw, dated February 26 1610, beseeches the Earl of Salisbury, Lord High Treasurer, to send him one of each kind of 'popishe books newly taken and now in his Lordships disposition'. Another aspect of the matter appears in the correspondence of Isaac Basire, the Caroline Divine, who, writing to the lady to whom he was engaged, sends a present of two Catholic Manuals of Devotion: 'two books which next to God's owne my soule hath been much taken with.

The first was made by a French Bishop, yet is the booke free from Popery, (for I have read is aforehand for your soule's saecke): only where you see a cross at the margent, there it may be mistaken by some: else, all is safe'.[1] In the British Museum copy of *The Angel Guardian's Clock* of Hieronimus Drexelius (Rouen) 1621 those portions of the book exhibiting grossities of dogma are excised by a thin and monitory pen.

In Lewis Owen's *The Running Register....* (1626) there is a moody glimpse of Jesuit publishing affairs on the Continent. 'In the English Colledge of *St Omer*, the Jesuites haue a printing Presse, to print such Popish bookes and seditious, (yea, blasphemous) Pamphlets, as are written by any English Jesuite.' Owen continues by giving details of the presses themselves. 'Their Presse is worth vnto them more than foure hundred pounds yearely. For they themselves are the Authors, Correctors, Composers, and Pressmen; in so much that it doth cost them nothing but Paper and Inke, and these books they doe sell at an vnreasonable rate for they are not ashamed to sell a booke that contains not a quire of paper, for fiue or sixe shillings; and to that purpose they haue their Factors, and Brokers in *London*, and all parts of England, to disperse and sell these Books and Pamphlets.'

The Emblem lies in the tradition of ideographical writing. Its non-naturalistic bias has roots in the 'descriptive geometry' of Egyptian art. Among the Medievals a precursor can be noted in the heraldic use of 'canting arms', which allude to the name of the bearer either by a pun in the motto, or by representation if his name is also the name of an object.

The first recognisable Emblem Book—*Emblematum Liber* of Alciati —dates from 1531. In 1571 occurred the earliest application of the Emblem to Christian uses. The *Emblemes ov devises chrestiennes* of G. de Montenay embodies a hundred Emblems, including one which became widely patent: that of Christ's wounds as a fountain of waters.

The Emblem itself may be properly defined as an harmonious union of picture, motto and poem. The emblematic design itself is, in effect, allegorical, and the accompanying poem reciprocally interprets it. While the Device, its obverse form, is essentially dynamic, the Emblem is essentially static. In the Emblem all is given: the imagination does not operate.

---

1 *The Correspondence of Isaac Basire*, D.D. ed. W. N. Darnell. 1831. p. 21.

Emblem Books presented the Jesuits with curious technical equations which they succesfully solved. For those whose diversions were many, such as Princes and the young nobility, who delighted in being amazed by what was subtle and spectacular—*casuistique galante*—any form of symbolic representation must be visually seductive and ingenious: must be the apt exemplar of life lived on an heroic, indeed a grandiose plane. For the barely-educated the aim must be simplicity: to touch the heart of the mystery, to lay it bare. Here also, perhaps, there must be a certain forcible naturalism.

Some persons, however, worship mystery and relish intellectual caprice. For them another mode of the emblematic was already in existence. This was the *Impresa* or Device. While the purpose of the Emblem was to reveal, the purpose of the Device was to conceal: to conceal, at all events, the intricacies of emblematic art from the understanding of the vulgar. The Device sustains the mind as well as the eye. The Emblem is enriched with an inscription, the Device with a motto. It may be permissible for Device to function as Emblem and Emblem as Device by the transposition of motto and inscription.

Stringent conditions were established for the Device. It might not embody the human form; the accompanying motto might not be in the native tongue of its owner, although essentially its purpose was to define graphically the character and intention of that owner. Academically such distinctions might separate the Device from the Emblem, in practice they were rarely enforced.

The relation between poetry and the Emblem had been vivid from the beginning. In early Emblem books the verses were often derived from some classical, or prior source. An Emblem of this type was nothing more than the illustration of a given poem, although it might not be confined only to the factors of that poem. Nevertheless, in some sense, the Emblem is also an extension of the poetic conceit. Whereas the conceit in poetry may perhaps use abstraction towards a concrete end, the converse is readily true of the Emblem. The notorious compasses are opened by Donne to express, in the last analysis, a physical situation of human bodies. In Emblematic art the purpose is often to realise abstractions. Attempts are made to depict graphically as rareified an object as a state of soul. The tension between the palpable and the impalpable, the material and the spiritual, which is manifest in many religious Emblem Books arises largely from just such a visualisation of metaphors, mostly of a scriptural order. Moreover, the symbols

deployed by writers of Emblem poetry are not calculated to bear
emotional weight. The images which comprise the total symbol, taken
as they are from a prior source, can give nothing to the poem since they
already exist homogeneously and independently. They are inevitably
taken by the poet without any of their emotional connotations being
worked out.[2] A symbol becomes poetically valid only when it is
identified with what it represents. It is not valid to the same degree
when, as in much Emblem poetry, it is merely equated with the real
object.

The influence of the Counter-Reformation mystics on the imagery
of Emblem-Books is to be noted. Paradoxically enough in many
respects the incidental imagery of mysticism parallels that of the
Jesuits not only in its symbolic, but even in its physiological form. The
latter had a tradition of length and honour particularly in so far as
feminine mysticism was concerned. An example of the visualied
metaphor is S. Teresa's description of the Devils playing tennis with
her soul. Originally such visualised metaphors with their incongruous
hardness and crudeness did not appear exact to the sensibility; but after
being assimilated within the judgement by repetition, they invaded
poetry proper. To an age whose habit of mind was allegorical, an age
which saw, for example, the production of Filère's irenic poem
Hermaphroditus—in which the naiad and the youth representing the
warring Churches, embraced with such passion that they grew into a
single body—the invasion proved irresistible.

The prose-content of most Religious Emblem-Books was dense with
quotations and paraphrases from the Fathers and supported by the
elaborate rhetorical devices of pagan orators. The Alexandrian school
of exegesis had licensed the multiform interpretation of any given text.
There were four types of meaning to be found in any one text: the
Literal, the Allegorical, the Tropological, and the Anagogical: 'The
Allegoricall is the mystical signification of the Literall, The Tropolo-
gicall, the fruit of one and the other, the Anagogicall, the end of them
all.'[3]

Between the different Emblems which taken together form the
Emblem-Book there is generally a latent connection, which is often

2 This relationship of poem and Emblem is discussed in full by R. Freeman. *English
   Emblem Books*. 1948. Cap. II.
3 From *Holy Pictures of the mysticall Figures of the most Holy Sacrifice and Sacrament of the
   Eucharist* tr. into English by C.A. (1619). The original work is by Fr Richeome, s.j.

one of theme. The Emblems do not necessarily develop one from the other, nor are single Emblems axial.

Partheneia Sacra is attributed to Henry Hawkins. One of the seven sons of Sir Thomas Hawkins of Nash Court, Kent, the date of his birth is given variously as 1571, 1572 and 1575. In 1609 he was admitted to the English College at Rome, joined the Society of Jesus in 1615, and, with one intermission, laboured chiefly in the London district for twenty-five years. Two or three years before his death, which took place on August 18, 1646, he withdrew to the House of the English Tertian Fathers in Ghent.

Although the publication of Hawkins' other books is, with one exception, confined to the years 1630-36, it appears from internal considerations that they were in fact written earlier and not necessarily in the order of publication. In the preface to the *History of S. Elizabeth* mention is made of the translation from Fr Binet's *La Vie Admirable de la Princesse St Aldegonde*. This was not printed until 1636, four years later.

Within the last few years a new claimant to the authorship of *Partheneia Sacra* has been presented by Fr Gervase Mathew, O.S.B., and this claim has been repeated with a variant by Doctor Mario Praz. There is one inconsistent element in the Hawkins canon: the multiplicity of initials attaching to the books. If he were their author why should Hawkins pass three books into the world under the initials H.A.? Certainly some psuedonym was only reasonable for a priest working in an heretical country; but why should the other books adhere to the comparatively flaunting H.H.?

Fr Matthew's suggestion is Herbert Aston, the third son of Walter, first Lord Aston of Forfar.[4] Hawkins' claim is fairly robust. Alegambe in *Bibliotheca Scriptorum Societatis Iesv*, which appeared in 1643, and during Hawkins' lifetime, ascribes *Partheneia Sacra* to him, and Marracci in *Bibliotheca Mariana* (1648) is equally unambiguous. So far as the initial question is concerned it is worth noting that *A Survey of the Apostasy* purports to be written by M.A., the reversed initials of De Dominis. W. C. Hazlitt quotes an inscription from the copy of *Partheneia Sacra* before him: 'For Dame Benidicta Hawkines w(r)itten By her Borther Henery Hawkines of the Societie of Jesus'.[5] Benedicta is given as the

---

4 Vide Appendix 1 for Aston, also R. Freeman *op. cit.* p. 243f. for discussion of Aston's claims.

5 W. C. Hazlitt. *Bibliographical Collections* and Notes. 1st Series 1876. p.205. R. Freeman. *op. cit.* p. 246.

name of one of Hawkins' six sisters by Hasted in *The History of Kent*.[6]
The History of S. Elizabeth (1632) is dedicated to Lady Mary Tenham.
The Tenhams were a recusant family and near neighbours to the
Hawkins of Nash Court. Finally, as R. Freeman notes,[7] Hawkins'
alias was Brooke, and this name may have been chosen in commemora-
tion of the friendship between the Hawkins family and Sir Basil
Brook, who collaborated with Sir Thomas Hawkins, Henry's elder
brother, in his translation of Nicholas Caussin's *The Holy Court*. Brook
was also the dedicatee of *Fvga Saeculi*. The pattern seems to be fairly
complete. The only continuing mystery is that of the H.A. initials.

None of the extant poetry of Herbert Aston reveals distinctive
affinities with the poems assigned to Hawkins. Moreover, when
Partheneia Sacra was published Aston was barely nineteen, and only
eighteen when *The History of S. Elizabeth* appeared. At that date he
would already have translated Binet's *Vie de St Aldegonde*. Abraham
Cowley and John Hall must admit an equal in precocity.

Partheneia Sacra itself gives no indication of having been written
by a young man: whoever wrote it not only moved with ease among
the Patristics and Scholastics, but had an acquaintance with the
ritualistic poetry of the Middle Ages, was haunted by the symbolic
science of Pliny and Isidor of Seville, quoted from Southwell and
Sidney. The poems of the last named would perhaps come more
naturally to the mind of a man of Hawkins' generation, than to a
contemporary of Aston's. The *Tixall Poems*, of a religious cast, reveal
the authority of Caroline rather than Elizabethan modes: Crashaw has
replaced Southwell as the Parnassian coadjutor. Further, what learning
there is in *Partheneia Sacra*, and this is secular as well as theological,
practical as well as academic, is not of the florid character proper to a
young man. Hawkins is described more than once as a man of mature
learning and abilities.

The three Catholic Emblem books in English: *The Devovt Hart;
Partheneia Sacra* and the *Ashrea* of E.M. (1665) occupy, in relation to
other English Emblem Books of Catholic and Reformed, and of
merely Reformed type, a somewhat isolated position. The intention
in books of this type was to unite the function of the Emblem book
with that of the devotional manual.

6 E. Hasted. *The History of Kent*. Vol III, p. 4.
7 R. Freeman. *op. cit.* p. 246.

The Devovt Hart, both in style and arrangement of content, closely resembles *Partheneia Sacra*. Both were written for a Marian Sodality. The theme of the later book is that of the preparation of the human heart for its heavenly guest:

> Altho' I be unworthy
> Of so divine a Guest

yet Christ will come, as he comes to *The Devovt Hart*, will knock at the heart's door, will enter, will search out 'the monsters lurking in the darke corners', and 'the closet of my hart being wholy vacant', He will rest. Resting, He rejoices: 'the Sonne of Dauid Playes on the harp in the hart, while the Angels sing'. Having rested, having rejoiced in the house which He has now clarified, Jesus 'crownes HIS DEARE HART WITH Palmes and Laurels', celebrates the Heavenly Nuptials in the heart, and in the mirror of the heart 'manifestes Himself and the MOST holy Trinity'.

Assuming then the translation to be by Hawkins, the poems which he added have the naive tenderness of those in *Partheneia*. IESVS BRINGS IN THE CROSSE *into the hart, and easily imprints it on the louer* (p.149) is typical:

> Hast thou no Harbinger to bring
>   Thy furniture, so great a King,
> But must thy self in person come
>   To order al, and hang this roome?
> My hart alas! it hardly brooks,
>   To be transfixt with tenterhooks;
> For nayles and hammer, now I see,
>   And ladder, al prepar'd for me.
> And without sheets I see thy bed;
>   Thy Crosse, no bolster for thy head
> Except it be a crowne of thorne,
>   Thy canopy is Heauen forlorne.
> Al things lament thy paynes to see,
>   IESV come in, I'l mourne with thee.

The emblematic nature of the *Hymne* can be noticed, and the delicate but solemn ambiguity of 'the sheets' forever unwound.

Apart from the composition of the devotional act there are emphatic similarities between the diction of both books. In *The Devovt Hart*, unchastened by metaphrastic necessity, there is the same richly latinated prose. Jesus, 'curious and elegant IESVS stand in the midst (of the angels), not only a singer, but a Rectour of the Quire'.; S. Mary becomes the 'great *Chorist* and *Retrice* of the Angelic Quire',[8] in *Partheneia Sacra*. There is a passage curiously reminiscent of the *Essay* on *The Nightingal*: 'With how admirable a pleasure the numbers quauer and iump with al.... For to this purpose IESVS the prime Christ, records his ancient loues to the humane hart, & now mixing with admirable skil flats with sharps, sharps with flats, the tenour with the base, and running diuersly diuisions, he touches with a sweet remembrance....'[9] This whole passage elaborates the Latin original. There is also a garden-scene in *The Devovt Hart* which nearly resembles the floral amphitheatre of *Partheneia Sacra*.[10]

Mention should be made of the colour symbolism which appears to have esoteric significance in Hawkins writings. The passage:[11] 'Thy bloud, o sweet IESV, is alwayes red with purple, and white with lilies intermixed. For these two colours thou affect'st, the purple red and snowy white. (*Cant.* 5.)', should be compared with both the gloss on *My Beloved is white and red* in *Partheneia*[12] and *The Poesie* of *The Rose* and of *The Iris* where Christ is seen of his Mother 'al black & blew, pale, wan, & red'.[13] and again with the poem prefixed to T. Wright's *Passions of the Minde in Generall* (1604) and not present in the editions of 1601, 1620 and 1630.

> Centrally drewst my heart to one faire head
> Enamelled with browne, blew, white and red;[14]

In *Partheneia Sacra* the scope of the act of devotion is considerably increased. Here it becomes more complex, but no less intense. Its ground-base, the Garden, is only one in the dense tradition of symbols devoted to S. Mary. For example, Maximilian Sandaeus sees Our Lady as symbolically present in the whole of creation. Six jewels are collected to represent her life in *Maria Gemma Mystica*; a hierarchy of flowers in *Maria Flos Mysticus*; fowls congregate in *Aviarum Marianum*, while the other sequels are *Maria Sol Mysticus*, *Maria Luna Mystica*, and,

---

8 P.S. p. 150.
9 vide *Devovt Hart*, p. 174f.
10 *D. H.* p. 111f.
11 Idem. pp. 163-164.
12 *Partheneia Sacra*. p.204. also pp. 136-137 'for as the Oliues are first green, then red, then brown....' Hildebertus Turonensis has a poem on *Mary the Rainbow* rather more ingeniously applying noumenal colours.
13 *Partheneia Sacra* p.100.
14 This poem is signed H.H. and by some attributed to Hawkins. *vide* Appendix II and L. I. Guiney: *Recusant Poets*. p. 366, p. 370.

exclusively and triumphantly, *Maria Mundus Mysticus*. Among these may be found a community of images with *Partheneia Sacra*: The Dove, Hen, Swan, Nightingale, Rose, Violet, Lily, Sunflower. The dates of Sandaeus' books parallel the dates of Hawkins' literary activity.

The Garden is a symbol justly applicable to S. Mary. Eve has from the time of Justin (*Trypho.* 100) and S. Irenaeus (*Adv. Haer* v. 19) been associated with her as her anti-type: so the Garden of Eden is anti-typal of those other gardens: Gethsemane and that Garden from the midst of which the Gardener Himself rose out of Hell and went up into Heaven. And—*Hortus Conclusus*. In the tableau at the beginning of *Partheneia Sacra* where all the symbols are formally grouped the whole extent of the enclosed garden can be viewed, fertilised by the subtle breath of the Holy Ghost, but fortified by its wall of virginity, since S. Mary conceived 'without the fellowship of man'. Beyond is the *Sea* whose *Star* She is, and the *Heavens* than which she is greater since in her womb She bore Him who sustains them. One singular *Ship* sails this unique *Sea*. S. Mary is reverenced by S. Andreas as 'thou new Arke of Glory'; in the Proverbs of King Lemuel the rarely-found virtuous woman is compared with the merchant-ships: she also brings her food from afar.

Of the twenty-four symbols in *Partheneia Sacra* a number were deduced from the Fathers, from *Physiologus*, Pliny, Isidor of Seville, and others from Medieval Latin poets and mystics. The Fathers applying the allegorical method used symbols from the Old Testament as types of the New: the Stone not cut with hands; Gideon's fleece on the threshing-floor, wet while the ground about it was dry; dry while the ground about it was wet.[15] Such are distinctive symbols of the Virgin Birth; but the Fathers also multiplied vocative images of their own as the cult of Mary grew from its simple beginning in gift-offerings. Some of the 'starre-like salutations' which were bestowed upon Our Lady are paralleled in *Partheneia Sacra*.

'Golden Urne, which contains the heauenlie Manna; the most precious pearl of His Kingdom; the soft dew which comes to refresh my aridity; all haile, O Ocean, most full of pearles and precious stones; Hail, shady and fertile Mountain where has been nourished the spiritual Lamb,[16] mountain from whence came that stone cut without hands; and which has overthrown all idols....; Glorious House; Hail, Vessel of purest gold, which containest.... ever chast our Manna; Virgin

15 This symbol is explicitly mentioned on p. 66 of *Partheneia Sacra*.
16 cf. *Partheneia Sacra.* p. 199, p. 203.

earth, flowering earth, fruitful fount of waters; Hail, Dove which hast brought the olive branch; Hail, Paradise where is found the unfading Rose; O beata Virgo, columba pura et sponsa coelestis Maria coelum, Templum at Thronus divinitatis....; Virgo est lilium immaculatem, quae rosam.... genuit Christum' from Ephipanius; 'Fair and fruit-laden Olive-tree' from S. Ildephonsus' Litanies. 'The Violet of humility; *Oliva* figurat misericordiam: fuit ergo Beata Maria oliva per misericordiam', and in 'the mellifluous Doctor' S. Bernard: 'For the holy Ghost wishing us to understand by the House the Virgin Mother.' There is also the Nightingale: and one which may well have been the proto-Nightingale for Hawkins, is that celebrated by Fr Strada in his well-known poem: *Jam sol a medio prenus deflexerat orbe* published in *Prolusiones Academicae* (1617). This poem was fairly popular, and there are a number of versions,[17] of which the most accomplished is Crashaw's. Doctor Praz makes the suggestion[18] that its influence is revealed in Hawkins' description of the Nightingale in *The Essay*.

I have alluded before to the complex structure of the devotional act in *Partheneia Sacra*. Beside *The Devise* and *The Embleme* there is a poem and a number of prose passages: *The Character; The Morals; The Essay; The Discourse; The Theories* and *The Apostrophe*.

The Character presents certain similarities and contrasts with much of the character-writing of the earlier XVII Century. In *Partheneia Sacra* it exists in essential relation to those other elements which taken together comprise the whole subject of meditation. In character-writing of a religious type the bias is towards satire. Most character writing is concerned with types of men and women, with 'humours'; 'wits descant upon any plaine song' is designed to proceed from unity to diversity, multiplying suggestions from the original definition without the necessity of referring them back to that definition. The 'wit' of Hawkins besides multiplying definitions which are consonant with the symbol, also renders them conformable with what will be predicated in other sections of S. Mary. Examples of his concise handling of the definition are: 'The *House* is an artificious *Plasme* framed by the hand of man....'; 'The *Moone* is the Dowager and Queen-Regent of the Firmament.' *The Rainbow* is 'the Camelion of the ayre'. Dews are 'the sugred stillicids of Nature falling from the Limbeck of the Heauens, as so

17 Ford: *Lover's Melancholy*; B.M. Add Mss 19,268; Landsdowne Mss. 3910; Sir F. Wortley. *Characters and Elegies*, 1646. p. 66f.
18 M. Praz. *Seventeenth Century Imagery* Vol. i p. 151.

manie liquid pearls.... They are liquifyed Cristal, made into so manie siluer-orbs as drops. They are the verie teares of Nature'. 'The *Lillie* is the sceptre of the chast *Diana*'; 'The *Ship* is the artificious Dolphin of the Seas.... It is a floating Castle..' ..

The Morals, which follows, is a verbal fugue whose subject is the motto of *The Devise*. This motto contains by definition a number of moral sentiments which are recapitulated in *The Morals*. For *The Sea* the motto is: AB AMARO MARE, A MARI MARIA: one of those acrostical permutations which were thought to have an internal truth and logic all their own. 'The *Egiptians*', *The Morals* begins, 'for characters, had pictures; of pictures made they books, wherein they had need to haue been excellent Morallists, and consequently good Naturallists, to know the natures and properties of al creatures.' Adam is then shown assigning names to the new-born creatures about him, affording an example of GOD Himself: 'he was called *Adam*, as signifying *de terra terrenus*, & she Virago, *a vira desumpta*'. 'And so', and inevitably, 'the Incomparable *Virgin* was Diuinely sorted with the name of MARIE, that fitted her so right. For she was indeed a Sea of bitternes, through the seauenfold sword of sorrow, that peerced her hart; and therefore rightly. AB AMARO MARE, A MARI MARIA.'

Next: The *Essay* or Review. This is sometimes more of an allusive prose-poem than anything else, particularly when Hawkins has a subject as aesthetically yielding as *The Rose* or *The Lillie*. R. Freeman has quoted extensively and with taste from the more 'gorgeous' passages and rightly points out the superiority of this section from the point of view of literature.

Hawkins' purpose in *The Essay*, which occupies a medial position between the analogical *Morals* and the relatively bulky *Discovrse*, is to solicit the reader's attention towards higher and more intimate passages of the devotional act. The *Character* was the first and 'slender glance' at the garden. In *The Essay* it is not a glance from under the gate; the reader, the devotee, like the novices whom Mario Praz refers to, stands in the middle of the garden. *The Essay* makes in fact a candid appeal to the senses: to sight and to memory; an appeal moreover which is made with force and virtuosity. In it can be noted the operation of a method which has already been referred to: that of heightening the senses both as a result of, and a palliative to, the biological and mystical tension of the religious life. In *Partheneia Sacra*, and most vehemently in *The Essay*, is realised an observation at once detailed, rich and precise, but without

the bloodless precision of the scientific eye. It has been suggested that
this minuteness, this faith that each object present to the senses if surveyed resolutely and humbly must surrender its hypostatic significance,
was passed on to Hawkins by Fr Louis Richeome,[19] another Jesuit. It
is also representative of the willingness of the Renaissance mind to
detect a web of analogies crossing the external world.

The reader passes on to the more solemn and definitive *Discovrse* or
Survey, where the secular shadows cast by *The Essay* are given their
theological substance. This passage develops from *The Essay* and what
appeared to be so much levity of decoration is now seen to represent the
point by point affinity between S. Mary and her Sybmol.

The Theories or *Contemplation* is a brief summary of the earlier
passages of the devotional act. The function of the Emblem is admirably
stated by R. Freeman: 'There remain *The Embleme* and its *Poesie*. These
are placed between *The Discourse* and *The Theories* to provide an
interval of rest and entertainment for the worshipper. *The Discourse* had
contained much learned reference and scriptural allusion and had
required considerable mental effort to follow; *The Theories* would also
demand concentration, so *The Embleme* or as Hawkins termed it the
Pause was included as a means by which strength and refreshment
could be gained before the final meditation and prayer.'[20] The same
writer continues by stressing the distinction between *The Embleme* and
The Devise, a distinction which had been denied by Doctor Mario
Praz. *The Devise* is, in fact, the matrix in which all the meditations
originate, and to which they are referred. It is 'the-thing-in-itself;' the
core of the symbol; the centre of the wheel. *The Embleme* is not,
composite: *per contra* it represents one moment of time, the passage of
a specific event. *The Embleme* of *The House* is a difficult, but rewarding
example. It represents a particularised house, far different from the
placid rectilinear house of *The Devise* which is the idea of *a* house.
The Embleme portrays *the* House, 'the virginal workshop of the two
natures', with Gabriel, the paranymph, courteously knocking on the
thick gate of a chateau with a deal of pleasing floriation. *The Apostrophe*
which follows is in the form of a direct address to her who has been
directing the addresses of the reader. *The Apostrophe* both consum-

19 Mario Praz quotes a warm passage about flowers. But in the books I have been able
     to consult: *Tableaux Sacrez des figures mystiques du tres auguste sacrifice et sacrement
     de L'Eucharistie DE DIEZ*. (1601), and others, Richeome is vivid about Manna but
     has no room for flowers.
20 R. Freeman. *op. cit.* p. 191.

mates and eviscerates the symbol, The symbol is now and at last related
to the inner life of the devotee. Mental prayer becomes manual and
ejaculatory prayer. The symbol vanishes before the majesty of what
it represents. The approach is made, the act of praise becomes explicit,
and the sun of devotion stands at the glory of its meridian.

Before summarising what the interest and importance of *Partheneia
Sacra* consist in, one or two things may be noted about the nature and
quality of its verse and prose. The prose varies from part to part of the
book, according to the necessity of the section involved. The prime
characteristic, however, is a curious union of formal rhetoric and
colloquial, but not incongruous, phrasing. Although as a Jesuit Hawkins
was a cultivated rhetor, the use made of the art in *Partheneia* is to
be found as much in the *ordonnance* of the book as in its actual prose
constituents. By this I mean the structure of the devotional act itself:
the secondary titles of the sections could themselves have a logical as
well as a psychological significance. *The Review, The Survey, The
Pause, The Contemplation, The Colloquie* are only names for *The Occasion*,
the *Coherence*, the *Principal Scope* and the other items of the *Index
Rhetoricus*. There is at least one example of *prooimion*: 'And the Eyes
(the Agents of Loue) like a payre of twin-like Doues haue set vp their
nests, and built their nests, as it were, in the hollow concaues of the
browes....'[21] The purely verbal conceit flourishes occasionally; this
from *The Character* of *The Palme*: 'The Male, that beares no fruit
himself, in a manner is endles and euerlasting, because Dateles, as
without dates; and the femal though fruitful & ful of dates, yet
bearing pulles her not downe, but is for al her dates as durable euery
whit as the other.'[22] Occasionally the artifice is rendered immediately
sensible as in this passage where the repetition 'Doue' or 'Doues', carries
with it its own solemn and subministrative effect: 'For lo, this Doue
with the rest of that desolate and mourning flight of *Maries*, her fellow-
doues, did nothing els, but sigh and groane, in beholding the onlie Pearl
of doues, her deerest Sonne, in so piteous a plight, so hampered and
entangled in the fowler's nets *Like Doues that meditate, they groned sore*, as
the Prophet sayth, especially this *Doue* aboue the rest, the incomparable
Virgin-Doue, being the natural dam and parent of the poore distressed
one....'[23] This passage illustrates another quality in Hawkins' writing:

21 *P.S.* p. 199.
22 *P.S.* p. 152.
23 Idem. pp. 204-205. cf. pp. 208-209, as quoted in R. Freeman *op. cit.* p. 197.

a quiet tenderness, an intimate but reverent tone as, for example, in *The Lillie* where after comparing the root of the flower, with S. Mary's heart, by one line he suggests her resting in, yet restless for, Her Son and God:

> The stemme, her right Intention.[24]

Contrasting with this is his use of an ingenious comparison out of S. Bernard: 'our glorious *Virgin*, the fountain, I mentioned aboue, of liuing waters, as an Aqueduct hath so great a length, so she reaches euen from heauen to the earth; according to that melliflouus *Doctour: Marie* is an Aqueduct, whose top like *Iacob's* ladder reaches to Heauen....'[25]

Hawkins' diction in *Partheneia Sacra* demands a brief mention. It is heavily Latinate, but the vocabulary is a mixture of the old and the new. Beside the use of theological terminology, i.e. 'impetrate', Hawkins uses several words, to all appearances, for the first time. e.g. 'perlustration' (1640 N.E.D.) and 'dilection' (1656 N.E.D.) Nor is it a question of adopting words for their euphony, or for their mythical and historic associations. Both of these underlying motives can be sensed in Sir Thomas Browne; although Hawkins is self-conscious in his choice of phraseology, there seems to be little evidence that they are common also to him. Nor, as in the case of many Catholic exiles, are there signs of a hesitating approach to the language. It is probable that it is simply the effect of intense classical studies, of residence abroad, and of Latin conversation affecting a style by nature self-conscious and rhetorical.

The Poesie is co-inherent with *The Embleme*. It is committed to no more elaborate purpose than that of a passive commentary. It cannot be judged, therefore, simply *qua* poem. All the verse in *Partheneia Sacra* is written in the same measure and, with one exception, is of identical length. On a first reading the impression of monotony is paramount. When, however, the limitations of the subject—together with the consequent lack of tension—are borne in mind, it must be conceded that 'H.A.' has, in two or three of the poems, contrived to achieve both movement and fire:

> Then more to glorify
> This *Heauen* from his, the *Sunne of Iustice* came,
> Light of the world, with his eternal flame.

The converse of this expression of God on earth:

24 Idem. p. 35.
25 Idem. p. 220.

The Holie-Ghost that nestles like a *Doue*
Betwixt the Father & the Sonne aboue
Is flowne from Heauen to seek a mate below....

is a heritage from *The Embleme* which is no embarrassment. This particular poem aims at describing in its first three lines the nuptuary element among the Holy Trinity. The almost bizarre detail of The Holy Ghost perching on the bar of Heaven serves to illustrate how the Emblem can be a visualised conceit. Within a narrow neck of meaning the metaphor is just.

In a number of poems, to escape monotony, the medial caesura is varied and used, too, as an indication of astonishment, of effort. The climax of each poem arrives invariably in the last two or four lines (once in the last four and a half.) The success of the climax must be judged from two points of view; whether it is a singing, but significant summary of *The Embleme* and its precept, and whether it does in fact— leaving *The Embleme* out of account—complete the internal logic of the whole poem. It may do this with the *concetto predicabile*:

> To her Sonne appeals
> Who signes the Pardon, and his Wounds are seales.

or with the radiating plea of:

> *Starre* of the *Sea*, thy Sun hath giuen thee light;
> Til he bring day, guide me in sinnes dark night.
> I seeke, what sages heertofore haue donne,
> Guided by thee a *Starre*, to find the Sunne.

A more professional example of the *concetto predicabile* finishes off *The Olive*:

> *Mercie* both
> (Like oyle) the Tree & fruit, produce: a *Priest*
> Messias in her Womb's annoynted *Christ*

Again, here is an example of the culminating conceit derived from Scholastic theology—that of S. Mary's *fiat*:

> One *Fiat* banished night,
> And now an other brings from heauen the light.

As an example of the fulfilment of the Emblem the last few lines of *The Heauens* may be cited, ending as they do with:

> *Empyreal Heauen*! For in her makes abode
> The first blest Soule, that had the sight of *GOD*.

which movingly interprets *The Devise*—as well as *The Embleme*—since its motto is *Capacitatis Immensae*: Whom the Heavens could not contain, thou hast held in thy womb.

Partheneia Sacra has both an appeal and a claim. Its appeal lies in its evocative prose which embodies the pattern of a new sensibility: a sensibility belonging to a non-scientific age, but able, nevertheless, to examine objects with scientific minuteness; in its poetry, which is not only 'above mediocrity'—the verdict of Oliver—but has in it a tender and 'mystical unction'. Its claim is based on its being an example —indeed one of the most notable in the period—of the Emblem Book and Devotional Manual combined, and on its variety and consistency as such.

The purpose of this synthetic essay and of the textual notes is to re-inforce both claim and appeal; to provide a compact *terminus a quo* for the further study of the book and for the augmentation of the bare details of Hawkins' life. Until an adequate Bibliography of XVII Century Recusant Literature is available—a Bibliography which includes the smaller libraries here and on the Continent—this small contribution may have its uses.

I should like to thank Fr Sebastian Redmond, s.j. and Fr C. D. Ford, s.j. for helpful discussion of several dilemmas; and Miss R. Freeman for permitting me to read her *English Emblem Books* in proof. My copious citations from this admirable study speak for themselves, and to far better purpose than their context— unless it happens that I am paraphrasing Miss Freeman instead of quoting her. Lastly, my gratitude to Mr H. Peschmann for the fear of his lurking *obstat*.

JANUARY 1948   IAIN FLETCHER

Η ΠΑΡ
ΘΕΝΟΣ

By Iohn Cousturier.
M·DC·XXX·III·

P. van Langeren fecit.

PARTHENEIA SACRA.

OR
THE MYSTERIOVS AND DELICIOVS

GARDEN

OF THE
SACRED PARTHENES;

Symbolically set forth and enriched
With
PIOVS DEVISES AND EMBLEMES

for the entertainement of
DEVOVT SOVLES;

Contriued
AL TO THE HONOVR

of the Incomparable Virgin

MARIE

Mother of

GOD;

For the pleasure and deuotion especially of the
PARTHENIAN SODALITIE
of her Immaculate
CONCEPTION.

By

H.   A.

Printed by IOHN COVSTVRIER.

M. DC. XXXIII.

THE ORDER OF THE SYMBOLS contained in this GARDEN.

Wherunto are annexed
the PHOENIX, and the SWAN
without the Garden.

THE
EPISTLE
TO THE
PARTHENIAN
SODALITIE.

Y deare PARTHENIANS,
When the Saviour of the world had passed the Torrent of *Cedron*, into the Garden of *Gethsemani*, there to commence the Tragedie, whose sad Catastrophe he was to finish on Mount *Calvarie*, he gave to understand, how much (no doubt) he was pleased with *Gardens*. But then especially, after the Tragick Scene was ended, and that doleful curten or veyle was rent asunder (a token of the period of the Jewish Theater) when al was voyded, and he vouchsafed to appeare familiarly againe to his deerest friends, in the forme and habit of a *Gardener*, he evidently declared his good affection, towards the *Garden* of their Soules, which then he came to cheer-up and refresh with his Divine presence, & to banish the clowdes of heavines, which so sad a spectacle had cast upon the Garden of their harts, when as no flowers or functions of their soules could chearfully yeald their luster, or send forth anie special odour of sanctitie, so drowned in teares. May it not therefore seeme strange unto you, if I, knowing the sympathie of harts,
between

between the Mother and the Sonne, the Blessed
J E S U S, flower of Nazareth, and his sacred Stem,
presume heer to personate, and make her appeare to
your viewes, not in the habit of fashion of a Gardener,
which office she rather yealds (as proper) to her Sonne,
but of a *Garden*, under the veyle of Symbols, to
deliciate a while with her Devotes, You, deerest
Parthenians, yet greeved and groaning with the burden
of your pressures, for his sake, who is the curious
Gardener indeed, that from the beginning planted the
same for himself, from al Eternitie. Now then the
winter past of melancholie thoughts, the showers
blowne-over and quite vanished, of teares of
persecution; I say, laying the memorie of them al aside,
as stormes already past, in conceit at least, you heer
behold our SACRED PARTHENES, who presents her self
for your delights in Garden-attire and cheerfully
receave her, with serene browes, in this coorse and
rural array, of hearbes and flowers, as if she were
clothed with the Sunne, crowned with the Starres, and
trampling the Moone, as once she was seen by her
holie Guardian, the deare Disciple, whom J E S U S
loved. Nor would I wish you perfunctoriously to
view her only, and passe her over with a slender glance
of the eye, but to enter into her *Garden*, which she is
herself, and survey it wel. Where, to the end you may
not erre, mistake, or goe astray, in wayes so new, and
strange, and (for ought I know) as yet untraced or trod
of anie, take heer, I pray, for Guide, my proper *Genius*,
wel acquainted with al passages of them. And you (O
SACRED PARTHENES) I beseech especially, to guide me
also, while in your service I take thus upon me to
guide the rest.

THE

THE PREFACE
TO THE
READER

Onsidering, Gentle Reader, *how much thou
art taken and delighted (as men are wont) with
change and varietie in al things: I have heer
endeavoured to serve thee in this Worke, according to thine appetite. Which being not my sole*
end, *but for thy devotion rather, I made* Varietie *the handmayd to* Pietie, *directing al, as you see, thereunto. And though
I am a most unworthie Client and Devote to the Immaculate
Virgin-Mother of God, I have presumed (as you see) to
direct both the one and other, to the honour of that Incomparable* Queene of Heaven. *Wherin though the instruments
I use, may seeme prophane, so prophanely used nowadayes,
as* Devises *consisting of* Impreses, *and* Mottoes, *Characters,* Essayes, Emblemes, *and* Poesies; *yet they may be like
that* Panthæon, *once sacred to the feigned Deities, and
piously since sanctified, converted, and consecrated to the
honour of the glorious* Queene, *and al the blessed* Saints *of
Heaven. And following the example of the Israelits,
warranted by* GOD *himself, I have borrowed but the silver
and golden vessels, of those profane Ægyptians, and not the
poysonous liquours they caroused in them; to convert them (I
say) to a better use, in service of my Ladie and Mistris, and
for the pleasure and devotion of her especial Familie; yea,
Gentle Reader, for thy solace too, if thou art pleased to
accept of my poore endeavours.*

THE PROEME
TO HIS
GENIUS
ON THE SACRED
PARTHENES
herself.

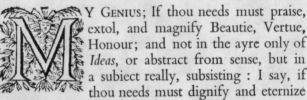Y GENIUS; If thou needs must praise, extol, and magnify Beautie, Vertue, Honour; and not in the ayre only of *Ideas*, or abstract from sense, but in a subiect really, subsisting : I say, if thou needs must dignify and eternize a pure creature above the skyes, praise then such an one, whose superlative praises, when thou hast sayd the most, can hardly so exceed, but that her due *Elogies, Encomiums,* and *Panegyricks,* stil shal farre transcend the facultie of thy tongue, and thou be acquit of the least imputation of flatteries. And if my *Genius* carrie thee (my pen) into daliances, as it were, to deliciat with thy self, upon thy plumes, in contemplation of that noble Sex, corrival with the Masculin; doe not, I prythee, with *Isocrates,* seeke a *Helena,* that fatal and most deplorable fire-brand of the *Troyan* Cittie, on whom that elegant and terse Sophister powred forth the musks and civets of his venal tongue, the riches of a wanton and luxuriating wit. Behold SHE is even now at hand, whom worthily thou
mayst,

mayst, and whom thou canst not prayse enough, so
farre from praysing her too much; who besides is able
wel to guerdon and recompence thy prayses given
her, with heaped and redoubled interest. Behold then
our SACRED PARTHENES, Virgin of Virgins, for
excellencie, is SHE, whom safely thou mayst prayse,
whom the impatient World for so manie Ages,
groaning under their pressing burden of their crimes,
with vowes and prayers had most incessantly begged
and importuned. A boon of wel-nigh fiftie Ages suit,
obtained at last with much adoe. So great a work it
was for Nature, albeit holpen by Grace, to bring forth
to Mortals a creature, worthie to be the Mother of God,
Ladie of the World, and the true Reparatresse of life.
Nor doe thou frame to thyself heer the *Mercuries* of a
counterfet and Sophisticat candour, couloured cheekes,
curled hayre, and wreathed knots with inexplicable
Meanders. Seeke not Vermilion or Ceruse in the face,
bracelets of Oriental-pearles on her wrist, Rubie-
carknets on the neck, rich pendants in the eares, and a
delicious fan of most exquisit feathers in her hand, nor
al that magasin of Feminin riches, or richest ornaments
of Beautie, enough to belye beauties rather, and destroy them quite, then to afford them, where they are
not found; they being nothing els then a precious
Scene of fopperies, which they only seeke with a
curious wastfulnes, who wil needs be wholy mad with
the greatest sumptuousnes and cost; wheras surely
true Beautie is but one, which even integritie of the
mind makes, being the livelie coulour of God; and was
no doubt that, which so much graced our PARTHENES,
and set her forth, whom the entire and intemerate
comlines of Vertues hath crowned with such a gloriet
on her head, and such splendour and glorie in heaven,
as in a pure creature nothing may be imagined more

c   magnificent

magnificent in riches, nor in suavities sweeter. And
surely when I think more attentively of her, it seemes
to me, the highest Architect of Al and great GOD, the
sole Moderatour of al, in creating this one Soule, hath
so admirably exprest himself in her, and with his most
exquisit fingars, hath bestowed so much art and
industrie in her delineation, and so pleased himself
with the delicat draughts he hath shewed in this one
image of himself, as if in the shop of human things he
would expose her to al, to be imitated. Wherefore
when as that Soule, farre purer then the Starres, and
flowing with so manie exquisit ornaments, glided
into the Tabernacle of her bodie, that impure Fire-
brand was not cast into her, which first was kindled in
the Authours of our kind, and flamed forth afterwards
farre and wide, to the waste and utter ruine of the
whole world, but as a Saphyr or purer Adamant,
appeares and growes up in pure and burnisht gold: so a
most chast Soule, by the hands of God disposing so
thereof, was put into her inviolable and sanctified
bodie, that no least stayne of her stock and progenie
might light upon her. Then, after SHE (that golden
issue of her Mother) was borne and brought forth to
light, I easily beleeve, that Nature recreated and
refreshed from the daylie miserie it lay in, even laughed
to behold her, supposing the light was newly risen to
her, when first she fixt her eyes on her, from whose
precious and Virginal womb, was the Fountain of
light itself to spring. The Virgin-infant heerupon was
nursed-up and trayned betwen chast walls, in a most
holie discipline of Patrial lawes, and instructed with
those studies of arts, that might addresse her as a noble
Sacrarie of God. Anticipating vertue, she urged and
pressed more hard the slower paces of her yeares,
which hardly could endure the long demurres of age,
of whom

of whom was Nature ashamed as it were to impose anie lawes of longer attendance. For even now in her first age, there shined manie *Dotes* in her, as starres in the heavens in a serene night, like sparkling gemmes fixed in their orbs; since SHE had in her whole life, as you know, a marvelous societie of al Vertues, wherewith SHE wove that loome of her age, as with singular and most excellent figures, in whom the absolute consent and harmonie of al Vertues have magnificently conspired, that Beautie should not violate Shamefastnes; gravitie, infringe lowlines; meekenes, gravitie; Simplicitie, Maiestie; facilitie, constancie; lastly (which til then was never heard of) that the name of *Mother* should be nothing iniurious to *Virginitie.* Al Vertues strove alike in HER, and al had the victorie. Nor yet was SHE destitute of the guifts of Nature likewise, while a certain Divinitie of beautie dazeled the aspects of men. The bashful forhead (seate *So Epi-* of shamfastnes) soft and gently arose; beneath the *phanius very* black and archie browes, shined forth the bright *nigh des-* lamps of HER eyes, which how powerfully they *cribes her,* pierced and penetrated the heavens, who knowes not? The nose most gracefully inflecting, made a handsome kind of pillaster to her forhead; lips somewhat thinner, the receptacle of a meeke elocution, and celestial graces; a great affabilitie of speach; a singular modestie of gate; a countenance, graceful without softnes or levitie, grave without statelines, set always in a perpetual sereanes, which hardly could admit the least impression of laughter. It were long to prosecute the rest; I shal have sayd al things, saying, SHE is the MOTHER of GOD. But this dignitie when al the tongues, I say not of men only, but even of the Angels them- selves, shal proclaime and set forth, doe what they can, shal be enforted to cry out: *De dilecta nunquam satis.*

THE PLAT-FORME
OF THE
GARDEN.

Herefore, my GENIUS, I would wish thee, to enter into the large, spacious, and ample GARDEN of our SACRED PARTHENES, and there behold those specious, and most delicious Obiects; al, so wholy consecrated to her service, that they seeme as borne to expresse her prayses; everie one, to help thee out, to accomplish and performe this task so hard to undertake, and impossible to be done so worthily, as SHE deserves. Goe, I say; survey her GARDEN, beset with the bashful ROSE, the candid LILLIE, the purple VIOLET, the goodlie HELIO-TROPION, sprinckled al with DEWES, which the busie BEE gathers as it falles from the HEAVENS, dressed with an IRIS, as with a silver MOON, instead of a torch, and enameled with miriads of STARRES, as lesser lamps, to afford it light, in the obscuritie of the night; enclosed round, and compassed-in with a wal, where on an OLIVE, you may behold the iollie PHILOMEL to pearch, chanting her Roundelayse; and on the other side, a flourishing and statelie PALME; and likewise see a

goodlie

goodlie HOUSE of pleasure, standing therein before you;
and if you mark it wel, you shal discerne that domestical and almost inseparable companion therof, the HEN,
there scraping in the dust for food, wherin She finds a
precious Margarit or PEARL; and on the top therof espy
an innocent and meek DOVE, as white and candid, as
the driven snow; for in this GARDEN are al things pure.
Where likewise in a place more eminent and conspicuous then the rest, you may behold a faire and
beautiful FOUNTAIN, artificiously contrived with pipes
so under ground, as waters al, when need requires.
And if, my *Genius*, al these wil not suffise, to make up
ful thy Quire of Laudes, to magnify thy SACRED
PARTHENES, ascend upon that MOUNT before thy face;
and with an Opticon discover thence, the Ocean SEA,
and invite it likewise with the rest, to beare a part; and
for a fuller complement of al, wave but a little banner
to some SHIP or other, to come-in with al her fraught
of magnificent prayses. For al within ken or view of
of that same MOUNT, are subiects and deare Devotes
of our Sacred and Incomparable PARTHENES.

But soft, my *Genius*; ere thou leade thy Reader into
the Maze or Labyrinth of the beauties therin contained,
pause heer a while, to consider how to behave thy
self, before (I say) thou let him in, to speculate that
Magazin of beauties; which being so mysterious and
delicious an Obiect, requires not be be rashly lookt
upon, or perfunctoriously to be slighted over, but, as
the manner is of such as enter into a Garden, to glance
at first theron with a light regard, then to reflect upon
it with a better heed, to find some gentle mysterie or
conceipt upon it, to some use or other; and then liking
it better, to review the same againe, and so to make a
Survey therupon to the same use. This would I have
thee punctually observe in al, to guide thy Reader
                                                    with,

with, in this present GARDEN of our sacred PARTHENES.
First then shalt thou presente him with the Symbol it
self, set-forth in manner of a *Devise*, with an *Imprese*
and *Motto*, expressing the allusion to the SACRED
PARTHENES herself, in some mysterie of hers, or attribute belonging to her. Then shalt thou take the *Imprese*
being the Symbol by itself, and dallie as it were with
some natural and apt *Character* upon it; being no more,
then certain superficial Glances, deciphering it in some
sort, but lightly only, for a first entertainment of thy
Reader. Then with *Morals*, on the *Motto*, shalt thou but
touch or reflect upon the *Paragon* herself for the present,
and no more. Then looking back with a fresh review
on the Symbol itself, by way of an *Essay*, shalt thou
make a fuller *Survey* therof, discoursing on the *Paragon*
herself, to match, compare, and paralel them togeather
to find out some *Elogies* or other, in prayse of our
SACRED PARTHENES. Thence to satisfy the Eye as wel
as the Understanding, for his greater delight, thou shalt
pause a while, to leade him to behold, as in a Tapestrie
the Symbol turned into an *Embleme*, piously composed;
where for the clearer understanding therof, the same
shal be indicatively expressed in a *Poesie*, made for the
purpose. Then shalt thou make him sit downe a while,
to ponder, consider, and contemplate some things
besides, conducing to the further discoverie of the
hidden mysterie, contained in the Symbol itself, to the
honour of our SACRED PARTHENES, as certain *Specula-
tions* or *Theories* theron. And after al, shalt thou invite
him to Apostrophize with the Paragon PARTHENES
herself, under the Symbol so handled, being the
utmost scope, and ful fruition of the whole; and so
conclude the peece with some boone or suite, corres-
pondent to the present occasion, in everie one. And
this method would I have thee keepe in al. Now then,
being

being thus admonished, I licence, and freely give thee leave, to leade thy Reader first into her private Garden (for Princes, you must know, and great Ladies too, besides their publick, have some private Garden of their owne) where, though enclosed, yet with the wings of Contemplation, may he secretly view, reflect, review, survey, delight, contemplate, and enioy the hidden and sublime perfections therin, and lastly obtaine, no doubt, anie reasonable suite at the hands of the SACRED PARTHENES in respect thereof, for his reward.

THE

THE I. SYMBOL.

THE GARDEN.

THE DEVISE.

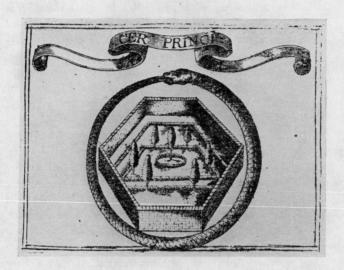

THE CHARACTER.

HE GARDEN is a goodlie Amphitheater of *The* flowers, upon whose leaves, delicious *Impresa.* beauties stand, as on a stage, to be gazed on, and to play their parts, not to see so much, as to be seen; and like Wantons to allure with their looks, or enchant with their words, the civets and perfumes they weare about them. It is even the pride of Nature, her best array, which she puts on, to entertaine the Spring withal. It is the

is the rich Magazin or Burse of the best perfumes or
Roman wash: A poesie of more worth, then a bal of
pomander, to make one grateful where he comes; the
one being sweetly sweet, the other importunely. It is a
Monopolie of al the pleasures and delights that are on
earth, amassed togeather, to make a dearth therof elswhere, and to set what price they list upon them: It is
the precious Cabinet of flowrie gems, or gems of
flowers: The shop of Simples in their element, delight-
ing rather to live delicious in themselves at home,
where they are bred, then changing their conditions,
to become restoratives to others; or to dye to their
beauties, to satisfy the covetous humour of everie
Apothecarie, to enrich himself with their spoyles. It is
the Pallace of *Flora's* pomps, where is the ward-robe of
her richest mantles, powdred with starres of flowers,
and al embroadred with flowrie stones. It is the
laughter and smile of Nature: Her lapful of flowers,
and the Garland she is crowned with in triumphs. It is
a Paradice of pleasures, whose open walks are Tarrases,
the Close, the Galleries, the Arbours, the Pavillions, the
flowerie Bancks, the easie and soft Couches. It is,
in a word, a world of sweets, that live in a faire
Communitie togeather, where is no envie of another's
happines, or contempt of others povertie; while everie
flower is contented with its owne estate; nor would the
Dazie wish to be a Rose, nor yet the Rose contemnes
the meanest flower.

THE

THE MORALS.

Sacer Principi.

 T is a Maxime in al Arts: *There is no rule without exception.* And Sanctuaries, we know, in al good Christian Common-wealths have been ever allowed of. Who is he so rude, that dares lay hands upon the vessels marked with the Prince's Armes? Or who presumes to disannul or cancel his Privie or Broad Seals? The Prince's closet is shut to al, but to the Prince himself. His Signet is a Key, that opens al the posterns of his Court. There is no Prince, who, besides his common treasure, hath not a privat casket of his owne. When the world was drowned, there was an Ark, that safely floted on the Mayne; nor al the Cataracts of Heaven, were able to overwhelme it. The Iewes indeed had their Citties of Refuge, and the King of Iewes no lesse his sanctifyed Cittie. It was a great *Piaculum* to violate the immunities of those; What think you then of his privat Cittie? Hath he a Cittie for himself, and not a Garden private to himself? Doubtles he hath. He hath then a private Garden of his owne, and keeps the keys himself. Long live the Prince then, to enjoy his Garden; and cursed be he, that shal but with the mouth or hart seeme to violate the sacred closures of his Garden. *Quia* Principi Sacer.

The Motto.

Capie comme dessus.

THE

THE ESSAY.

 wil not take upon me to tel al; for
so of a Garden of flowers, should I
make a Labyrinth of discourse, and
should never be able to get forth.
Cast but your eyes a little on those
goodlie Allies, as sowed al over with
sands of gold, drawne-forth so streight by a
line. Those Cros-bowes there (be not affrayed of them)
they are but Cros-bowes made of Bayes; and the
Harquebusiers, wrought in Rosmarie, shoot but
flowers, and dart forth musk. Those Beasts likewise,
horrible there and dreadful to see to, are but in ieast; al
that menace they make, is but a shew only. Al those
armed Men with greenish weapons, and those Beasts
al clad in skins of green, are but of Prim, Isop, and
Tyme, al hearbs very apt to historify withal. I wil
quite passe over those little Groves, Thickets, and
Arbours, and speake nothing of those Pety-canons
there and Quiristers, chanting their Complines in the
Evening, and Nocturnes in the Night, mingling their
prettie Mottets, which Nature learnes them, of their
owne accord. Nor wil I heer speake a word of those
Water-works, Conduits, and Aquaducts, which yet
might you heare to make a gentle murmur throughout,
affording an apt Base for the birds to descant on. I hast
me to the Flowers only most proper to our GARDEN
heer. Behold, I pray, those Bushes, al enameled with
ROSES of so manie sorts; these heer apparrelled with
the white of Innocencie; those there with a scarlet
tincture; one wel-nigh withered embalmes the ayre
with its perfume, and makes a shew with its golden
threads, and al its treasure; that other is yet in its folds,
and dares not hazard so much as to peepe forth; this
heer

heer puts forth the bud, and now half-open smiles withal, and shewes forth a glimps of its purple, through a cliff of the green Case, wherein it is; which the theevish birds would soone come to steale away, were it not for the Garrison of thornes, that serves for a Corps-de-guard to that Queene of flowers. Behold there the Lillies of ten sorts; some yet hidden in their green cups; others half borne; and the rest newly disclosed. What think you? are they not exceeding faire? You would say, they were of white Satin, streaked without, and al embroadered within with gold; you can hardly tel, whether they be milk condensed into leaves, or figured snow, or silver flower-de-lis'd, or a starre al musked. Those yellow ones, would you not verily think them to be golden bels? and that red one, a little purse of crimson-satin? and those others, some goodlie vessels of Emeralds, or the like? But marke a while; see you not those beds strewed with a thousand *Violets*? some yellow, some purple, some white, some speckled, and some party-couloured, some Carnashion, and some changeable. Behold those faire and beautiful Tulips there; those rich Amaranths, cerulean Hiacinths, Pansies, the gemmes of the goodlie IRIS; the scarlet Gilloflower, the Pinks, the Marygolds, and a thousand other flowers. O what a Paradice of flowers is this! What a Heaven of muskie starres, or Celestial Earth al starred with flowers, empearled with gemmes and precious stones! A land of promise, ful of milk and honie! Behold, I say, the ROSE, dedicated (they say) to that little elf *Cupid*; whose threads are as golden hayres; whose thornes instead of arrowes; whose fire, a flash of luster; and whose leaves are wings; few can touch it, without touch of love unto it; and it costs them deare, who meddle with it. The LILLIE hangs the head downe; for modestie, I suppose; though it can not

not blush, for having nothing to blush at; her flower being al so white and without spot. They say, She was borne of the milk of *Iuno*; howsoever she is called the Royal flower, the *Rose of Iuno*. Note there the humilitie of the VIOLET, how like to the strawberrie she keeps by the ground, hiding, what she can, her beautie in her leaves, but is discovered whether she wil or no; partly by the flashes of her luster, breaking forth unawares betweene the leaves, not so reserved as they ought; and partly with the odour she can not choose but send forth. The Tulip is a singular ornament to this Garden; looke and observe it wel. How were it possible, one would think, so thin a leaf, bred and nourished in the same ayre, and proceeding from the same stem, should be golden in the bottome, violet without, saffron within, bordered on the edge with fine gold, and the prickle of the point blew as a goodlie Saphir? and a hundred others of several fashions, as if they had striven to dresse themselves to put the eyes into paine, not knowing where to bestow themselves. There againe, may you note another, not unlike to a Columbin, very gracious to see to, enameled with drops of gold, and a thousand other the like varieties; so as of necessitie we must needs confesse, that GOD *is very admirable in his works*, since on so poore a thing, as a slender stalk, grow such a number of excellent varieties. And now I addresse myself to Thee, the Soveraigne and *Mystical* GARDEN itself, the Paragon of Gardens.

THE

THE DISCOURSE.

 Speake not heer of the *Covent-Garden*, the garden of the *Temple*, nor that of the *Charter-house*, or of *Grayes-Inne Walkes*, to be had and enjoyed at home; nor of the *Garden* of *Padua*, or of *Mountpelier*, so illustrious for Simples. I speake not of the Garden of *Hesperides*, where grew the golden Apples, nor yet of *Tempe*, or the *Elizian fields*. I speake not of *Eden*, the Earthlie Paradice, nor of the *Garden* of Gethsemany, watred with Bloud flowing from our Saviour's precious bodie: But I speake of Thee, that GARDEN so knowne by the name of HORTUS CONCLUSUS; wherein are al things mysteriously and spiritually to be found, which even beautifyes the fairest Gardens: being a place, no lesse delicious in winter, then in Summer, in Autume, then in the Spring; and wherin is no season to be seen, but a perpetual Spring; where are al kinds of delights in great abundance, that can possibly be devised; where are faire and goodlie Allies, streight and even, strewed al with sands, that is, a streight, vertuous, and Angelical life, yet strewed with the sands and dust of her proper Humilitie; where are Arbours to shadow her from the heats of concupiscence; flowrie Beds to repose in, with heavenlie Contemplations; Mounts to ascend to, with the studie of Perfections: where are hearbs, and Simples, soveraigne medicines of al spiritual maladies, where (I say) are the Flowers of al Vertues: The LILLIE of spotles and immaculate Chastitie, the ROSE of Shamfastnes and bashful Modestie, the VIOLET of Humilitie, the Gilloflower of Patience, the Marygold of Charitie, the Hiacinth of Hope, the SUN-FLOWER of Contemplation, the Tulip of Beautie and gracefulnes. In this

GARDEN

GARDEN ENCLOSED are certain risings to be seen of Hils
in elevations of mind, and Valleys againe in depressions
and demissions of the same mind, through annihilation; heer likewise are Vines of spiritual gladnes, and
Groves of a retired solitude, to be found. Heer whole
Quiers of Angels are accustomed to sing their Alleluyas
at al howers, in lieu of the Philomels in the silence of
the Night; in steed of the Larks, at the hower of Prime;
in place of the Thrush, the Linet, and Canarie-bird, at
al Howers. Heer spring the limpid fountains of al
Graces; whence streame the little rils and brooks
watering the Paradice on al sides, and thence abundantly flowing to the rest of Mortals. Heer are Pooles for
the harmles fry of her innocent thoughts, like fishes
heer and there to passe up and downe in the heavenlie
Element of her mind; heer and there certain labyrinths
formed in the hearbs of Her endles perfections. Heer
lastly are statues of Her rare examples to be seen,
Obelisks, Pyramides, Triumphal Arches, Aqua-ducts,
Thermes, Pillars of Eternal Memorie, erected to Her
glorie, in contemplation of her Admirable, Angelical,
and Divine life.

But that which sets forth and adornes this incomparable and mysterious GARDEN most, is the special
Priviledge and Prerogative it hath, not only over al
the Gardens of the world besides, but even also of the
Terrestrial Paradice itself; for that the Garden of *Eden*,
or Terrestrial Paradice, was not so exempt from Sinne,
but the place where Sinne began; and was not so free
from the Serpent, but that he could get-in and work
the mischief; so as for avoyding more ensuing dangers,
it was necessarie to place at the gates therof for ever
after, an Angel-Porter of the Order of the *Cherubins*,
with a fierie and two-edged sword, to guard the same.
Wheras this GARDEN (our LADIE) was a GARDEN shut-up
indeed

indeed from the beginning, and divinely preserved *Immaculate*, from Her first Conception, adorned with al those sorts of flowers and plants of Graces, Vertues, and Perfections I mentioned above; whereto no Serpent, nor Original sinne, much lesse Actual, could have acces, but was alwayes even from her first beginning, a most delicious Paradice and GARDEN *shut-up* from al invasions of Enemies.

THE EMBLEME.

THE POESIE.

He Virgin *was a* Garden *round beset*
With Rose, *and* Lillie, *and sweet* Violet.
Where fragrant Sents, without distast of Sinne,
Invited GOD *the* Sonne *to enter in.*
But it was clos'd:★ Alma's shut up, *we know,*

D

The Pause,

★Alma *signifyes* Inclosed *& a* Virgin shut up *in* Hebrew.

What

What Gard'ner then might enter in to sow?
Or plant within this Eden? *Or, what birth*
Might be expected from a virgin-earth?
The Holie-Spirit, *like a subtile wind,*
Peercing through al, only a way could find.
As th' Earth brought forth at first, how't is not knowne:
So did this Garden, *which was never sowne.*

THE THEORIES.

The Con-
templation.

Ontemplate first, how our Lord GOD had
planted a *Paradice of delights*, that is, the
Virgin MARIE, from the beginning, to wit,
in the *East*; wherin he placed *Man*, whom
he had framed, because indeed he put
CHRIST in her womb, through the operation of the
Holie-Ghost. Which place in truth is very pleasant;
because whatsoever is delightful in a *Garden*, was
abundantly found in Her: there being the Cedar of
high *Contemplation*, the *Cypres* of odoriferous *fame* and
sanctitie of life, the *Lawrel* of *Constancie*, the *Palme* of
glorious *Victorie*, the *Mulberrie* of *Patience*, the *Myrtle*
of *Mortification*, the *Olive* of *Mercie*, the *Almond* of *Fruit-*
fulnes, the *Figtree* of *Deliciousnes*, the *Plane-tree* of
Fayth; for the *Plane* hath leaves like to our Escuchions,
or Targets, and therefore signifyeth *Fayth*; for that
Fayth is a *Target* against the temptations of the Divel;
But especially the *Tree of Life*, wherof S. *Augustin*
sayth thus: The Virgin MARIE is sayd to be a *Paradice*,
in the midst wherof is the *Tree of Life*, with whose
leaves the sick are cured, whose odour revives the
dead, whose tast sweetens the bitter, whose shadow
refreshes the wretched, and whose aspect reioyceth
the Angels.

Consider

Consider then the amenitie and pleasure of this
GARDEN of our Ladie. For there were *Pomgranats*, that
is, an ordination of Vertues, and a wonderful sweetnes
of Devotion; for loe, Pomgranats have their graines
disposed in an admirable order, and are indeed most
delicious fruits; to which kind of Apples the *Spouse*
invites her *Spouse*, saying: *Let my beloved come into his
Garden, and eate the fruit of his apples.* There likewise
was the *Cypres* with *Nard*, that is odoriferous fame and
profound humilitie; because the *Cypres* is an oderi-
ferous tree, and the *Nard* a most humble hearb. There
was *Nard* and *Saffron*, to wit, fervent Charitie, and
Humilitie of Celestial Contemplation; because the
Nard is a hot hearb; and *Saffron* hath a golden colour.
There were *Canes* and *Cinamon*, withal the trees of
Libanus; because in her was a singular puritie of
Conscience, an excellent odour of good Fame, and
Incorruptibilitie of the flesh. For the *Cane* hath its
vertue in the pith; the *Cinamon* hath its odour in the
bark; and the wood of *Libanus* is incorruptible: And
lastly was there both *Mirrh* and *Alloes*, with al the
prime *Unguents*; because in Her was bitternes of
tribulation for her Sonne's passion, the bitternes of
compassion for the affliction of the miserable; and the
sweetnes of devotion was in Her mind. For *Mirrh* and
Alloes are bitter; and the *Unguents* sweet and delicious.

Ponder lastly these words of the *Canticles*: *Come* Cant. 4.
*Southern wind, and blow upon my garden, and the spices
shal flow forth.* Where by the *Southern wind* is understood the breath of the Holie-Ghost. For the South-
wind is a hot, humid, and fruitful wind; which even
blew in the Virginal *Garden* of our LADIE, for that it
made her hot through *Charitie*, humid through *Pietie*,
and fruitful through *plentie of good works*: and so
flowed She with odoriferous Spices, whose odour as
balme

balme did recreate GOD; and like *Cinamon* comforted the whole world: because· *Cinamon* comforts the stomack; and like unto *Mirrh* did drive away Divels; for that indeed the smel of *Mirrh* expels the wormes.

THE APOSTROPHE.

The Colloquie. SHAL be made to the INCOMPARABLE VIRGIN, as to the Abstract of perfections, in this or the like manner: O most Soveraigne Princesse, *Ladie of Paradice, yea a Paradice itself of al perfections: Most pure Virgin, most chast Spirit, Virgin ful of grace, Mirrour of puritie, Pattern of sanctitie, Sunne of chastitie, Model of innocencie, Image of vertue, Example of perfection, Vessel of singular pietie, Mother and Mistris of Christian Religion, blessed Band, delicious Garden, the Devotion of the whole world: Be al Vertues.* O my dear Advocat, *afforded me,* O Ladie, *Soveraigne creature among the pure; obtaine them for me, I beseech thee from the bottome of my hart, through the sweetnesses of thy immaculate Conception, and thy blessed child-birth; through the sweet nourishment of the precious milk, given to thy Sonne,* GOD *and* MAN, *the King of Kings; by those sacred and divine kisses, which thou so reverently gavest him in his tender infancie. O grant me those flowers of thy delicious Garden, I beseech thee; and after al, to behold Thee triumphant in the Celestial Paradice.*

THE II. SYMBOL.
THE ROSE.
THE DEVISE.

THE CHARACTER.

THE ROSE is the Imperial Queene of *The* Flowers, which al doe homage to, as to *Impresa.* their Princesse, she being the glorie and delight of that Monarchie. She is herself a Treasurie of al Sweets, a Cabinet of Musks, which She commends to none to keepe, but holds them folded in her leaves; as knowing wel, how little conscience is made of such stealths. If anie have a wil to seeke Diamonds among flowers, he may seeke long enough ere he find them; but if a

Rubie

Rubie he seekes for, the ROSE is a precious Rubie. It
is the Darling of the Garden-Nimphs, and the cause
sometimes perhaps of much debate betweene them,
while each one strives to have it proper to herself,
being made for al, and is verily enough for al. It is
the Pallace of the flowrie *Numens*, environed round
with a Court-of-Guard about her, that stand in a
readines with iavelins in hand, and the *Qui va la* in the
mouth, with whom is but a word and a blow, or rather whose words are blowes, that fetch the bloud.
It is the *Metropolis* of the *Graces*, where they hold their
Comon-wealth, and where the Senat of al odoriferous Spices keepe their Court. It is the chiefest grace
of Spouses on their Nuptial dayes, and the Bride wil
as soone forget her fillet as her *Rose*. It is the maister-
peece of Nature in her garden-works, and even a
verie spel to Artizans to frame the like; for though
perhaps they may delude the eye, yet by no meanes
can they counterfeit the odour, the life, and spirit of
the *Rose*. When *Flora* is disposed to deliciate with
her minions, the *Rose* is her *Adonis*, bleeding in her lap;
the *Rose* her *Ganimed*, presenting her cups ful of the
Nectar of her sweets. It is even the Confectionarie-
box of the dantiest Conserves, which Nature hath to
cherish-up herself with, when she languisheth in Autumne: The Cellarie of the sweetest lickours, either
wine or water; her wines being Nectars, and her
waters no lesse precious then they, whose dryed leaves are the emptie bottles. In a word, the *Rose* for
beautie is a *Rose*, for sweetnes a *Rose*, and for al the
graces possible in flowers, *a verie Rose*; the quintessence
of beautie, sweets, and graces, al at once, and al as
epitomized in the name of ROSE.

THE

THE MORALS.

CASTO PERFUSA RUBORE.

T is a common Saying: *The honest Bride-* *The*
groome, and the bashful Bride. For so *Motto.*
when *Rebecca* first was brought to the
youthful *Isaac*, as a Spouse, she put
her scarf or veile before her eyes. So
Rachel did, and manie others. *Lucretia*
the Chast chose rather to wallow in her bloud, then to
survive her shame, wherin she blushed indeed, but yet
without cause; for yet stil she remaynes in al mens
mouths, *the Chast Lucretia.* The hart and cheeks have
their intelligences togeather, and the purest bloud is
messenger betweene them. The hart is put into a
fright; the obsequious bloud comes-in anon, and
asks: What ayle you, Sir? Goe, get you up, and mount
to the turret of the cheeks, my onlie friend, and cal
for help; the bloud obeyes, and makes the blush, that
rayseth such alarmes, in tender Virgins most especially. What feares the Virgin, when she blushes so?
The wrack of her honour; you wil say. How so? Is Honour in the Bodie, or the Mind? If in the Mind, the
Mind is a Citadel impregnable, not subiect to violence, nor to be betrayed, but by itself. Then blush
not, Virgin, for the matter; thy hold is sure enough,
and thou in safetie, if thou wilt thyself. But this of al
other Vertues, never is safe and secure enough; this
of al others feares the verie shadowes themselves,
and trembles like an Aspin-leaf at the least motions.
Now lookes she pale like a verie clowt; and now
through modestie, the colour mounts into her cheeks,
and there sets-up his ruddie standard, as if the Fort
were his; til feare againe prevayling, plucks it downe
And

And these were the vicissitudes our Sacred VIRGIN
had, when her glorious Paranimph discovered his
Embassage to her in her secret closet, presenting her
a shadow only, seeming opposite to her chast Vow;
wherat She trembled in his sight, CASTO PERFU-
SA RUBORE.

THE ESSAY.

Ehold heer the Princesse of flowers, the
Pearl of Roses, with al its varieties: the
Damask Rose, the *Musk-Rose*: The *Red*,
the *Cinamon*, the *Carnation*, the *Province*,
the *White*, the *Savage Rose* (which
growes in the *Eglantines*) and lastly the *Golden Rose*,
faire indeed to behold, but not so sweet. The Rose
growes on a speckled thorn, swelling into sharp or
pointed buttons somwhat green, which rives by little
and little, and opens at last, then unbuttons and discloses
its treasure, the Sunne unfolds it, and opens the lights
and leaves, making it display itself, and take life, so
affording it the last draught of beautie to its scarlet;
and now having perfumed it; and made the infusion
of Rose-water therinto, in the midst appeares, as in a
cup, certain golden points, and little threds of Musk
or Saffron, sticking in the hart of the *Rose*. But to
speake of the fires of its Carnation, the snow of the
white Satin, the fine Emralds, cut into little toungs
round about, to serve as a trayne to wayt upon it; of
the Balme and ambergrees, that breathes from this
little crop of gold, which is in the midst; of the
sharpnes of the thorns, that guard it from the little
theeves, that would be nibling it away with their
beaks; of the iuice and substance, which being
squeezed, embalmes al round about it, with its savour, of a hundred hidden vertues; as to fortify the
                                                hart,

hart, to cleer the cristal of the eyes, to banish clowds, to coole our heats, to stirre-up the appetite, and a thousand the like, were a world to deale with; but I hasten to the Mistris-flower herself, who mysteriously sits in this goodlie œconomie of Sweets and beauties, as in her Bower, wherin She delights to shrowd herself.

THE DISCOURSE.

wo things in the *Rose* chiefly doe I note: what inwardly it containes, and what vertue and qualitie the *Rose* outwardly gives forth. It is strange, the same should be hot and cold togeather; cold in the leaves, hot in the seed; so as passions proceeding of excessive heat, it alayes and qualifyes with its leaves; and with the heat and vigour of its seeds, it quickens and virifyes the frigid and melancholie affections of the bodie. Some men are tepid, yea cold in the love of God; they are so dul & stupid in Divine things, that they cannot rayse up the mind from terrene and earthlie cogitations, to sublimer thoughts; being immured with base affections. But our *Mystical Rose*, with the seed of Grace in her, wherewith She was replenished, inflames their harts to the love of God. Oh seed of our Rose! *She shal not feare her house for the colds of the snowes; for al her houshold are cloathed double.* This snow so cold, is a frigiditie of mind; but against this cold she cloathes her Devotes with double suites of charitie, to *God* and their *Neighbour*. Some also are hot, and most desperatly inflamed with the fires of Concupiscence; these heats she tempers and extinguishes with the deawes of her refrigerating grace, as with the leaves or mantle as it were of her gracious protection.

The Survey.

Trov. uls.

The

The *Rose*, the more it is wrung or pressed, the sweeter odour it sends forth, and yealds such a redolent fragrancie withal, that al are wonderfully taken with the odoriferous breath it gives: And this our *Rose*, the more she was wrung and pressed with the cruel fingar of tribulations and afflictions, the greater her sanctitie appeared. Being banished into Ægypt, she gave forth a most fragrant odour of *Patience*, wherewith she embalmed al Ægypt, and fructifyed afterwards into an infinit race of Deuotes, to her and her Sonne; witnes the *Pauls*, the *Anthonies*, the *Hilarions*, the *Macarians* of Ægypt. In the Passion of her Sonne, transfixed with the sword of sorrow, she yealded a sweet perfume of perfect *Fayth*. In other afflictions and tribulations she imparted the communicative odour of *Compassion*. For the torments which he suffered of the Iewes, she sent up the fragrancie of *Thanks-giving* to the heavenlie Father, from the Thurible of her Hart. And in the desolation she felt after his Ascension, for the absence of her Beloved, she powred forth incense of her holie *Desires* and incomparable Devotion. After al which odours, O give me leave, *most sweet and odoriferous Rose,* through *desires and devotion* to runne after *thee*; or, *doe thou but draw me after thee, unto the odour of thine oyntments.*

Cant. 1.

The *Rose* growes on thorns, but puts not on their nature; the thorns are churlish and rough, while the *Rose* is sweet and gentle. And *Our Rose* sprung indeed from the thornie stock of the Iewish race, but yet tooke nothing of the conditions of thorns with her. The Iewes were *prowd* and *haughtie*, She most *humble*; they ful of *vices*, she fully replenished with *grace*; the Iewes, we see, are Infidels, she the pattern and mirrour of *Fayth*; the

the Iewes *covetous* of earthlie and terrene things,
and she most *thirsting* after celestial. She sprung
likewise from the thornie *Eva*; but yet tooke not
after her nature. O thou *Virgin* (sayth *S. Bernard*)
most flourishing *Rod of Iesse*! through whom was re-
covered in the Branch, what had perished in the
Root! *Eva* was a branch of bitternes, *Marie* a branch
of eternal sweetnes. An admirable and most profound dispensation of the Divine Wisedome! that
such a *Rod* should grow from such a *Root*; such a
Daughter from such a *Mother*; such a *Free-borne* from
such a *Bond-slave*; such an *Empresse* from such a *captive*;
from so dry a *Thorn*, so flourishing a *Rose*.

What the *Rose* gives outwardly forth, are the
objects of three principal Senses: of Seing, Smelling
and Touching; and for the first, who sees not, that
hath the benefit of eyes, how gorgeous the *Rose*
is among al the flowers of the Garden, alluring and
attracting the eyes of al that enter into it? So our
incomparable *Rose, was exceeding faire; and with incredible beautie, seemed gracious and amiable to the eyes
of al.* She was a glad *spectacle unto* GOD, *Men and* Hest. 2.
Angels; to GOD, because so specious to her Sonne,
her Spouse, her GOD. *The King desires thy beautie,*
and sayes therefore: *Shew me thy face, for thy face is
comelie.* Unto men, she was so admirable for beautie Psal.
and grace, that *S. Denys*, that great light of the
Militant Church, beholding her, acknowledged himself to have been dazeled, and nigh transported from
himself. And for the *Angels* heare what the Prophet
sayes: *Al the rich of the people, shal implore thy countenance.*
And who are these rich, but the Angels, who beyond
others enjoy the riches of the heavenlie Kingdome?
Whence She is sayd to be the *Glorie of Hierusalem,* Iudith.
the *gladnes of Israel*, the *honour of her people*. 14.

As for

As for the odour she gave-forth of her Sanctitie, it is sayd: *The odour of thy garments*; which is of her outward vertues, being as the odour of incense, a grateful Sacrifice to God, which recreates those that are edifyed therewith.

And for the sense of *Touching* in the *Rose*, it is understood in a spiritual sense. Heare *S. Bernard*: Why feares human frailtie to approach to *Marie*? you shal find nothing terrible; She is wholy sweet and gentle; and being so sweet, is therefore to be sought-for, and embraced through devotion. *Take her then, and she shal exalt thee; when thou shalt embrace her, thou shalt be glorified by her.*

Cant. 4.

THE

THE EMBLEME.

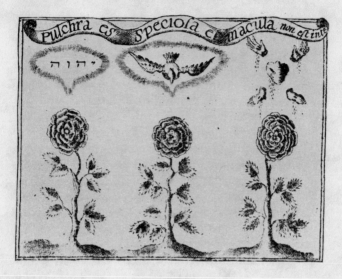

THE POESIE.

The Virgin *sprung even from the barren earth,*
A pure white Rose *was in her happie birth,*
Conceav'd without a thorne. This onlie Flower
The Father *rays'd by his Almightie power.*
When th' Angel said, she should conceave a Sonne,
She blushed, and asked, how it should be donne?
The Holie-Ghost inflam'd, and so the white
By him was made a Damask firie-bright.
Lastly her Sonne made her purple red,
When on the Crosse his precious Bloud was shed.
No Faith of Mortals then but had a staine,
Excepting hers; for she was died in graine.

The Pause.

THE

THE THEORIES.

 Ontemplate first, a gallant and odoriferous *Rose*, growing on a pricklie and
thornie stemme, and men with admiration to stand pointing at it, saying to one
another: What is that, there so shot-up, so
beautiful to behold, from so ragged, sharp, and harsh a
thorn? And then ponder, how the Angels stood amazed,
seing so our *Mystical Rose* transplanted from *Hierico*, into
the *Heavenlie Paradice*; or ascending rather so flourishing
from *the Desert*, when there was like questioning
amongst them, at her glorious *Assumption*, asking:

Cant. ult.

Who it was, that ascended flowing with delights?

Consider then the *Rose*, while it growes in the
Garden, and flourisheth, as it were alive; how it
cheeres and glads the eyes of al with its glorious
presence; and how, after it is cropt from its stemme
also, which is the death of the said *Rose*, what an odour
it hath with it, even after it hath been persecuted with
fire in the fournace of the Stil, as wel in the water, as
in the cake, and then think, what a mirrour and
pattern of sanctitie *Our Ladie* was, during her abode
heer in the garden of the World; and how she multiplied her favours to man-kind, especially after she was
translated thence, and had been proved and exercised
with infinit tribulations, leaving an unspeakable odour
behind, of miracles and graces; witnes the innumerable
Votes that hang on her Temples and Chapels through-
out the world.

Ponder lastly, that of *Roses* are made, sometimes
Electuaries, sometimes Oyles, sometimes Playsters,
and Conserves very soveraigne and medicinal for
manie diseases, namely foure: for first, the *Rose* forti-
fyes the stomack, and comforts the hart; secondly, it
stops

stops the flux of the venter; thirdly, it clarifyes the
eyes; and finally, heales the head-ach. So our *Mystical
Rose* comforts the hart, in affording it the Charitie of
GOD; restraines the flux of sinnes, through the Feare
of GOD, which she gives to eschew sinnes withal; clarifyes the eye of the understanding, by imparting to
it the knowledge of Divine things; and cures the head,
which is hope, *being the helmet of health,* when she *Thess. 5.*
rayseth our tepid hope, to desire Celestial things; and
therefore sayth: *I am the mother of fayre dilection, of feare,* *Eccl.* 24.
of knowledge, and of holie hope.

THE APOSTROPHE

Lower of flowers, O Rose *of roses,* O *The*
Flower of roses, O Rose *of flowers!* *Colloquie.*
Shore me up with flowers, because I
languish for love of thy love JESUS, *the
bud of thee* O Rose, *little in thy womb,
greater in thine armes, and then fayrest of
al, when opened throughly and displayed on the Crosse. By
that precious bud of thine, I beseech thee, and the sheading of
his most precious bloud, thou wouldst change my thorns into
roses; and present me, as a Rose of sweet odours, to thy
Sonne, and not as thorns for fuel of the fire of his indignation.
O grant me this, I beseech thee; and heer doe I present thee,
in honour of thee, the* Mystical Rose, *and thy* Sonne, *thy
soveraigne Bud, the Hymne that followes*:

> Salve CHRISTI sacra Parens,
>   Flos de spina, spinâ carens,
>   Flos, Spinati gloria.
> Nos spinetum, nos peccati
>   Spinâ sumus cruentati;
>   Sed tu spinae nescia.

THE

THE III. SYMBOL.
THE LILLIE.
THE DEVISE.

THE CHARACTER.

The
Impresa.

THE Lillie is the Scepter of the chast *Diana*; whose Flower-deluce, the crowne; and stemme, the handle; which she chastly wealds amidst the Nimphs of flowers. It is a Silver-Bel, without sound to the eare, but ful of sweets to the brim; and where it can not draw the eares, the eyes it wil; and inebriats the curious with its over-sweets. It is a Box of Civets, which opens to the *Zephirs*, and prodigally powers forth its spices to the standers round-about, though they

they come not very nigh it. *Flora* it seemes hath no
other Purse, then this of candid saffron, without strings
to shut it up; so prodigal she is of her sweets which she
wel knowes can never al be disbursed. Who had not
seen a *Lillie* heertofore, especially the Flower-deluce,
the Prince of Lillies, would start (no doubt) as with the
sight of a Garden-Comete, and cal in his friends
perhaps to gaze on a Blazing Starre or Garden-Miracle.
It is the ensigne of *France*, even vying with the *Brittish*
or *Lancastrian* Whiter Rose; if not so happie for her
Union with the Red, the Ensigne of Peace, yet in this
more happie, that she never was divided, to have need
of such a Union, as ever standing of herself. It is a
Quiver of amourous shafts, with golden heads, which
some cal hammers rather, against lust, to blunt the
thorns of lewd Concupisence. A verie Purselin cup,
replenished within, with the rarities of Nature, enough
to stupify and astonish the curious in the search of
secrets. It is besides a precious Pot of the purest Ala-
blaster, filled with the invaluable Spicknard of *Arabia*;
for sent and odour, as it were, fellow unto that, the
blessed *Magdalen* powred on her Maister's head; and
if you wil not beleeve me, approach but to the vessel
itself, and you shal feel it streight. To say no more, no
snow is found to be more white then it, nor gives a
greater flash of lightning in the eyes then it, that
sweetly dazels and not duls the sight.

E   THE

THE MORALS.

NIVEO CANDORE NITESCENS.

Hey are truly chast, whose mind and bodie never yet admitted stayne in the virgin-wax of their pure integritie, in either part. Chast is she held to be, and so is truly, that vowes her chastitie, and keepes the same, howbeit once stayned perhaps, at least with impurities of mind, and washed againe with the Laver made of the purest Bloud of the immaculate Lamb, she seemes indeed to follow the Lamb, wheresoever he goes. The Turtle-Widowes are accompted chast, and so they are, that having lost their virginal integritie, are re-borne anew, as it were, both in mind and bodie, with a chaster purpose, never more to choose another earthlie Mate, or Turtle-Dove, to follow and consort withal; but instead of such, make choice to linck themselves from thence-forth to a heavenlie *Spouse*; and who, trow you, but the *Spouse of Spouses?* and that for ever. The *Vestal-Virgins* were esteemed such by al their *Flamins*, though they had a bodilie integritie, and no more, while the mind perhaps was secretly a Prostitute to al impurities. And if there was anie of them, as some there might be, who kept both the one and other sort of purities indeed, yet were they not vowed perpetually to be such; and so were chast, though they shined not with that snowie chastitie; which, if it be, were, and ever shal be so, is not yet the perfectest chastitie of al, nor anie way such, as the *Queen of Virgins* was, and therefore worthily sayd to be : NIVEO CANDORE NITESCENS.

THE

THE ESSAY.

WHEN Nature is in her cheefest iolitie, she tapistryes the whole Univers *The Review*. with a world of delicious flowers. And to say truth, these flowers are even the smiles and laughters of the Earth, that sees herself now delivered of the cruelties of the Winter, and long captivitie. She seemes therin to take pleasure, recreate, and disport herself; to diaper the face of the earth in a thousand fashions, enameled with as manie rarities; while the gentle breaths of *Zephirus*, with the sweet influences of Heaven, mixing their moystures, with the heats of the April-Sun, make that whole diversitie, which is in the bosome of the earth, al sowed-over with a thousand seeds, now mortifyed with the austerities of the winter. When they are come forth, Nature solicitous of these treasures so odoriferous, seekes to guard them carefully, and adorne them curiously; arming some with thorns, others with prickles; covering these with rough, and others with large and shadie leaves, to conserve their luster. Among the which the *Lillie* carries hers very long, and green; the stem, high and round, streight, united, fat, and firme, al clothed with leaves. On the top wherof, grow out as it were certain wyers, with heads theron, or buttons somewhat long, of the coulour of the hearb, which in time grow white, and fashion themselves in forme of a bel of satin or silver. From the bottome and hart therof, grow upright, some litle wyers of gold, with heads like hammers of the same. The leaves wherof, of an exquisit whitnes, al streaked and striped without, goe enlarging themselves, like a bel, as before is sayd. The
seed

seed remaines in these hammers of gold. The stem to
carrie the head the better, is knotted and strengthned
through-out; for that the *Lillie* is ever with the head
hanging down-wards, and languishing, as not able to
beare up itself. There are some of them red, some of
them azure. These are al so delicious, that even to
behold them were a great delight.

THE DISCOURSE.

*The
Survey.*

THE *Liseron* is a *Lillie* also, though a bastard
of that kind, without odour and those
wyers above, made as an essay, or practice,
and first draught of Nature, endevouring
so to forme patterns, to frame some maister-piece of
the true *Flower-deluce*, the *Prince* of *Lillies*. Our incom-
prable VIRGIN is this *Flower-deluce*, that Princesse of
Lillies, for the manie sympathies and faire resemblan-
ces it hath with it. The *Lillie* is white without, and gold
within, and both within and without, most fragrant
and odoriferous; and the Blessed VIRGIN was most
faire and beautiful in her flesh, through the candour of

Sap. 7.   her virginitie: *She, the candour of the eternal light; and
the glasse without spot.* In mind she was al inflamed, as
the burnisht gold. *Gold* (as *Aristotle* sayth) can not be
corrupted; nor could Her *Charitie* be ever extinguished.

Cant. 8.*c.*   For, *manie waters*, as it is said, *can not extinguish charitie.*
And how sweet She was both inwardly and outwardly,
who sees not, that considers her Humilitie, in the
lowlines of her hart within, and outwardly in her
conversation? Which Humilitie of hers sent forth such

1. *Cant.* 1. an odour unto God, as allured and attracted him to her:
*When the King was in his seaty, my Nard gave forth an
odour:* to wit, her Humilitie: And these are the *Lillies*:
Virginitie, Humilitie, and Charitie, which cheefly
                                           invironed

invironed the *Blessed Virgin*, while her litle IESUS was hanging at her breast, being *fed among Lillies*; for if these be not *Lillies*, what are they?

Againe the *Lillie* hath a streight stem or stalk, tending wholy and directed upwards, but the leaves pendant and hanging downwards; and the Virgins mind like a staf was alwayes streight, and tending to GOD, in yealding him thanks for his benefits, and ever magnifying his holie Name. For as the *Lillie* whatsoever odour and candour it hath, directs it to heavenwards: So MARIE, what sanctitie or grace soever she had, offered it up al unto GOD. But for the leaves, her words, they were alwayes bent to the earth, in speaking perpetually most humbly of herself. Whence sayd she so affectuously: *My soule doth magnify our Lord*; behold the stem of this *Lillie*, how streight it was, and how directly ascended to the Heavens: But see the leaves now, and marke how they looke downwards: *He hath regarded the lowlines of his handmayd*, and the like.

The *Lillie* besides is always fragrant, and of a most sweet odour: and our *Lillie* was perfumed with an odoriferous oyntment, which made her so fragrant and redolent, composed of three odoriferous spices: *aromatizing as Balme, Mirrh, and Cinamon*. For she was *Embalmed* by the *Divinitie*, when the Deitie was lodged in her; spiced with *Mirrh*, through the guift of Angelical puritie and Virginitie; and enflamed with a sweet Divine love, which is as the powder of Cinamon heer understood, hot in smel, and tast; hot in smel, and therefore as love, *draw me with the odour of thy Oyntments*, to wit, with the love of thy heavenlie graces; hot in tast, and therefore Divine; because we are bid to *see and tast, how sweet our Lord is*. Of which oyntment it is sayd in the Canticles: *The odour of thine oyntments, is beyond al spices.* *Eccl* 24.

Cant. 1.

Besides,

Besides, the *Lillie* hath the root and stem, six-square or corner-wise. So the root of *Charitie* in this *Paragon*, hath six points with it: the first, a love of GOD above al things; the second, wherewith she loved her owne soule, conserving the same in al sanctitie; the third wherewith she loved her bodie, keeping it entirely for the Divinitie; the fourth, wherewith she loved her domesticks and familiars, instructing them in al vertue; the fift, wherewith she loved her friends, in GOD; The last, wherewith she loved her enemies, for GOD.

And to conclude, as the Bed-chambers of Kings are adorned with *Lillies*, that they may rest more deliciously among them: so the *Virgin*, not the Chamber only of a KING, but of GOD also, was dressed-up and beset al with *Lillies* round-about; according to that: *Thy womb as a heap of corn hedged-in with Lillies*; for she was al encompassed with *Lillies*: above, being enclosed with the *Lillie* of eminent *Charitie*; beneath, with the *Lillie* of profund *Humilitie*; inwardly, with the *Lillie* of internal *Puritie;* outwardly, with the *Lillie* of *Virginitie*; on the right hand, with the *Lillie* of *Temperance*, in prosperitie; on the left, with the *Lillie* of *Patience*, in adversity; before, with the *Lillie* of *Providence*, in future things; behind, with the *Lillie* of *Gratitude*, for passed benefits. And since she was so environed and enclosed with *Lillies* of al sides, the Church sings of her: *As the dayes of the Spring, doe the flowers of the roses environ her round*. Among which *flowers* of Roses and *Lillies*, the *Beloved*, that is CHRIST, is feeding: *My beloved to me, and I to him, who feeds among the Lillies*.

Cant. 7.

Cant. 2.

THE

THE EMBLEME.

THE POESIE.

The
Pause.

A Pure-white Lillie, like a silver Cup,
The sacred Virgin humbly offers up.
Her constant, stedfast, lowlie Hart (the foot,
Which al supports) is like this flower's root.
The stemme, her right Intention; and the bole
(The flower itself) is her chast spotlesse Soule.
The yellow knobbes, which sprowting forth are seen,
Is radiant Love, which guild's her Cup within.
In lieu of liquides, is a fragrant sent:
Her vertues odours, which she doth present.
Her Sonne accepts al, that she offers up,
GOD, Part of her inheritance, and Cup.

THE

THE THEORIES.

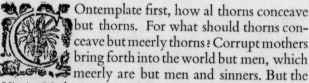Ontemplate first, how al thorns conceave but thorns. For what should thorns conceave but meerly thorns? Corrupt mothers bring forth into the world but men, which meerly are but men and sinners. But the *Virgin-Mother* conceaved the Holie of Holies. *She* now a *Lillie* conceaved, and afterwards produced the *true Lillie of the vallies*; a Lillie of Virginitie, the Lillie of Maiestie: through whose candour is darkness expelled; with whose odour, are raysed the dead; with whose touch, are the leaprous cleansed, and al the infirme and diseased cured. And therefore how much this *Lillie* of ours, is to be exalted above al the other Daughters, iudge you, and ponder it wel.

Consider then, that though there were manie other Virgins besides, conspicuous and eminent for sanctitie, yet were as thorns; for that they had some blemish in them; since howbeit they were pure in themselves, yet the *fomes* of sinne was not extinguished in them; who were indeed as thorns to others, that have been touched and incited with concupiscence towards them. Wheras the *Virgin-Mother* was wholy priviledged from al guilt, in whom was that *fomes* altogeather extinguished, and was accomplished with so intense a Chastitie, that with her inestimable Virginal puritie, she so penetrated the harts of the beholders, as she could not be coveted of anie; but for the time rather extinguished al lust of concupiscence in them. O beautie of Virginitie and Humilitie, wherewith the Sonne of GOD was so allured and ravished!

Ponder lastly, that as the *Lillie* hath a most efficacious vertue against leaprosie, ulcers and the holie-fire, as also against the stinging of serpents: So the *blessed Virgin*

Virgin being conceaved as a *Lillie*, was endued with such vertue of the Divine grace, that neither the leaprosie of Original sinne, the fire of concupiscence, nor the biting of the old Serpent, could anie wayes hurt her.

THE APOSTROPHE.

Lillie of Lillies, *and next the* Lillie (*thy dearest Sonne*) *the purest of al* Lillies. *Alas! most pure and immaculat* Virgin, *shal I alwayes live in the slaverie and servitude of this impure flesh of mine? And shal I ever be troubled and vexed with these unchast cogitations, and impure apprehensions, which so macerate my unwilling soule? Oh, thou elevated and raysed above al pure creatures,* most blessed Virgin, *I say* Blessed *with al benediction! how long? Alas! how shal I sustaine* the bodie of this death, this impure thistle of the bodie, with its thorns? Alas, when shal I be delivered and rid therof?

The Colloquie.

THE

THE IV. SYMBOL.
THE VIOLET.
THE DEVISE.

THE CHARACTER.

HE *Violet* is truly the Hermitesse of flowers, affecting woods and forests, where, in a lowlie humilitie mixt with solicitude, she leads a life delicious in herself, though not so specious to the eye, because obscure. She is a great companion to the Primrose, and they little lesse then sworne sisters; with whom, when she is disposed, she wil recreate herself whole nights and dayes: and you shal likely never find them

them farre asunder. When they are so in companie in
the wood togeather, where she is bred and borne, they
make an excellent enamel of blew and yelow; but
being by herself alone, as in her celle, she is a right
Amethyst. Had *Juno* been in quest, to seeke her Bird, as
strayed in the woods, she would easily have thought
these purple *Violets* had been her *Argoe's* eyes, as
shattered heere and there, and dropt downe from her
Peacocks trayne; and so wel might hope to have found
her Bird againe, as Deere are traced by their footing.
She is even the Wanton among leaves, that playes the
Bo-peep with such, as she is merrie and bold withal;
whom when you think you have caught, and have
now already in your hand, she slips and leaves you
mockt, while you have but her scarf only, and not her
self. She is the Anchoresse, sending forth a fragrant
odour of her sanctitie, where she is not seen; which she
would hide ful faine, but can not. She is the Herald of
the Spring, wearing the Azure-coat of Armes, and pro-
claiming sweetly in her manner to the spectatours the
new arrivall of the wel-come guest. She is the *Primitia*
or hastie present of *Flora*, to the whole Nature.
Where if the Rose and Lillie, be the Queene and Ladie
of Flowers, she wil be their lowlie handmayd, lying at
their feet, and yet happely (for worth) be advanced to
lodge in the fayrest bosomes, as soon as they; as being
the onlie Faire affecting obscuritie and to lye hid,
which other Beauties hate so much.

THE

THE MORALS.

HUMI SERPENS EXTOLLOR HONORE.

The Motto.

Irginitie indeed is a specious and glorious thing, and hath somewhat of the Angel with it: but yet nothing so happie as Humilitie is, which hath in truth somewhat els withal, as it were Divine. Virginitie and puritie invited the Word to take up his lodging in the *Virginal womb*; but Humilitie was it, that strook-up the bargain between the Immaculat *Hostesse* and the Divine *Guest*. And hence arose the source of al her advancements. The Angels are pure indeed, but lower then their nature is, they can not stoop; since *Lucifer* himself even after his fal retained his nature stil, which he could not forgo: thrice happie they, had they not aspired higher then they were indeed. But the *Eternal Word* could stoop so low, and really did, to be lesse then Angels. If *Puritie* then be a glorious, specious, and Angelical thing, *Humilitie* is a vertue more then Angelical, as being Divine. The Angels would faine have risen higher, but could not; they tryed their wings, and with that *Icarus* (that daring youth) had a shameful fal. But the purest of al Virgins in contemplation of the Eternal Word, readie to stoop so low, wheras she was to be truly the *Queen* of *Angels*, stiles heer herself *the lowlie handmayd of our Lord*; when creeping on the ground as low as might be, she came to be exalted to the highest dignitie next her Sonne, in human nature, and might worthily say: HUMI SERPENS EXTOLLOR HONORE.

THE

THE ESSAY.

ONE would think, the Authour of Nature had *The*
made choice of the *Violet*, to couch his *Review.*
enamel, and to make the delicatnes of his
pencil shine therin, and the fairest coulours of the world, to border the mantle
of the Spring withal. There are some purple, but with
the finest purple; some as snow, fashioned into litle
flowers, like curdled milk, and blazoned as with
Argent leaves, al sowen thick with little odoriferous
starres: Others are of *Ore musked*, or of *Violets* meta-
morphosed into most sweet gold, cut into blossomes.
There are some deckt with a hundred and a hundred
leaves neatly fitted togeather, and al as grafted into
one stemme, which casting themselves into a round
and folding within one another through a sweet
œconomie, agree to frame and compose a very dayn-
tie and delicious *Violet*, as faire as sweet, mingling,
with a gentle confusion, a thousand coulours, which
simpathize exceeding wel, and glad the eye. Behold
the *Violet* of *March* and *April*; *May* and *June* have theirs
a-part, being of a changeable coulour, having the top
and edge of purple, white in the midst, and guilded
beneath in the bottome. What a marvelous enamel to
see the *argent*, the *purple*, the *Ore*, and *azure* of the
leaves, which shade round-about, al coming forth of
a litle green tuft, from a litle sprig, with a string, that
serves as a pipe for Nature to distil her musks, that
breathe from thence. The leaves are somewhat round
in their peering forth, and jagged; and then after
extend they in length, and spread themselves. Their
great vertue comes from a litle fire wel tempered in
them, and a sweet heat, which is the predominant
qualitie

qualitie of their complexion, and makes them sweetly
bitter. To renew their forces againe, when they are
decaying, they steep them in vinagre; and it is incredible, the vertues these little flowers have; for they
mollify hardnes, alay heats, and extinguish inflama-
tions: the juyce softens the venter, dissipates and
evacuats choler, sweetens the asperitie of the lights,
alayes the fire that burns the breast; with infinit other
things, most soveraigne for use.

THE DISCOURSE.

EHOLD now the *Violet*, which after the
Rose (the Queene of flowers) and the
Lillie (the honour of gardens) I should
think might follow wel in *Our Ladyes
Garden*, as an excellent Type or Symbol of
her. It is a flower wel knowne to al, familiar and domestical with al Nations. For where have you a Garden,
that hath not store of them? yea the woods togeather
with the Primrose seeme to be as strewed with them
as tapistryes; they are so diapred al-over with those
flowers. And our glorious VIRGIN is as easie and familiar
to approach unto, as it. The honour of this *Violet*, is in
the Spring; or rather is the *Violet*, the honour of the
Spring. Because the hoarie and horrid Winter now
passed over, and the rigid frosts and snowes dissolved,
the pleasant season of the Spring returning, the Earth
seemes to put forth the *Violet*, as the *primitias* of flowers,
togeather with the Primrose her inseparable companion, to welcome it with; a hastie present indeed,
but yet a rare one. The Spring of Grace so appearing,
and opening the breast, after so tedious a Winter
overpast, of horrid Sinne and frozen Infidelitie, our
MARIE the *Violet*, or the *Violet-Marie* rather, is put forth
as a joyful present to glad the time withal.

This,

This flower I find now to affect the hils and mountains, though there want no store and plentie of them
in the plaines and vallies also; and, as gardiners use to
say, it loves to be transplanted to and fro. And so our
Violet heer was no lesse transplanted in her *Visitation*,
when she *Rising up, went hastily into the mountains.*
For loe, this *Violet* sprung at first and grew in the
vallies, to wit, of herself; but was then transferred and
removed into the mountain of Perfection, to the
mountain of Glorie, mountain of Fame, Honour, and
Exaltation: but yet was admirably planted in the valley
of Humilitie. A strange thing truly, and more then a
Garden-miracle, that our *Violet* should stil remaine in
the valley, and yet be placed on a Mountain! yea the
higher she was exalted on the Mountain, the better she
was rooted in the Valley: both on the same Mountain,
and in the same Valley, at one and the self-same time.
Now, Philosopher, tel me, what would you more?
can not the same thing be in two places at once? It
may; MARIE on the Hil of exaltation, and the self-same
MARIE in the Valley of demission, fulfilling therin the
precept of the Wise-man: *How much greater thou art,
do thou humble thyself in al.*   *Eccles.*

And now see, I pray, the haste the *Violet* makes
above al flowers, to entertaine the Spring; and then to
behold our *Violet* made to clime the mountaines,
would make you wonder, to see her in such haste. For
who would not admire to see a tender Virgin, great
with child, to fly from the valley, over hils and dales,
through thick and thin, to the mountain-tops? But yet
wonder not, while we dayly see great engins moved,
and that most swiftly too, by force of fire: GOD *is our
consuming fire.* This fire then the *Virgin* carried in her   *Deut. 4.*
bosome; She is stirred and excited with the blast of the
Holie-Ghost, unto offices of pietie. The fire breaks
forth;

forth; what marvel then, if it carries so the engine of
the bodie with it? I say, what marvel, while the Spirit
of GOD, whose Symbol is Fire, carries her so fast
through publick places, to shun the aspect of men (so
contrarie to the inclination of Virginal modestie) to
hide herself in the house of her *Cosen?*

The *Violet*, as the Rose also, being planted neer the
leck, or garlick, becomes more fragrant in odour; so
as the ungrateful sent of the one, gives a sweeter
favour unto the other; and therefore the Gardiner
plants it neer unto them, to have it send forth a greater
odour. Now the *Virgin-Mother* being in herself a most
odoriferous *Violet* above al other *Violets* and roses of
the world, breathed from herself the sweetest odour
of al vertues. *The odour of her garments were as the odour
of the fulfield.* But in her house at *Nazareth*, which
signifyes *Flowerie*, this *Violet* shined lesse, and, as a
Violet, lay hid within her leaves. Wherefore it seemed
good to the expert *Gardiner*, her heavenlie Spouse in
her womb, to transferre this *Violet* with his Spirit into the mountains of *Judea*, being places al set with
garlick and leeks, as I may terme it; Where *Zacharie*
and *Elizabeth* sat sheading of teares for the Redemption
of *Israel*, the proper effect of those hearbs; which
She through her coming wiped away, and further
gave forth a greater odour of sanctitie, then ever; for
loe, she filled the whole house with the odour of her
Vertues.

THE

THE EMBLEME.

THE POESIE.

I N Heaven the humble Angels GOD beheld; *The*
And on the earth, with Angels paralel'd, *Pause.*
The lowlie Virgin viewd; Her modest eye,
Submissive count'nance, thoughts that did relye
On him, that would exalt an humble wight,
And make his Mother. Alma, ne're in sight,
With vertues, fragrant odours, round beset,
Close to the earth lay like the Violet;
Which shrowded with its leaves, in covert lyes,
Found sooner by the sent, then by the eyes.
Such was the Virgin rays'd to be Heavens Queene,
Who on the earth neglected, was not seene.

F   THE

THE THEORIES.

The Contemplation.

Ontemplate first, how, as *Plinie* sayth, the *Violet* is soveraigne against the *Squinzi* in the throat, the *Catharre* in the eyes, and *Impostumes* in the bodie. So *S. John Baptist* was before his Sanctification, being as ulcerous and *impostumat*, as we al before Baptisme, through Original Sinne: *Elizabeth* continually powring forth teares, for the barrenes and sterilitie as wel of the Sinagogue, as of herself: and *Zacharie's* throat being stopt with the *squinzi* of Infidelitie, so as he could not speake. MARIE the *Violet* entering into this Hospital, the *impostumes* of *John* vanished, the *defluxions* of *Elizabeth* ceased, and *Zacharie's squinzies* were unstopt; and finally health was restored to the whole house.

Consider then againe, how, as *Plinie* sayth, the seed of the *Violet*, is the infallible destruction of the *Scorpion*; then which, what more expresly in Symbolical Theologie declares the *Mother of* GOD to be a *Violet*? For this malediction was given by GOD against the accursed Serpent, from the first beginning: *I wil put enmities between thee and the woman*; *and thy seed and her Seed*; *and she shal tread (or it shal tread) thy head.* No seed more opposit to the Scorpion, then that of the *Violet*; nor none to the Serpent so much, as the Seed of the *Virgin*, JESUS.

Ponder lastly, how the *Violet* by some is called the *Flower of the Trinitie*; perhaps for the triple coulour which is found therin: for that, as in the *Violet* are seen the violet, the purple, and the golden coulour; and as those coulours in the natural, so in the *Violet* MARIE may you consider, the *Violet* coulour of *Humilitie*, the *purple* of her *Chastitie*, and the *golden* coulour of **Maternitie**

Maternitie or *Charitie* in her; since her *Charitie* was the cause of her *Maternitie*, and consequently, she the *Violet* of a *Trinitie*.

THE APOSTROPHE.

Faire and goodlie Flower, *the true* Aurora *of*   *The* *the* Spring, *the gladsome* Herbinger *of the* *Colloquie.* Spring *of grace, thou fairest of al flowers, and yet who holdst the lowest place, stil grounded in thy Nothing!* O *that this true contempt of my-self were planted once and rooted in the ground of my hart! that this lowlines of hart, I say,* O Ladie Violet, *and humilitie of spirit, were imprinted for ever in my soule!* Oh *obtaine for me.* Alas! *doe. I conjure and beseech you to it, by al the reverences and respects, which the* Sonne *of* GOD, *the* Wisedome *of the* Father, *hath yealded you in heaven; and which the* Great GOD *your* Sonne *no lesse hath afforded you on earth.*

THE

THE V. SYMBOL.
THE HELIOTROPION.
THE DEVISE.

THE CHARACTER.

The Impresa.

THE *Heliotropion* is the loftie Cedar of flowers, wherin the Sun, could he nestle himself, would choose of al the rest to build his neast; for birds, we know, breed where they hant most, and delight to harbour and converse in, al the day. It is even the Eye, and nothing els but Eye, to behold the Sun; which she never shuts, til he sincks down in *Tethis's bed*; where being drowned over head and eares, she wincks and shrowds herself the while, in the thin eyelids of her leaves, to meditate upon him. It is the Arsenal of

crimson-

crimson-flags displayed to the *Pithian Apollo*, in despite
of *Mars*, whom she adores as God of Armes as wel
as Books; wheras *Mars*, if you take him from his speare
and shield, can neither write nor reade. It is the
Gnomon of the Garden, a Dial artificially made in
hearbs, to expresse al the howers of the day; a verie
needle, pointing to its radiant Starre; which being so
restles as it is, makes her as restles everie whit; with
this difference only, that he measures infinit degrees of
Heavens, and she as manie points. It is a verie Mart of
silks, sarcenets, taffeties, and satins, al of Gingeline in
graine, because in fashion. If the Rose excel in savour,
which she professes not to utter in her shop, she vowes
to be more loyal and constant to her Paramour, then
it. She is so amourous, and dotes so much upon him,
that she can not live without his conversation; which
she hath so much, as she almost is turn'd and quite
metamorphosied into him, and now become already
in the Garden, what he is in his Zodiack, the true and
real flower of the Sun, or Sun of Flowers, as he himself
the Sun of starres, or that great Starre they cal a Sun.
It is the true *Alferes* of hearbs, bearing up the standard
of *Flora*, amidst the rest of flowers; the *Pharus*, to direct
the Garden-Nimphs, when they loose themselves in the
labyrinth of flowrie knots or Maze of flowers: the
Beacon al on fire, to give warning to the rest of flowers
of the arising of the Sun, to beware of his parching
rayes, for feare of withering before their times. It is
even the *Daphne* of flowers, whom *Phœbus* followes
al the day; and, if she fly, she hath her eye on her
shoulder, to looke behind her, as she runnes.

THE

THE MORALS.

AD ME CONVERSIO EIUS.

Ictures likely are so framed, that be you in the roome, in anie part, they wil seeme to look upon you. Looke where the Panther is, in woods and forests, there wil commonly other beasts resort, to look and gaze upon him; whether it be the beautie of his spotted coat, or sweetnes of his breath, which attracts, I know not; but this is sure, the effect is so, as I have heard. The Turtle seemes to have no eye but for his mate; and where they sit togeather, their eyes wil be as glued upon each other. The *Pole* that drawes the *Needle* to it, the load-stone that attracts the iron, the ieat that puls the fescue, what is it els but a natural instinct, or Moral rather I may say, of more then mutual love that makes the one so powerfully to allure, and the other to be so easie and willing to be drawne? This I am sure of, *Vertue* is so specious, and so goodlie a thing, that it drawes the eyes of al to look upon her; and where they have not harts to follow her faire steps, yet wil they stand to gaze upon her, and admire at least. The litle JESUS lying in the Crib, like a *Loadstone* drew the *Shepheards* from their flocks, *Kings* from their peoples, a *Starre* from the rest of the fellowship of starres, yea even the *Angels* from the Heavens, to sing a *Gloria in excelsis* unto *God*, and *peace* to *men*: What trow you, but a secret instinct, that could be no lesse then Heavenly and Divine, made so great a conversion of Terrestrials and Celestials to a *litle Infant?* And as for the *Mother* her self, that held him in her lap the while, she before

sitting

sitting in her little *Nazareth* obscure, drew so the eyes of the *Almightie* to her, that He could not choose, but so convert himself unto her, as to descend and lodge within her, and she truly say: AD ME CONVERSIO EIUS.

THE ESSAY.

HE honour of our Gardens, and the miracle of flowers, at this day, is the *Heliotropion* or *Flower of the Sun*; be it for the height of its stem, approaching to the heavens some cubits high; or beautie of the flower, being as big as a man's head, with a faire ruff on the neck; or, for the number of the leaves, or yellow, vying with the marigold; or, which is more, for al the qualities, nature, and properties of the Flower, which is to wheel about with the Sun; there being no Needle, that more punctually regards the Poles, then doth this *Flower* the glorious *Sun*. For in the morning it beholds his rising; in his journey, attends upon him; and eyeth him stil, wheresoever he goes; nor ever leaves following him, til he sink downe over head and eares in *Tethis's* bed, when not being able to behold him anie longer she droops and languishes, til he arise; and then followes him againe to his old lodging, as constantly as ever; with him it riseth, with him it falles, and with him riseth againe. Nature hath donne wel in not affording it anie odour at al; for with so much beautie and admirable singularities, had there been odour infused therinto, and the sweetnesse of odoriferous flowers withal, even men, who are now half mad in adoring the same for its excellent guifts, would then have been stark mad indeed, with doting upon it. But Nature, it seemes, when

The Review.

when first she framed a pattern for the rest, not being throughly resolved, what to make it, tree or flower, having brought her workmanship almost unto the top, after a litle pause perhaps, at al adventure put a flower upon it, and so for haste, forgot to put the Musks into it. Wherupon, to countervaile her neglect heerin, the benigne *Sol*, of meer regard and true compassion, graced her by his frequent and assiduous looke with those golden rayes it hath. And as the Sun shewes himself to be enamoured with her, she, as reason would, is no lesse taken with his beautie, and by her wil (if by looks we may guesse of the wil) would faine be with him. But like an Estrich, with its leaves as wings, it makes unprofitable offers, to mount up unto him, and to dwel with him; but being tyed by the root, it doth but offer, and no more. It is like the *Scepter* which the *Paynims* attribute to their Deitie, that beares an Eye on the top; while this flower is nothing els but an Eye, set on the point of its stem; not to regard the affayres of Mortals so much, as to eye the immortal Sunne with its whole propension; the middle of which flower, where the seed is, as the white of the eye, is like a Turkie-carpet, or some finer cloth wrought with curious needle-work, which is al she hath to entertaine her Paramour.

THE DISCOURSE.

The Survey.

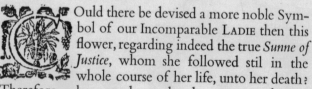 Ould there be devised a more noble Symbol of our Incomparable LADIE then this flower, regarding indeed the true *Sunne of Justice*, whom she followed stil in the whole course of her life, unto her death? Therefore, whom we have already represented, as a *Rose, Lillie,* and *Violet,* let us now contemplate, as a true
Heliotropion.

Heliotropion. Compare we then, first, by certain Analogies, the Sunne, being the king of Planets, with the *Sunne of Justice*, King of the Sunne and Planets; and the *Heliotropion*, with the *Virgin Marie*. The *Sun chief of Planets*, fils the earth with his influences: the *Sun of Justice*, the world, with the effects of his power. The *Sun of Planets* is the First cause, among the Seconds; the *Sun of Justice* the First before them al; that traverses al places, this penetrates al harts; that lends his light to the moon and starres, this gives both life and being to al creatures. The *Sun*, the Planet, is the origin of life, the *Sun of Justice*, life itself; that is soveraignly visible, this most soveraignly intelligible. In the *Sun of Planets*, is fruitfulnes, light, and heat, essentially but one and the self same thing; and the *Sun of Justice*, with the *Father*, and the *Holie-Ghost*, substantially is but *One God*. The *Sun of Planets* was never without these properties; nor the holie Divinitie of the *Sun of Justice*, without these Three eternal Persons. And for our *Ladie* herself; our faire *Heliotropion*, as the *Sun of Planets* illumines the Starres, so the *Sun of Justice* enlightened her thoughts. The *Sun of Planets*, is the eye of the world, the joy of the day, the glorie of heavens, the measure of times, the vertue of plants and flowers, the perfection of the starres: and the *Sun of Justice*, is the eye of her thoughts, the joy of her hart, the glorie of her soule, the rule of her desires, the vigour of her spirit, the maister of her loves, and even the center of her propensions. He was, I say, the object of her looks, the Monark of her wils, the thought of her thoughts, the light of her understanding, and the absolute Moderatour of al her passions.

Looke where the *Sun* is, the *Heliotropion*, being nothing els but eye, hath the same stil cast upon it: and so the *Virgin* had the eye of her soule, stil on the
Sun

Sun of Justice. I to my beloved, and his conversion to me.
Examine each day of her blessed life; runne over the
howers, tel the quarters, discusse the moments, and
you shal alwayes find *her* turned to the *Sun*. In her
Nativitie, an *Heliotropion;* in the *Presentation*, an *Heliotropion*; in the *Annunciation*, an *Heliotropion*; in the
Purification, and everie action, a true *Heliotropion*. For
she never sayd, did, or thought anie thing, which she
directed not to God as to the Authour, which she
reduced not to him as to the last end, which she began
not for his service, and finished not for his glorie, and
lastly, wherin she followed not *her Sonne*, that true
Sun of justice, which is to be *a true Heliotropion* indeed.
And for her bodilie eyes, she was directly so, when
she stood dolourous by the tree of the Crosse, on
the top wherof was Christ the true *Sun* indeed in the
height of the *Zodiack*, as in his proper Orbe, when
not only with the face, but with the whole bodie also
she regarded her *Sonne*, and with eyes fixt attentively
indeed, beheld him fully: and as the flower *Heliotropion*
is wont to flag with the leaves at the setting of the Sun,
so likewise was she (had she been left only to the
strength of nature) readie to fal and sinck to the ground,
when her *Sonne* drooped.

   Plinie wonders at the *Heliotropion*, for converting
itself to the Sun, even under a clowd, and that in the
night also; but Marie, our true *Heliotropion* heer, takes
not her eye of *Contemplation* of from her *Sonne* so much
as in the night. For manie *Doctours* most constantly
hold her *Contemplation* was never interrupted so much
as in her sleep; and that she slept in bodie, but waked
in hart. *I sleep, and my hart wakes.* There was never
knowne a time more clowdie, nor ever night more
obscure then that, wherin the *Sun of Justice* being set,
the whole light seemed quite extinguished; nor anie,

Heliotropion

Heliotropion appeared in the Garden of the *Church*, so to gaze on the Sun under a clowd, but only those two beautiful *Heliotropions*, *John* and MARIE; never creatures better resembled that flower, being of the self-same posture, of the same pale sad coulour; and with the whole countenance cast stil upon him, and she especially, not taking off her eye from him, who was enwrapped in the clowd of Death.

Behold now this rare *Heliotropion* of *Ours*, even at the point of death, as she lay a-dying; dying, doe I say, or sleeping rather? For if the death of anie mortal wight may be tearmed a sleep, surely that of the *Mother* of *God* is not to be called a death so much, as a sweet Sleep. She lyes in her death-bed, as burning al with love, like a true *Heliotropion* turning to her *Sonne*, stil casting her eyes upon him. *I to my beloved, and his conversion unto me.* The *Eternal Father*, like the Sun, darts most radiant beames of love upon her: she endeavours of the other side, with reciprocal looks of love, as darts, to returne to him the like, but sincks and fayles in the midst of the endeavour, and like a flower hangs downe the head, and dyes. With this kind of death, the Fathers of the *Church*, clients of that great *Mother*, affirme, she was translated from the earth, and assumpted into heaven.

THE

THE EMBLEME.

THE POESIE.

The
Pause.

Eer you behold the handmaide of the Sunne,
That waites upon him, as his stallions runne.
There in the Moone an other flower attends,
And followes her, that borrow'd brightnes sends
Upon its gazing eyes. Eve, like this flower,
Was al for change. Her happines an howre
Continued not. Alas! 'twas altred soone;
Affected Deitie, was like the Moone,
Which she beheld, But Marie's thoughts were high,
Upon the Sunne of Justice fixt her eye;
Her Soule, with al her powers were stil theron,
As flowers and leaves of Heliotropion.

THE

THE THEORIES.

ONTEMPLATE first, how as soone as the *The* golden Sun peers and puts forth his head *Contem-* in the morning, the *Heliotropion* displayes *plation.* itself to the Sunnie beames, circles with the Sun, and when he comes to the West, bowes downe the head, and sits with him. So MARIE, as soone as CHRIST, the *Sun of Justice*, arose in his nativitie framed and composed her countenance to his, with him fetching her compas in the *Zodiack* of his life, she ordered her course, as it were, by the same coasts: by the *South of Love*, when he redeemed mankind; by the *North of Patience*, in so manie adversities; by the *East of Resignation*, when he satisfyed the Eternal *Father*, by his passion; and lastly in the *West*, in the setting of her *Sonne* the *Sun*, in her solitarie retirement til his glorious *Resurrection*, the new *Aurora* of the Eternal day.

Consider then, how we first convert not ourselves to the *Sun of Justice*, nor attract the rayes of the Divine benignitie unto us: but he with a gracious cast of his beames, upon the *Heliotropion* of our Hart, excites the flower, and allures it to turne the face unto it back againe. *Convert me, and I shal be converted*, sayth the *Ierem.* Prophet. But the *Mother of God*, the true *Heliotropion* 31. 18. indeed, doth otherwise; and therefore, *I to my beloved*, that is, I convert myself unto him; and so it followes: *and his conversion unto me.*

Imagine you behold artificially painted, a JESUS sporting in his *Mothers* armes; looke which way you wil, of anie side, he alwayes seemes to have his eyes cast upon you. So surely the most sweet face of JESUS, whose eyes shine like starres, of their parts are

always

always converted towards thee; so as if thou per-
ceavest not thyself to be especially regarded by them,
it proceeds no whit from them, but from thyself, who
turnest away thy face, or dost not marke or eye them
at al. Wheras our *Heliotropion* heer never takes off her
eyes from her *Sonne*, but hath them alwayes cast upon

Cant. him: and therefore truly may say: *I to my beloved, and
his conversion unto me.*

THE APOSTROPHE.

*The
Colloquie.*

Fairest Virgin-flower! *Thou most specious and
amourous* Heliotropion, *more happie then the
rest of flowers, for those especial favours from thy
Spouse, being no lesse then the glorious and
radiant* Sun of Justice. O gracious Queen of flowers!
O *Sacred* Prodigie *of al Gardens, and most stupendious*
Heliotropion, *the miracle of Paradice, the amazement of
Philosophie, wonder of Nature, fruitful Virgin, Virgin-
Mother! O mediate for me, with thy amourous* Sun, *thy*
Sonne, *and obtaine for me, through thy example, I may
become a true* Heliotropion, *with mine eyes stil cast upon
thee my object, and may receave like glances from that
al-seing Eye.*

THE

THE VI. SYMBOL.
THE DEAW.
THE DEVISE.

THE CHARACTER.

THE *Deawes* are the sugred stillicids of Nature, falling from the Limbeck of the Heavens, as so manie liquid pearls, and everie pearl as precious as the truest Margarits. They are liquifyed Cristal, made into so manie silver-orbs as drops. They are the verie teares of Nature, dissolved and soft through tendernes, to see the Earth so made a *Libian* Desert, which she supplies of meer compassion with the ruine of herself. No teare she sheads, that stands her not

The Impresa.

not in as much, as a drop of her deerest bloud. They are the grayne and seed, once reaped from the Ocean fields, and sowne againe upon the Earth, for a better harvest. They are the sweatie drops of *Tethis* face, which the benigne *Sol* exhales and wipes away for the use of *Tellus*. They are the *Manna* of Nature, to vye with those Corianders, food of Pilgrims, made by Angels: with this unhappines, they could not be congealed, to make a food so much for men, as a Nectar for the plants to drink. They are the *Protheus* of fresh waters, diversifying into as manie coulours, as they light upon; and are so courtlie withal, as they wil easily comply with everie thing they meete with; and likely seeme to put-on the forme, the garb, and qualities of everie one: so as I verily beleeve, had they but toungs to speake, they would say the same with everie one, that can so temporize with al. And as the showres were wrung and drawne from *Magdalen* through contrition of her sad and clowdie hart: so these *Deawes* are wrung and strained from heaven, through compression and mutual collision of the clowds. The Bees are the most laborious and industrious Factours for these Pearls; and they wil venture for them, as farre into the ayre, as any Moor shal dive into the seas for the best pearls. In fine, they are the Milk of Nature, wherewith she is disposed to suckle creatures at her owne breast.

THE

THE MORALS.

RORE MADENS, RORE LIQUESCENS.

HE sweats of that great Monark, were *The Motto.* held to be perfumes; and why? Perhaps because they took some Deitie to be in him, for his so strange and prodigious Conquests. The trees that have a gummie and viscous lickour in them, looke what they have within, the same they oft put forth; and if they sweat at al, they sweat but gummes. The *Spouse*, when he knockt so long at his *Spouses* doore, and could not be let in, was al wet with *Deawes* from heaven; and no marvel, that *Deawes* should fal on him, from whom al *Deawes* proceed; since *Deawes* exhaled from the earth, do thither distil againe. When the *Saviour* of the world was borne, arose a Spring of oyle, to signify the infused Oyle of Grace was then powred forth into the world. And what is Oyle in drops, but *Deawes* of oyle? and what is it to spring, but to ascend upwards? what to *Deaw*, but to spring downe? Our *Saviour* then being *Oyle* of *Grace*, was dissolved al into *Deawes* of graces, when he was borne. In this, looke what the *Sonne* was, the same the *Mother* is, with this difference, He the Fountaine of Grace and Mercie essentially the same, she the fountaine likewise, but participant of his; and as He through her distils downe *Deawes* of Grace and Mercie: so she from him distils the selfsame *Deawes* of Grace and Mercie; and therefore rightly RORE MADENS, RORE LIQUESCENS.

G THE

THE ESSAY.

EER now, must I needs confesse mine ignorance; for otherwise should I loose myself, in considering of the one side, the accompt which GOD and Nature make of the *Deaw*, and of the other, the poornes of this litle creature in itself. The voice of men, that set it forth, is more rich and copious farre, then what soever is in the *Deaw* itself; it is but even a litle fume, and oftentimes an unholesome exhalation raysed from some corrupt marishes or other, drawne-up to the second stage of the Ayre (being the Matrice as it were of Nature, whence hayls, snowes, frosts, and the like proced) if it arrive so high; where being dissolved, and recollecting itself, within a litle after thickens and turnes into litle teares, which falling downe againe, affords us nothing but a meer Seren infected, and breeds often very mortal catharres, lighting on our heads. See now a trim and goodlie thing, for us to make such reckoning of. And yet how manie treasures doe I see enclosed within these litle drops, within these graines of Cristal liquifyed? What think you then, is it ought els, then a litle water! Oh, do not think so of it; for if *Plinie* say true, that the *Deaw* takes the qualitie of the thing it lights on, that which to you seemes to be a water only, is Sugar in the Reeds of *Madera*, Hypocras in the vine, *Manna* in the fruits, Musk in the flowers, Medicines in the Simples, Amber in the Poplers, the verie milk of the breasts of Nature, wherewith she nourisheth the Univers. The *Deaw* it is which falling on our gardens, empearls them with a thousand muskie gemmes: Heer it makes the Rose, there the Flowerdeluce; heer the Tulips, there the

violets;

violets; and a hundred thousand flowers besides. It is
the *Deaw*, that covers the rose with scarlet, that clothes
the lillie with innocencie, the violets with purple,
which embroders the marygold with gold, and
enriches al the flowers with gold, silk, and pearls, that
metamorphosies itself, heere into flowers, there into
leaves, and then to fruits in sundrie sorts; it is even the
Protheus and *Chamæleon* of creatures, clothing itself
with the liverie of al the rarest things; heer scarlet,
there milk, heer the emerald, the carbuncle, gold,
silver, and the rest.

THE DISCOURSE.

Ut now come we to the mystical *Deaw*   *The*
indeed, the Incomparable *Ladie* and *Queene* *Survey.*
of al the Meteors of this Region of
ours, or of the other, the Æthereal or
Celestial. Who if she were not the *Deaw*
itself, she was the *Fleece* al steept in *Deaw*, and consequently may wel be held for *Deaw*; for she is sayd to
be *ful of Grace*, which is a kind of *Deaw*. The *Deaw* is
properly engendred in the spaces and regions of the
Ayre, tempered with heat and cold. Three Regions
there are: The Heavens, the World, and Hel. This
Deaw of Grace, was not engendred in the upper Region
that is, in *Heaven*; nor was the work of the *Incarnation*
of CHRIST effectually wrought therin, because he
assumed not the Angelical nature: *He apprehended not* 2 *Pet* 2.
the Angels; Nor beneath, that is, in *Hel*: because he redeemed not Divels, or spared them, or shewed mercie
to them: *God pardoned not the Angels sinning*; But it was *Gal.* 4.
engendred in the midst, that is, the *Incarnation* was
wrought in this *middle Region*, because therin the *Divine*
hypostasis assumpted human nature to itself. *God sent his*
Sonne

Sonne made of a woman. Now was this *Deawing* or *Incarnation* made, as I sayd, of hot and cold. For *God* vouchsafed to become *Man,* for two respects, that is, out of abundance of charitie, of the one side, which was excessive heat, and out of a general miserie of ours, which was a kind of benumming cold. From this heat therfore, to wit, from this Charitie of GOD, and from this cold, the general miserie of mankind, was wrought roration or *Deawing,* that is, the *Incarnation* of the *Sonne* of *God*; with this onlie difference, that there, was a temperate heat and cold togeather, but heer a heat, *Ephes.* 2. with a great excesse, *through his too much charitie, where- with he loved us,* and a great frigiditie of languour in us, *Psal.* or a languishing frigiditie: *Because al have declined, and are become unprofitable.*

Moreover, this roration or *Deaw* we speake of, was made in our Virgin-earth, who being watered with Celestial *Deaw,* brings forth the *Nazaræan flower,* that sayth of himself: *I am the flower of the field.* Againe: *Let flow thy speech like Deaw, and as drops upon the gras.* To which the Church alluding sayth: *Let him descend into* *Osee* 14. *the Virgins womb like Deaw therin.* This earth therefore so moystned and watered with *Deaw,* produced the *Lillie* of *Paradice. I the Deaw of Israel budding like the Lillie.* This *Israel* is interpreted *a man seing God,* and heer signifyes our incomparable *Ladie,* who was truly Masculin in al her actions, beholding, as it were, the Divine Essence, through *Contemplation.*

I wil now then marvel no more, that GOD leaving al other creatures, should take complacencie as he doth to be the *Father* of *Deawes,* the Scriptures saying: *Iob* 38. *Who begat the drops of deaw? and who is the Father of rayne?* You would say, he meant that there is nothing, which better represents the Divine generation of the Sonne, which is begotten of the Father by way of

Understanding;

Understanding; from whence as from a fruitful clowd,
distils the Divine *Deaw* of the Word: *Let my word flow
like deaw*. But for the *Incarnation* itself, it seemes to be
just the verie same. For the *Sun* of the *Divinitie* therin
united to the little poore vapour óf our mortalitie
hath fertilizd this beautiful *Paradice* of the *Church*,
the *Deaw* watering the same, which fel from the Five
Wounds of JESUS, that deawie clowd suspended in the
ayre, and hanging on the tree of the Crosse.

Hence it is, that GOD makes so great accompt of
this *Deaw*; for when he would make a feast for his
people, in the wildernes, he did it by meanes of the
Deaw, which was then converted into *Manna*, and
Manna virtually into al meats. And if GOD would
make him a chamber al of gold, or a cabinet for himself, surely he would choose the *Deaw* to be his house:
Who puts the clowds his bower, etc. God makes as exact Psal.
esteeme of a simple drop of *Deaw*, as of al the world
besides. *Before thee* (sayth *Salomon*) *is the whole world as a
drop of morning-deaw*. You wonder now at a smal matter;
but I wil tel you yet a thing more strange, which
is, that since the Sonne GOD of a litle graine of mustard
sayes: *The kingdome of heaven is like to a graine of mustard-
seed, etc.*, me thinks, I might say as wel: *The kingdome
of heaven is like to a drop of Deaw*: For the *Saviour* of
the world, who is the graine of mustard-seed, is likewise this same rich drop of *Deaw*. For as the *Sonne* of
God in outward apparance was, as it were, no bodie,
nor seemed to make anie shew, yet when the *Sun of
the Divinitie* once began to appeare in him, he shewed
himself to be the vertue of Paradice, even so a little
drop of *Deaw* falling from the heavens, for example,
on the Flowerdeluce, would seeme perharps to you
but a little round point of water, and a meer graine of
Cristal, but if the Sun do but shine upon it, Ah! what
a miracle

a miracle of beautie it is? while of the one side it wil looke like an Orient-pearl, and being turned some other way, becomes a glowing Carbuncle, then a Saphir, and after an Emerald, and so an Amethist, and al enclosed in a nothing, or a litle glasse of al the greatest beauties of the world, that seeme to be engraved therin; so manie drops, so manie Orient-pearls, so manie drops of *Manna*, wherewith the Heavens seeme to nourish the earth, and to enrich Nature, as being the Symbol of the Graces, wherewith GOD doth water and fertilize our soules.

For what should that *Fleece* of *Gedeon* signify, but the Grace of graces, the admirable grace of the *Incar-nation* of *Christ* to be wrought in the conception of the Divine Word, in the virginal womb or *fleece* of the said *Gedeon*, which was replenished with the *Deaw* of the Holie-Ghost, in liew of the verie *Deaw*; that is, where descended the fulnes of the Divinitie, she being worthily called and compared to a *fleece*, since she hath cloathed the *true Lamb of God with her flesh, who takes away the sinnes of the world*? O *Virgin* worthie of al grace! How art thou graced indeed, and favoured above al the Daughters of *Jerusalem*! since thy head, JESUS CHRIST, came so to thee, ful of *Deaw*, and reposes in thy chast bower?

THE

THE EMBLEME.

Benedicta inter mulieres. luce. c.1.

THE POESIE.

The Pause.

Ot like a duskie clowde, which Sol *exhales*,
Nor like a gloomie mist, that shrowdes the vales:
But from the Earth, the Sunne of Justice *drew*
A purer vapour, which dissolv'd the Deaw,
Distilling from the Limbeck of the skies,
Our drie and barren Earth doth fertilize.
The barren womb erst was accurst; but she,
Though Virgin, was a faire and fruitful tree.
Women bring forth with paineful throbs and throwes;
She was a Mother, but not one of those.
Mongst women blest, *drawne by heavens radiant beames,*
Twixt clowd and mist, pure Deaw *twixt both extreames.*

THE

THE THEORIES.

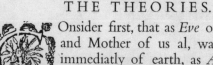

Onsider first, that as *Eve* our first Parent and Mother of us al, was not created immediatly of earth, as *Adam* was, but taken from his rib (it being a priviledge only due to *Adam*, so to be framed of virgin-earth) and was therefore called *Virago*, fetching her extraction as it were *a Viro*: So our second *Eve*, our Spiritual and Celestial *Mother*, adopting us, and engendring us as children, through the *Deawes* of Celestial graces procured us from heaven, was not made of virgin-extraction herself, that is, was not framed of the Divine or Angelical nature, as a *Deaw* exhaled from the virgin-element of waters, but of the pure human nature, as drawn from the mixt, bitter, and brackish waves of the Sea, by that great *Architect* of heaven, the *Sun of Justice*, giving her the name of MARIA, to wit, *a mari amaritudinis*, as it were, fetcht from the Ocean of bitternes of human kind. And now with her graces and favours, as *Deawes* falling from heaven, perpetually doth nothing, but showre downe upon her children and Devotes.

Consider then, how our *Ladie* became as a marine *Concha*, or Oyster of the Sea, which opens itself to receave the *heavenlie Deaw* into her *Lap*, that so the precious Gemme might be engendred in it, which when it hath received once, it closeth up again, not to loose so precious a *depositum*, til it be fairely delivered, and brought forth in time prefixed. Even so our incomparable *Ladie*, the precious vessel of so heavenlie and Divine a *Deaw*, having once conceaved the same within her virginal Womb, retires herself into her *Nazareth*, to ruminate on the mysterie she had within her, until necessitie drew her to *Bethleem* and the time prefixed of the deliverie of her *fruit* was come;

for

for then as purely as she receaved it, she gave it up most perfect and compleat, and made therof a rich present to the world.

Ponder lastly, how the *Deaw* being a meer extract from the Seas, exhaled by the vertue of the Sunnie rayes, which when he can hold no longer, lets it fal to comfort and refresh al sublunarie things, and drawing it againe unto himself, lets it fal againe for the same end; and so wil do, to the end of the world, for the comfort and solace of man-kind. So the humanitie of our *Saviour Christ*, as a waterie *Deaw*, being extracted from the virgin *Marie* (*amaro mari*) and through the Sunnie rayes of the Divinitie assumpted up to heaven in the glorious *Ascension*, through love not able to stay any longer, descends againe in the blessed *Sacrament*, to recreate and refresh us Mortals, and so as often as we desire, is readie to visit us with his supercelestial and divine *Deaw*, and thus til the consummation of the world.

THE APOSTROPHE.

O *Thou* great Ladie, Mother of grace and mercie, *who in a strange and marvelous manner hast been replenished with the* Deaw *of grace in a soveraigne degree*; *I beseech thee, intercede for me, that I may likewise be replenished and filled with grace, fervour, love, and the Divine delights of thy* Sonne, *whom thou receavedst from heaven as the* Deaw *fallen into thy virgin-lap. And this I beg O blessed* virgin-Mother, *through the virginal milk, wherewith thou fedst that little great* GOD *in person; and by the teares of joy thou shedst for the deare embraces of so great a* Sonne *of thine, and by al the sweetnesses of his Divinitie, which made thy blessed soule to liquify with joy. O Ladie, O virgin-Mother, O my sweet Advocate, to thee do I recurre to impetrate these grates for me, at his hands, who sitting on thy lap, and hanging at thy breasts, can deny thee nothing.*   THE

The Colloquie.

THE VII. SYMBOL.
THE BEE.
THE DEVISE.

THE CHARACTER.

The Impresa.

THe *Bee* is that great little Architect of houses made of wax, as of playster of *Paris,* al ciment, and no stone, while you find not a stone or rub in al his works. He is a great Enginer in that mould, working his subtle mines til he be al in a sweat, which in truth is no more then a moisture he hath with him through his so much padling, and medling with deawes. It is a world to see, what mines and counter-mines they wil make amongst them, to supplant one another,

another, whereupon manie suits of law arise between them. For you must know, they have a notable goverment, and a wise and politick reason of State with them, which though it may seeme to partake of al, yet is in truth a pure Monarchal rule, and surely the best. As the *Venetians* have their Duke or Doague, they have their King, enthroned doubtles and invested with a more absolute authoritie then he, and yet not apt to slide or degenerate to Tyranie, as some would imagine. And if the *Venetians* have their Senat and Magnificoes, they have the same. The King for sword of justice, hath his sting, which he weares for terrour rather then use, whose best armes is a certain sweet and serene Majestie with him, which makes him loved rather then feared, if not feared for love: yet were anie so refractarie as not to love so sweet a Majestie, he could tel, how to bend the brow. He is then the great Dictatour above al, and true *Augustus Caesar* of that great Common wealth of little *Romans*. The *Bee* of al others makes his vintage in the Spring, because his chiefest harvest is in the sugred deawes, that fal upon the tender blossomes, at that time, wherof part they tunne up in pipes, for the purpose, to brew their meade with, against the winter; and churning the rest as handsomly as they may, they make it into a kind of butter, we cal honie, which they crock and barrel up for greatest marchandise. They are but Pigmies, in respect of the Giants amongst them, whom for their thundring voice, they cal *humble-bees*. Nor can you know the rest by their voices only, while the least wil carrie as great a horn about him, as the biggest of them. They are notable husbands abroad, and good huswives at home; for so they are both, or neither, as having no sex amongst them; which if they have, they are Mayds, or Bachelours everie one, because they
have

have no marriages with them, as living very chastly togeather like so manie Angels.

THE MORALS.

OPEROSA ET SEDULA.

Labour and Industrie are Brother and Sister, dwelling in the same house. He is strong and robustuous with *Atlas* shoulders; She as quick and nimble of the other side. It is incredible, what these two are able to do, when they joyne togeather; they wil work wonders, move mountains, and runne through stitch with everie thing. *Rome* indeed *was not built on a day*, but yet with labour and industrie in short time became the Metropolis of the whole world. What a work was that, which the infamous *Incendiarie*, to eternize his name, ruined in a moment, which Labour and Industrie had reared-up from the verie foundation to the roofe? The great Mausoleas, Amphitheaters, Piramids (and what not?) have al been built and finished by them. If Labour once fayle, Industrie anon rouzes him up: and then wil they roundly fal to their work as fresh as ever. Wheresoever they meet, he is the Bodie, and she the Soule; and as the Bodie and Soule cannot be divided without ruine of the person, so Labour without Industrie is no bodie, and wil presently come to nought. The Grace of the *Holie-Ghost* wheresoever it is, is Industrie itself, and knowes no delayes; it is as gunpowder set on fire, which carries the bullet, though of lead, more swift then an arrow, where it goes. The tender *Virgin-Mother* of *God* had this powder of Industrie in her, when conceaving with fire, through the

the match of *Fiat*, she flew so nimbly over hils and dales to her Cosen *Elizabeth*, the subject of *Charitie*; wherin truly she shewed herself OPEROSA ET SEDULA.

THE ESSAY.

He *Bee* is the greatest Politick in the world; the goverment of their litle common-wealth is most admirable. The King is he that hath the best presence with him, and a Royal looke; al his subjects obey him with submission and reverence, not doing anie thing against their oath of alleageance. The King himself is armed with Maiestie and beautie; if he have a sting, he never makes use of it, in the whole manage of his estate. He carryes nothing but honie in his commands; one would not beleeve the great severitie and courtesie there is amongst them, living in communitie, with good intelligences abroad, al goes with them with weight and measure, without errour or mistakings. In the winter they keep wholy within, not knowing otherwise how to defend themselves from the force of the weather and violence of the winds, and hold their little assemblies, in some place deputed for that effect, and keep correspondencies one with another; but for the drones and idle bees, they banish them quite from their common-wealth. They commit not themselves to the discretion of the weather abroad, until such time as the beanes begin to blowe, and from that time they wil loose no day from labour. They frame the wax from the juice which they suck from flowers, hearbs, and trees; and for honie they derive it also from trees and gommie reeds, having a glue and viscous lickour on them. They wil make their wax likewise of everie herb and flower; save only,

The Review.

only, they never light on a dead or withered one.
Their sting is fastned in their bellie; and when they
stick it so, as they cannot draw it forth againe without
leaving the instrument behind, they dy of it; and if
the sting remaine but half, they live as castrat, and
become as droans, not being able to gather either honie
or wax.

THE DISCOURSE.

The
Survey.

THE mellifluous *Doctour S. Ambrose*, in his
sweet *booke of Virgins*, sayth: the *Bee* feeds of
the deaw, engenders not at al, and frames the
honie. Which three properties peculiarly and singularly
appertaine to *Virgins*; but most expresly and sublimely
of al to the *Sacred Virgin* herself, the *Queen of Virgins*.
For as al other creatures live of the earth or water,
as birds, beasts, and fishes, some few excepted, to
wit, the Camæleon of the ayre, and the Salamander
of the fire; the *Bee*, as a choicer creature, more curious
then the rest, feeds no worse then of the deaw, that
falles from Heaven; and wheras al other creatures
(not bred of putrefaction) are subject to libidinous
heat in their kinds, the *Bee* is free therof, and multiplies
by a way more chast; and where other creatures are
wholy maintained at their Maister's charge, and some
wil eate you more then their bodies are worth, or
their labour comes to, the *Bee* makes its owne provision of itself, and leaves his owner rich with the
bootie and spoyle they make of the flowers of the field,
without anie cost or charge of the Maister; so industrious they are, to the great confusion of men.
Just so our *Ladie*, not taken with the bayts and allure-
ments of this world, for spiritual life, lived not but of
the heavenlie deaw of Divine grace; being capable of
no other

no other heat, then of the chast and amourous fire of
Divine Love; not conceaving Fruit, but by an admirable, mysterious, and miraculous way, through the
work of the *Holie-Ghost*, remaining a Virgin before, in,
and after her Child-birth; and lastly framed without
anie cost or merits of ours, that Honie of honies, that
Honie-comb distilling, which carries the honie in his lips.

The honie indeed is engendred in the ayre through
the favour and influence of certain starres; as in the
Canicular dayes, we may note betimes in the morning,
the leaves to be charged and sugred with it. Such as
go forth at that time, before day, shal find themselves
to be moistned therewith, which the *Bees* suck from
the leaves and flowers, and tunne-up in their little
stomaks, to discharge againe, and to make it perfect
honie in al points, for the use of men. So our incomparable *Virgin* receaving this *Dew* or honie of the
Eternal Word, as it came from Heaven into her
Virginal womb, so wrought it in *her*, as being delivered
therof, it proved a honie most apt for the use of man;
the true *Bread of Life* indeed. Most happie *Bee*! and a
thousand times most blessed HONIE!

Where it is to be noted, that *Bees* are exceedingly
delighted with these things: first, with faire and serene
weather; for then those deawes more plentifully fal and
are more delicious: and of the contrarie in the raynie
and more boysterous weather they are wholy hindered
from their vintage, as it were, or gathering those
sugred deawes. Secondly, they are pleased much with
abundance of flowers; from whence they gather
their purest honie; for though the deawes fal upon
the leaves, and they gather it no doubt from them also,
yet is it not so delicious and pure; for the nature of
deawes participats much of the places they light on,
which makes the *Bee* farre more busie and industrious
on the

on the flower, then on the leaves. Thirdly, they are
wonne with a sweet sound. For *Aristotle* sayth, they
are exceedingly allured with the harmonie of musick
and sweet sounds; which we ordinarily practise now
adayes, to stay them with, when they are in a great
consult to take their flight and be gone, for then with
the striking of a pan only insteed of other musick are
they brought to settle themselves neer home; so
Musical they are. And lastly, they joy greatly in sweet
wine, as we find by experience and daylie practise, as
often as they begin to swarme, and are now on the
wing and point to travel into forren parts.

Al these things the *Blessed Virgin* was exceedingly
affected to, and had them al, as it were, within her;
as first a serenitie in the internal conscience, where
appeared no clowd in the ayre of her Mind, and where
the pacifical *Salomon* sat peacefully indeed as in his
Ivorie Throne, *Al the glorie of the King's daughter, was
wholy within her*. Then had she the flowers of al Vertues
and Graces within *her*, to wit, the diversities of al
vertues, the *lillies* of *chastitie*, the blush and *modestie* of
the *rose*, the *hope* of the *Violet*, the *charitie* and Divine
love of the *Heliotropion*, and the like. *Her soule was a
Garden* of al flowers, and no lesse then a Paradise, which
had the Archangel as Paranimph and Guardian thereof,
with the two-edged sword of Humilitie and the chast
Feare of God. O delicious Paradise, and more then
terrestrial, even when she was dwelling on the earth!
Thirdly she was affected to Musick, and very rare and
singular therin, as appeares by that excellent and
melodious Canticle of *hers*, the Divine *Magnificat*, so
chanted now adayes in the world, and taken-up in the
Church, for an admirable peece of that Art, to vye with
the Angels, the Cherubins, and Seraphins themselves,
to frame the like. Not yet was *she* so pleased, to heare
herself

herself sing only, as to listen to her *Spouse, the voice of her beloved knocking* and saying: *My sister, open unto me*; to whom she would answer againe: *Behold, my beloved speaks unto me. Oh let thy voice stil sound in mine eares*! and a thousand other affects of her Musical hart would *she* dayly sing besides to the Angelical troups, which environed her round. And lastly for her love to wine, that is, to the Angelical Nectar, *she* was dayly feasted with, of spiritual gladnes, as tasts before hand, of her future joyes, which might appeare by the quantitie *she* tooke of those wines, and the qualitie againe by the frequent extasies of love *she* would breake into, remaining in her Closet, as we may piously beleeve, being inebriated therewith.

H

THE EMBLEME.

THE POESIE.

The
Pause.

TO Bethlem's sillie shed, me thinkes I see
  The Virgin *hasten like a busie* Bee;
  Which in a tempest subject to be blowne,
  In lieu of ballast, beares a little stone;
As 'twere with oares beats to and fro his wings,
Collects heavens deaw, which to the hive he brings.
Within that store-house lyes the daylie frait.
Lets fal the stone. Even so of greater weight,
Cut without hands, *the* Virgin *now is gone*
To lay the prime and fundamental stone,
Heavens Deaw condens'd was in the honie-comb.
She was the Bee, the Hive her Sacred Womb.

                           THE

THE THEORIES.

 Ontemplate first, how little soever the *The* Bee seemes, yet how great its excellencies *Contem-* and eminencies are; and measure not *plation.* the singular properties it hath, with the outward shew it gives forth. For though it seeme no more indeed, then as raysed but a little higher than an ordinarie fly; yet is it a miracle in nature, an astonishment to men, and a livelie Symbol of our *Blessed Ladie*; who being so singular and eminent in al prerogatives and graces, Celestial and Divine, made no greater a shew, then *she* did in being so private in her Closet or Oratorie, where *she* was, as a *Bee*, in her Cel a-framing the delicious honie of *her* admirable examples of life, to sweeten the world with, for after-ages. Where you may note her stupen-duous humilitie, that seing herself elected the *Mother* of *God*, and consequently the *Queene* of *Angels* and *men*, yet held herself to be no more then as a serviceable *Bee*, to worke the precious honie of Man's Redemp-tion, in her Virginal Womb, when *she* sayd: *Behold the hand-mayd of our Lord*.

Consider then, that as one of the properties of the *Bee* is, when it is on the wing, and feares to be carried away with the winds of the ayre, to take up a stone, to keep itself steadie therin, through the poyse therof: So our blessed *Virgin*, in her highest contemplation of heavenlie mysteries, which was frequent and ordinarie with her, would take herself to her little *Jesus*, the mystical stone (for *Christ was a Stone*) for *S. Paul.* feare of being carryed away with the wind of vanitie; *she* would fly and soare aloft, but yet hold *her* to her little Nothing, which she ever tooke herself to be.

O admirable

O admirable humilitie of our incomparable and industrious *Bee*!

Ponder lastly, that if the *Bee* is so admired for its singular guifts of Continencie, of Policie, and Industrie, and especially so affected by al men for the benefit of the honie they receave from it; how admirable needes must the *blessed Virgin* be? so chast, as to be the first, and onlie patterne of al Chastitie, both Virginal, Coniugal, and Vidual; so wise, politick, and welgoverned in herself, to have Sensualitie so obedient to Reason, and Reason to GOD, as to have no deordination in her, either of the inferiour to the superiour part; and so industrious withal, as to work so exquisit a loome of al Perfection, as wel Human as Angelical, in the whole course of her divine life. Yea how ought she to be honoured and worshipped of us al, for the Celestial and Divine fruit she brought us forth, that mellifluous Honie of the Divine Word Incarnate and made Man in her most precious and sacred Wombe?

THE APOSTROPHE.

The Colloquie.

O Great *Monarkesse and Princesse of intercession in heaven, most constant and immoveable in thy Virginal purpose, who hadst rather not to have been so great in the kingdome of* God, *then to falsify thy promise and vow of perpetual Virginitie, if in being the* Mother *of* God, *the same had been put in the least danger*: O help me then to guard *this inestimable treasure of* Chastitie *in my state of life! by that sweetest* Honie-comb *thou bredst within thee, and broughtst into the world, thy deerest* Sonne. *Ah, let me not be perfidious, disloyal, or a breaker of my faith, nor rash in my good purposes made to His Divine Majestie. For that,* O soveraigne Ladie, *displeases him highly, and offends thee likewise, deare* Princesse *of Virgin-soules.*

THE

THE VIII. SYMBOL.
THE HEAVENS.
THE DEVISE.

THE CHARACTER.

THE *Heavens* are the glorious Pallace of the *Soveraigne Creatour* of al things; the purple Canopie of the Earth, powdred over and beset with silver-oes; or rather an Azure Vault enameld al with diamants, that sparckle where they are. And for that there is aloft above this seeling, they make a paviment likewise for the Intelligences and Angelical Spirits, strewed, as become such inhabitants, with starres. It is a Court, where those blessed Spirits, as Pensioners, stand continually assisting in the

The Impresa.

the King's presence, with the favour to behold him to face in his greatest glorie, while the Starres as Pages attend in those spacious Hals and lower roomes. If al togeather, should make up the bodie of an Armie ranged and marshalled in the field, the Spirits themselves would make the Cavalrie, and the Infanterie the Starres, *S. Michael* General of the one, and *Phoebus* of the other; where even as the Foot, that are as the Corps of the whole Batallions, make a stand; so remaine the whole multitude of Starres al fixt in the Firmament, while the Planets, which are as the Collonels of the rest, with the speedie Coursers of their proper Orbs, fly up and down to marshal the Legions, and to keepe the Companies in their due squadrons. If they shoot, their shafts and darts, they send, are but their influences they powre on mortals and terrene things, good and bad; some sweet, of love; as those which *Venus* shoots from her Regiment, headed with gold; some with steel, as those of *Mars*, and his troups; and some againe, as more malignant, dipt in venome, as those of *Saturn* and the *Caniculars*. As the Earth hath beasts, the *Heavens* have their Lion and Beare, the great and lesse. Where the Sea hath fish, the *Heavens* have theirs, and waters enough, as wel above as under the Firmament. As the Ayre hath birds, the *Heavens* have Angels, as birds of Paradise. And if the upper Region of the Elements be of fire, the Seraphins are al of amourous fires of Divine love, and the highest order of the blessed Spirits.

THE

THE MORALS.

CAPACITATIS IMMENSAE.

Hat great Galleasse or Argosey of *Noe* The clapt under hatches the Epitome of the *Motto.* world; which yet virtually contained that vast volume or tome of the greater World. The *Troyan* horse held a whole Ambuscado in his bellie of warlick *Grecians* in compleat armour. Yea the Eye of man, though *de facto* it reach no farther then the Hemisphere only, yet of it-self is able to extend to the ful immensitie of the whole Sphear, were it placed as Center therof. But that were to make the *Heavens* the visible Object of the Eye only: I wil then go further. The Hart of man as it is, how little soever, if it be wel purged, is able to walke through the heavenlie vaults, both above and beneath; I meane, contemplate the Starres and Spirits themselves, with the immense capacitie of that wast dwelling of theirs. But what were al this but a meer extension and perlustration of the mind only, wholy occupyed in measuring Intellectual Objects? It is the Local continencie, I meane, as the kernel is contained in the shel, and the like. I say that great Amphitheater of *Pompey* was but a nutshel, as it were, of so manie sonnes of men, compared with the Globe of the Earth, and the earth with the Zodiack of the Sun, and the Sun againe being paraleld with GOD himself. It is GOD only, who truly beholds al Objects, both Intellectual and Visible; and truly containes them al, being present to al, comprehends al, is Al in Al. And yet this great Al, whom the *Heaven* of *Heavens* can not containe, hath the Virgin-Womb of the immaculate *Mother* of *God* conceaved

conceaved and held in *her* lap, as the *Church* sings;
and therefore is sayd to be, and that most rightly, and
worthily too, CAPACITATIS IMMENSAE.

THE ESSAY.

He *Heavens* with their circuit, cloathe
and mantle al the world, and with the
sweetnes of their influences nourish the
same, and distil a life into it. They are
the House of GOD; the floare and pavi-
ment of Paradise; the Garden of the Angels, al beset
with starres instead of flowers, with an eternal Spring;
the Temple of the Divinitie; and the azured Vault of the
Univers. The number of the *Heavens* hath not alwayes
been agreed upon; for one while they beleeved, there
was but one onlie, wherin the starres did sweetly glide
heer and there, and glance along, as in a liquid cristal
floud. Sometimes have they allowed of eight, by
reason of so manie divers Motions and Agitations
very different in them; then nine; then ten, and then
eleven; and if perhaps some new *Galilæus* should
devise and frame us other spectacles or opticons to see
with, we are in danger to find out yet some new
Starres and *Heavens* never dreamed of before. This
round Machine makes its circular revolutions through
an unspeakable swiftnes. But that is a meer tale, which
Plato tels, to busie mens braynes with, to say, the
Starres and *Heavens* yeald a sound or delicious melodie
through their motion and stirring up and downe;
whereas truly the sweet sliding and shuffling of the
Heavens, the accords so discordant of contrarie
motions, those sweet conjunctions and divorces of
Starres, is it truly which is called, the sweet harmonie
of the *Heavens*. They would likewise make us beleeve,
the

the *Heavens* were al engraved over, because the *Zodiack* is composed and distinguished into twelve Figures of Beasts, therin cut, as with a chisel; and the whole Figure and face of *Heaven* were as fully stockt with beasts, carved and fashioned so to beautify the *Heavens*; and therefore wil some have *Cœlum* to take its denomination from *cœlatum*, as much to say, as *carved* and *engraved*; But in effect are nothing els but certain assemblies and congregations of Starres togeather, which the fantasies of men hath fashioned in Figrues and Constellations; which being so taken, resemble some kinds of beasts, but in truth have so smal resemblance with them, as that which they cal a Beare, might as wel be tearmed an Ape; and Necessitie makes us to accept it for good coyne, and GOD himself with *Job* makes use of such manner of speach, in naming them *Orion*, the *Hyades*, and the like. This great Bowle of the *Heavens*, roules and turnes about an Axeltree, fixt in a certain place, and flyes with the winged swiftnes it hath; the Angel gives it the whirle about, and makes it turne round according to the Divine providence, crowning the world with its vaulted Arch enameled al with starres.

THE DISCOURSE.

Hus are the *Heavens* expressed in themselves; and now let us seeke another *Heaven*, these ancients never dreamed of. One Authour divides the *Heavens* into seaven parts; the *Aerean*, *Aetherean*, *Olympian*, *Firie*, *Firmamental*, *Waterie*, and *Empyreal*. But we wil content ourselves with these three only, the *Syderean*, the *Cristalin*, and *Empyreal*. And for the first, we shal find our *Queene* of *Heaven* to be so the

The Survey. Barth. Angl. l. 8. c. 2.

Queene

Queene therof, as *she* is a *Syderean* or *Starrie Heaven* herself, if we regard but the ornaments *she* is decked with, as so manie starres. For as that *Heaven* is adorned with varietie of Starres; so *she* with diversitie of al Vertues. The beautie of *Heaven*, to wit, of *Marie*, is the *celestial glorie of the Starres*, that is, the glorious varietie of al Vertues. For as for the ornaments of this *Heaven*, it is sayd in the *Apocalyps*: *She had a crowne of twelve starres upon her head.* Now in this number of *Twelve* is a double number of *Six*, which is the number of Perfection, and signifyes the *Saints*, as wel those which are in glorie and Celestial Paradise, as those, who are as yet on their way thither; who al honour, crowne, and adore this *blessed Virgin*, as their *Queene* and *Ladie*. For as the *Heaven* with its proper Orb and certain revolutions, carries al the moving starres along with it, so *she* induceth al the *Saints*, to joyne in intercession with *her*.

The *Cristalline Heaven she* is, being a *Heaven* as composed of the waters above the *heavens;* which is hardned, as it were, and made solid, like *Cristal*; the matter being nothing els but waters hardned and condensed, as some think, not much unlike to the crust of *Cristal*, which is solid, lucid, and most pure: And so the waters of our *Ladie* were solid, that is, her Vertues were confirmed; and lucid, that is, transparent, because through them she might contemplate and behold the glorie of GOD; according to that: *But we with face revealed, shal speculate the glorie of* GOD. The forme of this *Cristalline Heaven*, is Spheral and round, which is truly the most Capacious, the Perfectest, and Fairest of al figures; and so is *she* most Capacious, as becomes the habitation of GOD, according as the *Church* delivers: *Who the Heavens could not containe, hast thou held in thy Womb*; the Perfectest, because endued with al vertues:

In me

Eccl. 4.

Apoc. 12.

1. *Cor.* 3.

In me is grace, of the way and veritie; most Faire, because *Eccl. 24.*
stained with no blot nor ever touched with anie
blemish, so much as Venial: *Thou art wholy faire, my* *Cant.*
friend, and there is no blemish in thee.

She is the *Empyreal Heaven*, which is the habitation of
the Saints, and a *Heaven* al of light, of an infinit capacitie, and immense sublimitie. The blessed *Virgin* then
is resembled to this *Heaven*: First, for her unspeakable
Claritie, because *she* is now wholy radiant and resplendent in Celestial glorie, having beneath, the Moone
under *her* feet, and on her head, a crowne of Starres;
and for the rest clothed with the Sunne. Secondly, for
her great *capaciousnes*; for as there can be thought no
place of greater capacitie, then the *Empyreal Heaven*, so
can no creature be found of greater *Charitie*, then
Marie. For *she* had an ample Womb, which was able to
receave GOD; *She* had an ample Understanding, which
had the knowledge of al Divine things; an ample
Affect *she* had, for her singular compassion on the
miseries of al the afflicted. Thirdly, for her *highnes* and
sublimitie; for as *Heaven* is the highest of al bodies, so
is *she* higher farre then al Spiritual creatures, as wel
Angelical as Reasonable. *Thy magnificence is raysed,* *Psal.*
that is, the *Virgin Marie*, to whom GOD hath shewed
very great things, yea above al the *Heavens*, as wel
Material as Rational, because appointed *Queene* over
al *Saints*; and therefore sayes of her self: *Who hath*
wrought great matters for me, who is potent, and holie is his
name.

Which things *S. Epiphanius* considering, in his
Sermon of the *Prayses of our Ladie*, breakes forth into
these words: *O impolluted Womb, having the circle of the* *Epip. in*
heavens *within thee, which bare the incomprehensible* GOD *laud.*
most truly comprehended in thee: *O Womb more ample,* *Marie.*
then Heaven, *which streightned not* GOD *within thee* ! *O*
Womb,

Womb, which art even verie Heaven *indeed, consisting of seaven Circles; and art more capacious farre then them al! O Womb more high and wider, then are the seaven* Heavens! *O Womb, which art even the eight* Heaven *itself, more large then the seaven of the Firmament.* So he. And *S.*

Chrysologus thus: O *truly blessed, who was greater then* Heaven, *stronger then the Earth, wider then the World!* For GOD, *whom the world could not containe,* She *held alone; and bare him, that beares the world; yea bare him, who begat her, and nursed the nourisher of al living things.* But yet heare what *S. Bonaventure* sayth heerof: *Thou therefore* (sayth he) *most immense* Marie, *art more capacious then* Heaven, *since whom the* Heavens could not hold, thou hast held in thy lap; thou art more capacious then the World: for whom the whole world could not hold, hath been enclosed within thy bowels, being made Man.

But especially indeed is the blessed *Virgin* sayd to be the *Empyreal Heaven,* because as that same being the proper place of Beatitude, where GOD cleerly manifests himself to the Blessed, face to face: so the Womb of the blessed *Mother* of GOD, was the first of al wherin GOD in a permament manner communicated to the soule of *Christ* our *Lord,* the cleare and blessed vision of *himself;* since certain it is, that from the beginning of his Conception, he was truly a comprehensour; and yet in this way, and a true viatour. Which no doubt is a singular prayse of the Virginal womb; that, where the wombs of other women are meerly the shops of Original sinne, as *David* lamented (*And my mother conceaved me in sinnes*) which makes one unworthie of the vision of GOD: the *Virgins* Womb of al others should be a place for the blessed Vision, and the only first shop of Beatitude. So as wel might the *Woman* of the *Ghospel* cry out: *Blessed is the Womb, that bare thee.*   THE

Chrisol.
Ser. 115.

Bonav.
in spec.
c.50.

Psal. 50.

THE EMBLEME.

THE POESIE.

THE Blessed Virgin, *even from her birth,*
Was like a Heaven *without a clowd, on earth;*
Where fixed Starres did shine, each in his place,
As she encreas'd by merits more in grace;
Til ful of Grace (*as is with starres the sky*)
Gabriel *salutes. Then more to glorify*
This Heaven, *from his, the* Sunne of Justice *came,*
Light of the world, with his eternal flame.
Lo, how the Angels from th' Empyreal sphere
Admire this Heaven *on earth, that shines so cleare,*
Contesting with their glorious Orbe above,
And with the Seraphins in burning love.
Empyreal Heaven! *For in her makes abode*
The first blest Soule, that had the sight of God.

The Pause.

THE

THE THEORIES.

Ontemplate first, that as the *Heavens* in their motions commit no errour, because they are alwayes obedient to the Intelligences or moving Angels that move and guide them: so likewise the *Blessed Virgin* could slide into no errour of sinne, because *she* punctually observed the *Holy-Ghost*, her Motour and proper Intelligence, as it were, in al things; while being moved with such motions, *she* was carried to God through fervent love, as being the wheel of GOD, wherof *Ezechiel* speaks

(*Which was carryed wheresoever the spirit went*; for the spirit of life was in the wheels) now in praying for us to her Sonne, now directing the Angels themselves unto our ministerie, and then exhorting the blessed Spirits to pray for us. Behold of what agilitie and motion this *Heaven* is!

Consider then, that even as from heaven, and its lights, we receave al the chiefest benefits of Nature, especially the growth and prosperitie of plants, without which nothing would succeed or come to anie thing: so from this glorious *Virgin-Mother* we likely receave the most notable favours and guifts we have from GOD. For as the *Heaven* visits the earth, affording its light by day and night, by meanes of the two great torches, Sun and Moon, and millions of lesser lights, which with their influences besides doe fructify the same, and with their sweet showers in a manner inebriate it, and coole it againe, when need requires, with dryer clowds, yea enrich it also, with gold, silver, and precious stones: so our incomparable *Ladie* visits and illustrats the whole universal *Church* with her admirable examples, and with the guifts of the *Holie-Ghost* inebriats the same, stores it abundantly with good works, and enriches it

with

with an infinit treasure of al vertues: and therefore is it
sayd: *Thou hast visited the earth.* *Psal.*

Ponder lastly, how among al things which have anie
stuff, matter, or dimension in them of length, breadth,
or thicknes, there is no incorruptible thing to be
thought on, but only the *heavens*; for al mixt things,
whatsoever they be, corrupt at last, and the Elements
we see continually corrupt; save only the Celestial
bodie, which is wholy incorruptible of its owne
nature: So in like manner, whenas al the Children of
Adam, begot according to Nature, are lyable, and
obnoxious to the corruption of Original sinne; and al
women loose in conceaving, the integritie of the bodie;
yet this *Heaven* of *Marie*, through especial grace and
prerogative of her *Sonne*, was made incorruptible,
according to either part, of soule and bodie: Of the
soule truly, because the contagion and corruption of
Original sinne touched not *her* so much as a moment
only; and of bodie also, because though indeed *she*
were a true and natural Mother, and conceaved *her*
Sonne most truly indeed, yet knew *she* no corruption at
al, observing and keeping perpetually the Virginitie of
mind and bodie. How worthily therefore, is *she* compared to *Heaven* for this so strange and admirable
incorruptibilitie in *her*?

THE APOSTROPHE.

O *Great Miracle of the world, or little world of miracles;*   *The*
not Queene *so much of* Heaven *alone, as the* Heaven   *Collo-*
of the King *of* thee, Queene *and* Mistris *of the* Heavens;   *quie.*
thou only maister-peece of the Almightie hand; O *Divine*
Throne, not second unto anie; Thou living Ark *of* Alliance;
and the Elder Sister of al creatures, who wast a Mother and
a Virgin, a Virgin and a Mother, al in one; a Mayden and a
Nurse,

Nurse, a Nurse and yet a Mayden, the Mother and the Nurse of God *and* Man, *a Virgin and a Mayd for ever. By that glorious* virgin-fruit *of thine, the astonishment of* Angels, *which so miraculously thou broughtst into the world, after thou hadst so long afforded him thy precious* Womb, *as a gratful and delicious Paradise of* Heaven: *Grant, we beseech thee, by that shower of grace in* Him, *which fel through thee,* O mysterious Heaven, *that we may come at last to that* Heaven *of his glorie, which he hath purchased for us with his more then precious* Bloud.

THE

THE IX. SYMBOL.
THE IRIS.
THE DEVISE.

THE CHARACTER.

THE *Iris* is the radiant and refulgent *Bow* *The* *of Heaven*, that shoots but wonders to *Impresa.* astonish the world with. It is the *Thiara*, or fayrest dresse of Nature, her shining Carkanet enchaced with the richest jewels. It is the Triumphal Arch of the heavenlie *Numens*, set-up in triumph as a Trophey of Beautie, to allure the eyes of al, to stare and gaze upon it. The *Protheus* of the Seas could never take so manie shapes upon him, as the *Iris* diversifyes its coulours. And for

J   **the**

the *Camelion* of the ayre, she doubtles used no other pattern then it, to coppie forth the great varietie of coulours she assumes. This Prodigie of Nature, lives in and by the Ayre, but hath its whole subsistence in the Eye only. Open the eyes, and there it is; but shut them up, and it wil vanish. It is indeed the faire and goodlie mirrour of the heavenlie Intelligences themselves, which they wil gaze on, as their leasure serves them, and breake at their pleasure, if they like it not, to make them new perhaps to please them better. If the Angels would lay aside their wings, and goe a-foote, I doe not think, they could have a better way to descend by, and ascend againe, then by this Causway, paved al with jewels heer and there, and where not, al strewed with tapistries; the Turkie ones are nothing like; nor those of *Barbarie* come neere them; while those the mothes wil eate, and time destroy their coulours, and they fade; but these, wil last til al be quite worne out. They seeme al as made by the same hand; they are so like; looke what you have to day, the same you have to morrow. And surely no other Artizan then he that made you this, can make you such another. They say, it is a nothing in itself; which if it be, it is a prettie Nothing, that so with nothing should make the heavens so beautiful, nay more, so rich, and al with nothing.

THE

THE MORALS.

PACIS FERO SIGNA FUTURAE.

HE *Scythian Tamberlan*, the terrour of the House of *Ottomans*, had in his warres, three Ensignes: the red, the black, and white; which he used to advance upon occasions: wherof the white especially signifyed Peace and a reconciliation offered; which if refused, the red, and then the black succeeded. *Castor* and *Pollux* in the Heavens, are held to be sweet, propitious, and pacifical Starres. The *Halcion* in time of a tempestuous storme at Sea appearing on the decks, is a comfortable, and little lesse then a certain signe of a calme and quiet Sea, wherat Mariners wil cheer up, as no such thing had ever hapned. The Spring immediately followes the bitter and sharp Winter; the signes are the buds appearing then, in the tender and green twigs. When the Lyon is in his chiefest rage, and when he roars most dreadfully of al, and for anger beats himself with his tayle in meer despite, let come but a tender Virgin, by, the while, and appeare in his sight, his courage wil fayle him, and he be a Lamb in a Lion's skin. The *Lion* of *Juda* roared then, when the *Lord* of *Hoasts*, to extirpate human kind, so let go the Cataracts of heaven, to drowne the world, with a total deluge of waters covering the earth; when lo, the white flag was spred in the Heavens, in forme of an *Iris*, representing the pure and immaculate *Virgin* of *Virgins*, which made the Lion to let fal his creast, and to enter into a league with al mankind, to drowne it no more; and therefore our *Ladie* herself was a true *Iris*, and may rightly be called, and truly is, that PACIS FERO SIGNA FUTURAE.

The Motto.

THE

THE ESSAY.

THE *Iris* or *Rainebow* is that goodlie mirrour, wherin the humane spirit sees very
easily its owne ignorance, and wherin
the poore Philosopher becomes Banck-
rout, who in so manie yeares can know
no more of this *Bow*, then this, that he knowes nothing to the purpose, and that it is a *Noli me tangere*;
since as manie as have mused therupon, have but
broken their braines about it to their owne confusion.
For of the one side, there is nothing of lesse being, in
the whole pourtrait of Nature, being framed of a goodlie Nothing, diversifyed and diaperd with false coulours, dressed-up with a feigned beautie, the matter
nothing, its durance a moment. It is a *Bow* without
an arrow, a bridge without a Basis, a Crescent not
encreasing, a phantasme of coulours; a Nothing, that
would faine shew to be somewhat. And yet is this
rich Nothing a miracle of beautie, among the fairest
things of the world, which being compared therunto,
are even as nothing. Would you have riches? The
whole *Bow* is nothing els then the carkanet of Nature,
enameled with al the precious Jewels she hath; some
are Pearls, others have the sparcle of the Diamant,
the flames of the Carbuncle, the twincle of the Saphir;
I should say rather it is the maister-peece, wherin
Nature had embrodered al her rarest stones, and placed the richest peece of her treasures, which she can
sever at her pleasure: It is the Collar of her Order, her
chaine of pearles, and the fairest of al her Cabinet,
wherewith she decks herself, to please her *Spouse*, the
Heavens. Good God! what a goodlie Nothing is this,
if it be no more, that carryes such beautie and riches

with

with it? It is said, that great High way of milke, which
appeares in the heavens, was the way of the *Gods*,
when they went unto the Consistorie of *Jupiter*; but it
is a fable: whereas I should think, that were there any
ordinary way for the Angels to descend down unto
the earth by, or for men to mount up to heaven, there
could be no fayrer then this *Bridge* alwayes tapistryed,
and paved with so bewtiful stones.

THE DISCOURSE.

OD himself takes such complacencie in *The*
the *Rainebow*, that when he is in the *Survey*.
highest point of his just choler, if he cast
but his eye therupon, he is suddenly
appeased. I wil *looke on my* Bow, *and wil*
remember &c.: sayth he. And no marvel surely; since *Gen.*
the *Bow*, he regards so much, is the Symbol heer of
his deerest *Mother*, the Incomparable *Virgin*.

Let us see then, how this *heavenlie Bow* deciphers the
Queen of Heaven, this mirrour of Nature, and the astonishment of man-kind. The Generation and extract
of anie thing discovers it most. This *Iris* then or
Raynebow, is caused by the reflexion of the Sunnie
beames, upon a lucid clowd, concave and waterish.
Clowdes are engendred of the marine vapours or
exhalation of the seas, where the vapoural parts of
the Ocean are attracted by the vertue of the Sun;
which conglomerated togeather, engender a clowd,
when the brackishnes of the Sea-water is turned to
sweetnes. And so was our *Ladie* a true clowd, since in
her were found these marine vapours, that is, incredible tribulations, bitter and brackish of themselves,
though to *her* made sweet, through the force and
vertue of Divine Love. The Sunnie beames therefore,
                                                   that

that is, the grace of GOD being a ray, as it were, of
the Divine Essence, reflecting on the purest *Virgin*, a
lucid clowd, concave and waterish, produced the
Iris or *Rainebow* in the Hierarchie of the Church, as in
the firmament of the Heavens; and therefore called
the *Iris* or *Celestial Bow*, a signe of the Reconciliation
of GOD with al mankind. She was concave through
humilitie, and therefore very apt to receave the rayes
of the *Sunne of Justice*, the influence of Divine graces;
as she was waterish no lesse through compassion and
pietie, because *her* hart was a Spring, and *her* eyes as
continual-standing pooles of teares.

A bow commonly hath a string, is bent with an
arrow in it, and hath the horns converted towards
us, as menacing the Foes. Our *Blessed Virgin* is a *Bow*
indeed, but without the string of severitie, because
most just; and without menaces and feare, because
most sweet; and hath two horns withal, to wit, Grace
and Mercie, which *she* holdeth towards us; while
grace *she* affordeth to the just, and mercie to sinners,
and is therefore called the *Mother* of *Grace*, and *Mother*
of *Mercie*.

Above al, the *Rayne-bow* hath its proper subsistence
in coulour, which it seemes to borrow (as *Bede* sayth)
of the foure Elements. For, of the fire it contracts a
ruddie coulour; from the water a Cerulean; from the
ayre, the coulour of the Hyacinth; and from the
earth, the green it hath: al which seeme spiritually
to be found in our *Celestial Bow*, the Incomparable
Ladie; for red *she* was, being wholy inflamed with the
fire of Divine love, which *she* tooke from the Divine
fire, *God being our consuming fire*: a fire indeed, that
burns and consumes others, but not *her*; because although *she* were a *bush*, and *burning too*; yet *incom-
bustible*. She might borrow that coulour likewise from
her

her dead *Sonne*, as *he* lay on *her* lap, being taken from the Crosse, al bathed with his precious Bloud, which mixed with *her* faire complexion, might wel appeare like to flames, in our *heavenlie Iris*.

She had the Cerulean, which is the coulour of the Sea, because *she* is properly the *Starre of the Sea*, and hath therefore a great correspondencie with that liquid Element; and through meer compassion, was become, as it were, al liquid, according to that of the Psalmist: *My hart is become as dissolved or liquifyed wax*; as wel for the abundance of teares *she* was wont to shed, as the puritie of *her* mind, which made them so limpid and cleare.

She had thirdly the coulour of the Hyacinth; which *she* tooke, as from the ayre; since al *her* conversation was in the ayre, as it were, abstracted from the earth, or terrene cogitations. *She* was wholy as the *Bird of Paradise*, which hath no feet to touch the earth with; and from the time that her Sonne ascended to heaven, from the mount Olivet, she could do nothing but cast up her eyes thither-wards, and so powerfully perhaps contracted that coulour, through the vehemencie of her attention, and application to that object, til her *Assumption* haply, when *she* left it by the way in her Bow, to remayne for ever, as a signe of her puritie.

But now to conclude with the green, which *she* tooke from the earth, what might it be, but a continual Spring of al Graces and Vertues, which *she* practised on earth? Looke into a garden, in that season of the Spring; and whatsoever your eyes can behold truly delicious there, in the greennes of the plots and arbours, both open and close, and in the green-sword allies and bancks; your understanding shal be able to paralel and find-out her vertuous conversation on earth. For if you consider *her* green walks, they were al as
streight,

streight, as garden-walks; for streight were the paths of *her* whole life. If on the arbours, you shal find *her* continually in her closet; her plots were nothing els, but how to become more gratful to her Sonne, *her* Spouse, *her* Lord; and those alwayes new and ever green; so as in the garden of *her* mind, was a perpetual Spring to be seen of al vertues, while *she* lived amongst us: no marvel then, the green was so dear unto *her*, to be put into *her bow*.

THE

THE EMBLEME.

THE POESIE.

Rom heaven the Father viewes his Sonne below,
Upon the Cross, as on a clowde a Bowe,
When vapours from the earth exhal'd arise.
The Mother likewise sees with mourning eyes
Her Sonne al black and blew, pale, wan, and red,
Green with a crowne of thornes fixt on his head.
Al which reflect, and by reflexion die
The Mother, like a Raine-bow in the skie.
To her for mercie when the Sinner sues,
The Sonne his Mother as a Raine-bow viewes,
That pleads for mercie, to her Sonne appeales,
Who signes the Pardon, and his Wounds are Seales.

The Pause.

THE

THE THEORIES.

Ontemplate first, that if Nature be able to frame so rare a peece of workmanship as the *Rayne-bow*; and that no wit of man can truly comprehend the reason of its forme and figure, with the admirable diversitie of coulours in it, so as among her other works most choice and rare, the same is accounted as a cheef miracle in Nature, in the visible Heavens: I imagin the while, what GOD himself is able to doe in his works of Grace, being disposed, as it were, to vye with Nature in framing an *Iris* likewise, in this Heaven of Heavens, to astonish not Mortals only, but the Angels and blessed Spirits themselves, better able to judge of the diversitie of coulours in *her*, to wit, the mysteries and graces, wherewith he hath adorned her.

Consider then, that as the *Rayne-bow* of it-self is no more than a meer Meteor in the ayre, if it be so much, whose whole luster it takes from the Sun, and vanisheth as soone as he is either in a clowd, or hath his aspect some other way, since it is wholy of him, and so of him, as without him it is nothing: So our Incomparable *Virgin-Iris*, whatsoever *she* was of herself, she esteemed as nothing, not so much as a Meteor, as it were, in the Celestial Hierarchie of Heaven, attributing al to the *Sun* of *Glorie* reflecting his rayes so powerfully upon *her*, to make *her* appeare so glorious as *she* doth, the most refulgent *Bow*, or Carkanet of Heaven, the delight of the Angels, and the gracious signe of Reconciliation to Mortals with *her* onlie *Sonne*, the *Sun* of *Justice*, whose *she* is wholy, and ever was.

Ponder lastly, how as the *Rayne-bow* of itself, is
nothing

nothing els, but exhalations and vapours extract from the Seas, and drawne-up into the Ayre, by the heat of the Sun. So this *Iris* is the Quintessence, as it were, extracted from the Sea of the generation of *Adam*, through particular favour and priviledge of the *Sun* of *Justice*, to become first a light clowd, that is capable of Celestial rayes; and then being concaved through humilitie, to beare him in her womb, and to have the forme of a *Celestial Bowe*, enriched with such diversities of al Graces.

THE APOSTROPHE.

H specious Iris! *Hand-mayd of the* Sun *of* Justice, *in thine owne account*; *and yet esteemed of al the world besides, the glorious* Queene *of* Heaven, *and placed as a radiant* Iris *or* Anckour *of our hope and reconciliation to* GOD *thy* Sonne, *whose unbent* BOW *thou art, sure* Signe *of* Peace. *Ah then*! *shal I alwayes live thus*? *Shal I alwayes walke the labyrinth of the fraylties and in-ordination of my soule, for want of a Clue to guid me forth, and to leade me unto the true love of my* GOD, *the only Lovelie and Amiable above al lovelie and amiable things*? *Shal I alwayes walke thus, by the brinck of Hel, unrulie, immortifyed, curious, sensual, and vayne*? *O my most deer Divine* Mother; *guard me with the bow of thy safeguard and protection, and make intercession for me, O thou proclaymed* Happie *through al nations*; *heare my desires, have pittie on my teares, let my sights mount up unto thee. O receave them, I pray, most gracious and auspitious* Iris *of the Empyreal Heavens.*

The Colloquie.

THE

THE X. SYMBOL.
THE MOONE.
THE DEVISE.

THE CHARACTER.

The Impresa.

HE *Moone* is the Dowager, and Queen-Regent of the Firmament, that rules that Monarchie by turnes with *Titan* her brother, with this happines above him, that his goverment over some of his provinces is found too hot and intolerable, and held as tyranous; but hers more benigne and sweet over al. She is so good, as she seems to spend her whole demeanes upon the poore and indigent. And as she is charitable to al, she is even prodigally profuse of the treasure of her influ-ences on her neerest kin about her, especially *Tellus* her

her Sister, more necessitous then stands with her gentle breast, to see her in; and therefore as made for her alone, she seemes to apply herself to her only. And to the end she may stil have to give, she is stil borrowing from her elder Brother new and fresher lights, from the rich Magasin of his greater splendour; wherof she spends so fast, as she is often forced to breake and become Bankerout, and as often by her Brother set aflote againe, with a new stock, as brisk as ever. She holdes besides very faire correspondences and good intelligence with the Seas, and those so good, as never fayle without some prodigie or other. They use to taxe her of inconstancie; but they doe her wrong; for She is constant stil, in that inconstancie of hers, they charge her with; how then inconstant? The spots they note her for, shew but how good a glasse representative she is, that so figures something, which they cal a Man, which I scan not heer. She is faire and beautiful, and yealds to none but to the Sun, and that for reverence, and good respects. She is a great riser in the night, which she doth to good purpose, stil obliging the whole world through manie favours. She is indeed the precious Diamant of the rest of Starres, cut round of the larger size, and sometimes Crescentwise, as she is pleased to communicate herself, and take away the veyle before her face.

THE

THE MORALS.

BENIGNA ET FACILIS.

The Motto.

He Children of *Israël* indeed, though they acknowledge GOD for the Authour and Creatour of al things, yet not to be dazeld with his glorie, were stil calling upon *Moyses* to speake to them, and not the *Lord*. The Kings of *China* are never seen to their Subjects, but negotiate their Royal affaires by the trustie hands of their Eunucks about them; and they dispense his favours heer and there according to his mind. By them gives he audience to Embassadours; and by their hands, receaves the presents, suits, and requests of al; and gives dispatches by them: and so his Subjects doe more sweetly tast his benignities and favours, and seeme more freely to communicate with him. The Understanding or Reason hath the common Sense for chief dispenseresse, and the Executive powers for ministers, while al things are not done immediately by himself. *Tyberius* had *Sejanus* as it were his right hand. He that would have a favour at the hands of *Alexander*, would apply himself streight to his deerest *Ephestion*, and he was sure to have his suit. Yea the great *S. Peter* himself, how great soever in his Maister's favour, would stil be pulling of *S. John* by the sleeve, to put forth his doubts and his requests to his Maister for him. And the great *Assuerus* had his gracious and benigne *Hester* alwayes by his side; who did nothing but communicate the Prince's favours to his people with a pious and prudent hand. This was the *Virgin-Mother* right, to our great *Assuerus* indeed; and therefore is *she* heer most truly and aptly stiled: BENIGNA ET FACILIS.

THE

THE ESSAY.

HE *Moon* of al others, is a Planet the neerest to the earth, and most familiar with it. It is the Sun of the night; her course and *The Review.* decourse never fayles; her glasse is cleer according as she lookes on the Sun; and sometimes do we see but a certain list, as it were, and Crescent of Silver; sometimes it waxeth againe, and makes a demie O or half circle, and then growes it to be wholy orbicular and round; her Argent is alwayes dimmed, with some shadowes and certain obscurities, that seeme to fashion a face with them. She supplyes the defaults of the Sun, and often shines in fellowship with him, and mingles her rayes with his, even at midday. The simplicitie of Painters heerin is discovered, in that ordinarily painting her in companie with the Sun, they make her horns, to looke to the Sun-wards; wherein truly are they quite mistaken; for the back is it, which is turned to the Sun, and not the horns; for she hath no claritie in her, but that which she borrowes of the Sun, presenting him in lieu therof, her mirrour and glasse to looke upon. She is the Sister of the Sun; and, as I sayd before, the Sun of the nights, which pearceth the thicknes of their darknes, with her silver rayes; somewhat moyst, and sweetly comforting the tediousnes of them, being otherwise gloomie and dark of themselves. A Starre she is, that lives but of loane, and hath the visage alwayes upon change: She is the Mistris of the Sea, the Queen of the Night, the Mother of Deawes, the sweet Nurse of the Earth, the Guide of Mariners, the Glasse of the Sun, the Companion of his travels, the Guardian of his light, and Depositarian of the day and treasures of the heavens: the second Glory of the firmament, the Empresse of Starres, of Starres, and Regent of this world beneath, where she hath her jurisdiction and demeanes. She marks-out the months and yeares, and the ages, as they runne, and through her sweetnes tempers the burning heats of her brother the Sun. When she is diametrally set under the Sun, and interposed between him and the earth, she eccclipseth him, and robs the earth of the beames of the Sun; and the shadow of the earth of the other side being cast over her, ecclipses her, and suffers her not to enjoy the Sunnie rayes: but the point of the shadow of the earth, not mounting neere so high, makes no ecclips at al in the other starres.

THE DISCOURSE.

The Survey. Cant. 5 *Eccl.* 53 *Psal.*

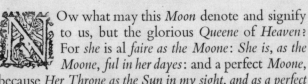 Ow what may this *Moon* denote and signify to us, but the glorious *Queene* of *Heaven*? For *she* is al *faire as the Moone: She is, as the Moone, ful in her dayes*: and a perfect *Moone*, because *Her Throne as the Sun in my sight, and as a perfect Moone for ever.* She is a *Moon* therefore, yea farre more beautiful then the *Moon* ever was, or ever like to be. For as the *Moon* indeed hath her light borrowed, very gracious to behold, but none of her owne, being meerly a light reverberated from the Sun: So the *Virgin* truly, though her light be borrowed, and none of her owne, as simply hers, yet hers it is indeed, though borrowed of her Sonne, the *Sun of Justice*, as daughter of the King. For *al the glorie of the King's daughter is within her* &c: not outwardly only in the voice of people, alwayes doubtful, ever uncertain, for the most part undeserved, and of little subsistence and permanencie, but intrin-secally in *her* most certain, meritorious, and for ever. Besides, the *Moon* hath her light often ecclipsed, and looseth wholy her light for a time; but the blessed *Virgin*, though *she* seemed to be ecclipsed, through the
vehemencie

vehemencie of her sorrow, when *she* saw her Sonne
so shadowed by a clowd, in the time of his Passion,
yet for her constancie of fayth *she* could not be ecclipsed
so, as to despaire of his Resurrection. *I wil not cease*   Eccl. 22.
unto the end of the world. Wel might the *Apostles* fayle
at that time, but *Marie* never. Moreover as the *Moon*
is variable and subject to changes, in the light it affords
to Mortals (an argument accounted of weaknes of
brayne, while *the foole*, as the *Wise-man* sayth, *is*
changed as the Moone) let us see, what changes and   Eccl. 22.
mutabilities they are. One is of the mind, which is
often moved through divers affections; another in the
bodie, which is subject to manifold alteration and corruption; an other of fortune, because temporal things
are alwayes a flowing or ebbing, a flux or reflux, the
losse of guilt and offence which is in sinners, who alwayes
are sliding from vice to vice. But our *Ladie* hath al
these changes and mutabilities under her feet, since the
Moon indeed is placed *under her feet*; while *she* alwayes   Rev.
retained the constancie of her mind, and Vow of
Virginitie; *she* put on the glorie of Immortalitie on her
bodie; *she* trampled al terrene and temporal things
under foot; and lastly through a singular prerogative
was ever priviledged from sinne. Furthermore, the
Moon hath her light all speckled over with little spots:
but our blessed *Ladie* had no blemish or spot at al,
either in her thoughts, because alwayes pure and immaculate; or in her bodie, because Angelical. *Thou art*
wholy fayre, my friend, and there is no spot in thee. I say,   Cant. 4.
most fayre in cogitations, affections, and intentions;
and spotles in al. Oh beautiful *Moon*, transcending anie
heavenlie Planet or Starre in the Firmament, as farre
in dignitie and excellencie, as so heavenlie a *Ladie* and
Queene of *Heavens* can surpasse her Rational, Sensible,
or Insensible subjects!

K   The

The *Moon* is sometimes wholy obscure, sometimes wholy lucid and bright, and sometimes partly obscure, and partly resplendent; wherin it resembles the *Virgin* right. For the *Moon*, as S. *Augustin* sayth, is obscured either when it is under a clowd, or when ecclipsed, or when renewed, as in the new *Moon*: So the blessed *Virgin* in this world, was thrice or three manner of wayes obscured. First, through her excessive humilitie, which was a kind of obscure clowd, that over-shad-owed her brightnes or splendour in the eyes of the world. *Black I am but beautiful*; as if she had sayd: I am outwardly black through humilitie, but inwardly beautiful in grace and majestie. Secondly, through acerbitie and bitternes of sorrow; and this in the Passion of her Sonne, as I sayd above, where she suffered an ecclips in the vehemencie of her greef. *The Sun*, that is to say, *Christ, shal be turned into darknes* through death; and the *Moon*, to wit, *the blessed Virgin, into bloud*, that is, into dolour. And thirdly, through corporal death; for then became she obscure in a sort, when her soule departed from her precious bodie so obscured, as it were to become a new *Moone* againe in her *Assumption*; and then indeed *was she a moone most perfect for ever*.

Secondly this *Moon* of ours, was wholy lucid, in her *Assumption*, because she was glorified in soule and bodie, and received there her double Stole; and like-wise shines upon us, with her infinit favours and graces, which *she* dayly sends us. For then indeed as the *Moon* is wholy bright and lucid, when *she* shines in the be-ginning, midst, and to the end of the night: by which night is tribulation both signified and usually under-stood: And as some *Saints* there are, who help the afflicted, in the beginning of the night as it were; others, who suffer men to fal into tribulation, and to be
tempted,

Cant. 1.

Joel 2.

tempted, in the beginning and middle, but help and succour them at the end: the blessed *Virgin* shines with her favours upon the distressed, as wel in the beginning, in affording courage; and in the midle in giving perseverance; as in the end, in placing the crowne on their heads. This is she, when others fayle, who never fayles; whom other *Saints* for sinnes justly forsake, she never leaves; and while others seeme to subtract their suffrages, she alwayes helps.

Thirdly, this *Moon* was partly lucid and partly obscure; and this truly in the Passion of her Sonne, where both she was obscured, and yet gave light; obscure, through intense sorrow, yet lucid by most firme Fayth. For as when the Sun is ecclipsed, the *Moon* being opposed between us and the Sun, appeares wholy obscure: so when the *Sun of Justice* suffered ecclips at his death, the blessed *Virgin* became wholy dark, that is, quite overcast and ful of sorrow; And yet not withstanding *she* shined even then likewise, because *she* kept the light of fayth unextinguished in her. *Her light shal not be extinguished in the night.* Surely two Heavens there *Prov.* are, which yet never lost their light, nor ever are like *ult.* to doe: to wit, *Christ* for one, who neither with death did forgoe the light of his Divinitie, but his Deitie was both with his bodie in the Sepulcher, and with his soule in *Limbus*: and his Mother the other, who never lost the light of grace and fayth within her.

THE

THE EMBLEME.

QVO TE CVNQVE SEQVOR

THE POESIE.

The
Pause.

He Empresse of the Sea, Latona *bright,*
Drawes like a load-stone by attractive might
The Oceans streames, which having forward runne
Calles back againe, to end where they begunne.
The Prince of darknes had ecclipsed Eves light,
And Mortals, clowded in Cymmerian night,
Were backwards drawne by Eve, *as in the Maine;*
'Twas only Marie *drew to* GOD *againe:*
O chast Diana, *with thy silver beames,*
Flux and reflux (as in the Oceans streames)
'Tis thou canst cause. O draw! and draw me so,
That I in vice may ebbe, in Vertue flow.

THE

THE THEORIES.

Ontemplate first, that if the *Moon* being *The Contemplation.* so faire, beautiful, and perfect, be so accounted of Mortals; and for the manifold influences and favours, which she continually imparts to creatures, be held in so great veneration, as to share in their opinion with the Sun himself, in the goverment of the world, whom the Paynim Gentilitie holds to be a GOD, and her Brother, and she his Sister, notwithstanding she hath yet so manie blemishes, defects, and spots appearing in her, who can except against the Churches devotion, in so magnifying our *Ladie*, who is truly so faire, beautiful, and perfect indeed, without any the least blemish, or spot in her; and so beneficial withal, as to communicate her graces unto us in a far higher nature, and those in a measure so immense? Or who can tax us, for stiling her the *Queen of heaven*, who is not only the *Sister*, the *Friend*, the *Dove*, and beautiful *Spouse* of the *Sun of justice*, but even his most immaculate *Mother*, the fountain of al her prerogatives besides; when especially we afford her no more honour, then may worthily be due to a meer creature?

Consider then, that as in the opinion of such as hold the *Moon* encreasing to have her horns directed towards the rising of the Sun; but decreasing, or being in the wayne, to have the horns pointing to the setting of the Sun: So our heavenlie, Angelical, and spiritual *Moon*, the Incomparable *Virgin-Mother*, had certain addresses and preparations, of humilitie and Virginitie, wherewith she disposed herself, to embrace her Sun in her armes, in the morning of his birth, as he lay in the Crib: And at his setting againe, that is, at his

Passion,

Passion, regarded him with two other horns as it were; to wit, with the sorrow she had for his death, of the one side; and the joy, she receaved of the other, for the Redemption of the world.

Ponder lastly, how though the *Moon*, while it is just over the earth, and the Sunne in opposition therunto, in a right diameter beneath the same, is shadowed, obscured, or ecclipsed: Yet our mystical *Moone*, when *Christ*, our true *Sun* indeed, descended and abid in hel, which is under the earth, and our *Moon* remayning there over it, lost not the light of Fayth, of his present Resurrection; for that the shadow of the earth, that is, the infidelitie of terrene things, could not ascend unto her, whereby the darkness of Infidelitie comprehended her not.

THE APOSTROPHE.

The Colloquie.

Empresse of the world, Ladie of the Univers, Queen of Angels, standing in the Moon, *and crowned with Starres in Heaven by* God Almightie; *most wise, most good! Oh regard me, I beseech thee, from the top of the heavens with thy sacred influences from thence; and have pittie upon me most miserable wretched sinner in al points. Present,* O *sacred Virgin-Mother, al my poverties to* God, *al my perils, al my miseries and necessities, to thy* Sonne. *For so will he take pittie on me, and open his hand, and afford me his Benediction, through thy gracious intercession. This grant, I beseech thee, most radiant and resplendent* Moone, *who shinest in heaven, and shal for al eternitie.*

THE

THE XI. SYMBOL.
THE STARRE.
THE DEVISE.

QUO TE CVNQVE SEQVOR.

THE CHARACTER.

THE *Starres* are the glittering lamps of Hea- *The* ven, set up as so manie lights, in the close or *Impresa.* upper seeling of the ample Theater of the world. They are as sparckling Diamants strewed in the Firmament, to entertaine the World with, as a goodlie maister-piece of the great CREATOUR. They are the silver Oes, al powdred heer and there, or spangles sprinckled over the purple Mantle or night-gowne of the heavens: the seed of pearle, sowne in the spacious fields of the Heavens, to bring
forth

forth light. Have you seen a statelie Mask in Court, al set round, and taken up with a world of beautiful Ladies, to behold the sports and revels there? Imagin the *Starres* then, as sitting in the Firmament, to behold some spectacle on Earth, with no other light then their owne beauties. If that great *Pan* they speake of, were that man sitting in the Cabin of the *Moone*, the *Starres* would be his Sheep and lambs, feeding in those ample downes of heaven; which not appearing by day (their proper night) you must suppose to be lockt-up in their folds for feare of those Beares and Lions in the Welkin. As *Cinthia* in the Heavens is even the very same that *Diana* is in the woods and forests, the *Starres* by consequence are her Nimphs, who encompas her about, and dance the *Canaries* in her presence, while so they seeme in twinckling to dance and foot-it in the same place. They are extremely given to mortification, and to a strange annihilation of themselves; that being so great as they are, they appeare to be so litle in the eyes of men; yea manie of them, are so passionatly addicted to it, as they appeare not at al. They affect equalities amongst them; and be anie of them never so great, they wil shew to be no greater then the rest. Their greater height and eminencie in degrees swelles them not a whit or puffs them up, but diminisheth their creasts, and abates them rather. In fine, they are a happie Common-wealth, devoyd of envie or ambition; where wel may you heare of conjunctions of Houses, but no jarres and discords amongst them, that ever I could heare of.

THE

THE MORALS.

IN ITINERE PHARUS.

Hen *Theseus* was puzled and entangled *The* in *Minos* Labyrinth, he found the twist of *Motto.* *Ariadne* to deliver him thence. The little Bird with the red breast, which for his great familiaritie with men they cal a Robin, if he meet anie one in the woods to goe astray, and to wander he knowes not whither, out of his way, of common charitie wil take upon him, to guide him, at least out of the wood, if he wil but follow him; as some think. This am I sure of, it is a comfortable and sweet companion, in such a case. It is the manner in al countries likely, in doubtful wayes especially, where they seeme to crosse one another, to set up Pillars with hands, directing and pointing this way or that way; and you wil not beleeve, what comfort it affords to wearie Pilgrims, whose everie step out of their right way, is a greevous corrasive to them. The Kings had a *Starre*, as companion in their pilgrimage, to the Crib. And the Pastours of the Church, are as so manie *Starres*, to leade their Sheep, and to guide their subjects in the pilgrimages of their owne salvation. When the havens are crooked and perilous to passe to and fro, the publick care of common safeties, in the night especially, provides some burning torch or other, upon some turret-top, to admonish the Marriners, where they are, and fayrly to guide and direct them into the wished port.   This same provision hath the Wisedome likewise of the great CREATOUR found out, to comfort and direct us, no lesse, in the open Seas, exposing a certain *Starre* among the rest,

as a

as a sure and infallible *Pharus*: But more truly and abundantly farre, in ordaining the Incomparable Virgin *Marie*, his blessed *Mother*, to be our *Starre* in the dangerous and tempestuous Sea of the world; and therefore is heer very truly sayd in the *Motto*: IN ITINERE PHARUS.

THE ESSAY.

He *Starres*, as sowne up and downe the Heavens, are the thicker and massive parts of Heaven, certain Buttons of Crystal as it were, which serve as a grace and entertainment to Heaven. By these silver channels, Nature distills her influences upon us, and insensibly distributes favours. They are the eyes of Nature, which without cease serve us as a Court-of-guard for watchfulnes; the Jewels of Nature, wherewith ordinarily she dresses herself. Sometimes they send forth their fire and rayes; sometimes they ecclipse their beautie, and strip themselves of al refulgence. There are some, who can punctually tel you, the course and travails of the *Starres*, their aspects, their encounters, and their fruits; the marriages and divorces of the Planets, their defects and ecclipses, their risings, their settings, their ascendants, their conjunctions, and the whole œconomie of the Heavens. For the swiftnes of their motions, it is a thing almost incredible, what they write, that one *Starre* in the firmament, should goe 200000. Italian miles in a minute of an hower; so as neither the flight of a bird, nor force of an arrow, nor the furious shot of a Canon nor anie thing of the world, can approach or come neere the imaginable swiftnes of these *Starres*; but yet most true. Besides al this, there is no *Starre*, that hath not a particular vertue with it, though

though unknowne to us. The clowded *Starres* cause
infallibly rayne; others, frost; some, snow; others shead
abundant deawes; some sow their hayle; others open
the mouths and gates of the winds; others fold the
world in clowds; others send downe mistie fogs; and
others contribute to the production and generation of
Minerals; and when the Sun and the Canicular *Starre*
are in conjunction, and match togeather, the world
burnes with outrageous heats. It is a dreadful thing,
to consider the greatnes of these *Starres*, their distance
in the Heavens, and the inexplicable swiftnes of their
courses and revolutions. You shal have a *Starre* which
shewes no bigger then a crowne, that is a 115. times
greater then the earth. Goodnes of GOD! Who would
imagin this beautie, to see such a Boule of Cristal al
of fire, to cast downe here beneath a thousand bene-
dictions on the earth, by meanes of its rayes, and the
sweetnes of its influences?

THE DISCOURSE.

HUS farre then of *Starres* in general;
which being thus decyphered, may seeme,
as so manie glorious Suns, in the Firmament of the Heavens, but are indeed as
the Common-people of that Celestial
Citie and Kingdome, compared with the Sun himself,
sitting in the midst of Planets, as the King of Heaven,
to whom al the rest of *Starres* make up a Court; among
whom, as a choice *Hester*, is one especially selected by
that great *Assuerus* of *Starres*, to cast his most amorous
glances and fayrest influence upon. This happie and
auspicious *Starre* is knowne and called by divers names,
according to the offices she discharges in the great
Assuerus his house. For first is she stiled by the name of
Venus, not as the Goddesse of Love, which the *Poets*
feigne,

The Survey.

feigne, but for that she disposes them to love, whom
she swayes, and exercises her vertues on. Secondly, she
is called the *Morning-Starre*, because she shewes and
declares the *Morning* now at hand, and even begins the
same herself with her burning torch, to glad the world
withal, who then begins to shake off sleepe, and disperse the mistie vapours, which so long had shadowed
and clowded over the Gemell *Starres* or Eyes of the
Microcosmes of men. Thirdly, they cal her *Lucifer*,
in that her light exceeds so much the other *Starres*;
so as wel she may be sayd, the *Hester* of them al. And
fourthly, she is tearmed the *Hesperus*, for as much as
she respects the ensuing night, and greatly illustrats the
same with her more then ordinarie splendour and light;
so as she glads the world therewith, and drawes al eyes
to gaze upon her.

Such is this special *Starre* indeed, the glorie of the
Heavenlie Orbs; but loe, we have another *Starre* in
hand, dwelling in the upper Region of the Empyreal
Heavens, that greatly symbolizes with this; but as
farre exceeds it (Analogically speaking) as the great
Assuerus, *Sun of Justice*, excelles the same of this our
Firmament; or as much as this same Firmament itself,
where GOD eternally raignes in his Empyreal and
Celestial Court: to whom, I say, these several titles
may aptly agree, according to these other things, which
are sayd of her: *I am the Mother of faire dilection, and of*
feare, and of knowledge, and of holie hope. This *Starre* is the
blessed *Virgin*, that may wel be tearmed *Venus*, because
she enflames mens harts with *Divine love*; and therefore
is sayd to be *the Mother of faire dilection.* Then the *Morning-*
Starre; for that she is the beginning of a new life; as
the morning is the commencement of the ensuing day,
and therefore, *of feare*. For feare is the beginning of
grace and of a new life; according to that of the
Psalmist:

Eccl. 24.

Psalmist: *The feare of* GOD, *is the beginning of wisedome.*
Againe she is sayd to be the *Lucifer*, for that *she* gives
the beginning of *Divine knowledge*, and so is the *Mother
of knowledge*; And lastly *Hesperus*, since *she* so piously
regards and illumines sinners, who are in the darknes
of wickednes and sinne; and for that cause is sayd to
be the *Mother of holie hope.* She is likewise called the
Morning-Starre, because appearing to Mortals, *she* is the
most certain and infallible signe of the approach of the
day of grace, and rising of the *Sun of Justice.*

This *Starre* besides is called *the Starre of the Sea*; and
that most fitly, if *Philo* most skilful of the Hebrew
tongue be worthie to be beleeved, to whose interpre-   *Phil. de*
tation *Beda* assents, and the Doctour *S. Bonaventure* in   *Mar no.*
his Glosse *of the Blessed Virgin*; yea the *Catholick Church*,
while *she* sings the *Ave Maris Stella*, and againe *Stella*   *Bonav.*
Maris, succurre cadenti. And truly, if *Stella* be sayd of   *in opera.*
stando for its stabilitie and immobilitie, then needs must
Marie be a *Starre*, whose firmitie and stabilitie in good,
is known to be such, as *she* never stept a whit from the
wil of GOD; which to no other creature once of riper
yeares was yet afforded, since (as the *Apostle S. James*
sayth) *We have al offended in manie things.* But for the   *Jacob.* 3.
glorious *Virgin*, as *S. Bernard* sayth, *She* was a *Starre*,   *Bern.*
because that as the *Starre* sheads its rayes without cor-   *Ser.*
ruption, so she powred forth her *Sonne* without im-   *Super*
peachment of her Virginitie; And as the *Starre* thereby   *Mis.*
looses no light: so the *Virgins* Sonne empayred not the
light of her integritie anie wayes. Reade but *S. Bona-*
venture in his foresaid Glasse, and he wil tel you how   *Bonav.*
fitly the *Virgin* heer bears the office of the *marine*   *in spec.*
Starre. For it is read (sayth he) and true it is, that the
custome of Marriners is, that when they determine to
sayle unto some land, to make choice of some one
Starre, by whose signe they may be lead without errour

into

into that part they desire to arrive unto. And such truly
is the office heer of *Marie* our *Starre*, who directs the
Marriners through the vast sea of the world, in the
Ship of Innocencie or Pennance, to the shore of the
Heavenlie countrey. And not unlike to this, Pope *In-*
nocent writes, being cited likewise by the sayd *S. Ber-*
nard in the same place. By what helps (sayth he) may
ships among so manie perils arrive at the shore of that
Heavenlie countrie? Surely by these two, that is,
through the Wood, and *Starre*, to wit, through fayth
of the Crosse, and vertue of that Light, which *Marie*,
that *Starre* of the Sea, hath brought us forth.

Now therefore as that *Starre* guides and directs the
saylers to their port: So this *blessed Virgin* is worthily
called the *Starre* of this tempestuous Sea of the world,
while in the midst of the stormes of this life, *she* lends
so her light to such as sayle to heaven-wards; and
through her example and patronage continually directs
them to the Haven of the Heavenlie countrie. Which
S. Bernard knew wel when he sayd: *This is the glorious*
and renowned Starre very needfully raysed upon this great
and spacious sea, shining with merits, and illustrious
in examples: if the winds of temptations arise, if thou
lightst upon rocks of tribulations, if thou beest tossed
by the waves of pride, and hoysed up with the surges
of ambition, looke on the *Starre*, cal upon *Marie*, let
her not depart from thy hart, let her not depart from
thy mouth; And sayth presently therupon: In following
her thou strayest not; imploring her, thou despayrest
not; in thinking on her, thou errest not; while she
protects, thou fearest not; thou art not wearie, while
she guides; and she propitious, thou landst securely at
the part; and shalt find in thy self, how worthily it
was sayd: *the Virgins name was Marie.*

Bern.
Ser. 20.

THE

THE EMBLEME.

THE POESIE.

The glorious Sunne withdrew his beames of light;   The
My sinne was cause: So I in dismal night   Pause.
Am sayling in a stormie dangerous Maine;
And ere the Sunne (I feare) returne againe,
Shal suffer shipwrack, where the fraite's my Soule.
My onlie Hope's a Starre, fixt neere the Pole,
But that my Needle now hath lost its force,
Once touchd with grace, and saile out of course.
Starre of the Sea, thy Sun hath given thee light;
Til he brings day, guide me in sinnes dark night.
I seeke, what Sages heertofore have donne,
Guided by thee a Starre, to find the Sunne.

THE

THE THEORIES.

Ontemplate first, that howbeit a *Starre* be sayd, by many degrees to be greater then the Earth, yet seemes it to be but a spangle or fierie point only in that immense and vast vault of the Firmament. So likewise the *Blessed Virgin* though she be the greatest *Starre* in the Heavenlie Hierarchie, yet thought she alwayes humbly of herself; and seemed the least and meanest of al the Daughters of *Hierusalem*, while she lived on earth. For she was humble in mind, in word, and fact: in mind, because she ever preferred others before herself; as *Joseph*: *Thy Father and I with heavines have sought thee*; In word, because she called not herself the Mother of GOD, nor Ladie of the world, nor Queene of Heaven, but the handmayd of CHRIST, when she replyed so: *Behold the handmayd of our Lord;* and agayne. *He hath regarded the lowlines of his handmayd;* And lastly in fact, because that after she was now become the *Mother of* GOD; she made herself the *handmayd of Elizabeth*, when she ministred to her for three months togeather that she remayned with her.

Consider then, how this *Starre* of ours is as the Pole-*Starre* or axeltree of the Firmament. For as the whole circumference of the lesser *Starres* encompasseth the Pole, and the wheel environs the axeltree round: So is the whole Firmament of Saintlie and Angelical *Starres*, about this singular and soveraigne *Starre*, that is, the whole Celestial Court of blessed Spirits, wheele, as it were; and beset the *Virgin* round, because they encompasse and environ her about as the Queen and Ladie of them al, according to that which the Church sings: *Like the dayes of the spring-time doe the flowers of roses and lillies of the vallies beset her round*, that is, the

Orders

Orders of Confessours and Virgins; and the *Prophet* sayth: *The Queen stood at thy right hand, in a garment al of gold with varietie beset round.* For the Saints are a certain robe or garment of the blessed *Virgin*, adorning her richly indeed like a Ladie or Queen, where the Apostles afford the embroderie of gold; Martyrs, the ground of scarlet, Confessours, Saphyrs and Emeralds; and the Virgins, the Orient Pearls and Diamonds.

Ponder lastly, that as this *Starre* is moved most swiftly by the motion of its Superiour, to wit, of the upper firmament or chief Mover, because it dayly carries it about the world; but moves most slowly of its owne motion, for that they say it moves but one degree in a hundred yeares. So the blessed *Virgin*, our delicious *Starre*, moved never of her proper motion, but through the motion of her Superiour, to wit, the *Holie-Ghost;* for as much as moved by the *Holie-Ghost* made she a vow of Chastitie, and kept her virginitie inviolable, and that perpetual; moved by the *Holie-Ghost*, she gave her assent to the *Conception* of the *Sonne* of GOD in an instant; being moved to goe to serve her *Cosen*, presently she climbed the mountains; being moved (so great with child, and neer her time) to goe to *Bethlem*, she went her wayes; and lastly moved to returne againe, immediatly she returned. Behold how she moved not of herself, but meerly of the *Holie-Ghost*, which was within her, and guided and directed her in al things: for other motion in moral actions had she none.

THE

THE APOSTROPHE.

The
Colloqie.

Glorious Starre! O *Mother of mercie! we have heard,
thou art ful of grace; and grace is it which we have
need of. O ful of grace! O radiant* Starre! *we, who are thy
humble Suppliants, present ourselves before thy* Sonne,
great King of Israel, *with sackcloth on our back, ashes on
the head, and cords about our necks, confessing our offences
in thy sight, that by thy meanes, we may obtaine pardon
of them. Look towards the North, heer of our affliction,
O* Starre *of the Sea; thou art our confidence; interpose thyself, between thy* Sonne *and thy servants; that of the one
side thou mayst appease his wrath, and of the other cancel
our sinnes; that through the heat of thy rayes, O Divine*
Starre, *the frigiditie of our soule may be warmed againe,
that by thy aspect, the heat of the* Holie-Ghost *may vivify
us. O grant the same, most Orient and bright* Starre *of*
Heaven.

THE XII. SYMBOL.
THE OLIVE.
THE DEVISE.

THE CHARACTER.

THE *Olive*, the Fig, and Vine, are the three *Triumviri*, that might wel have shared the Monarchie of trees between them; as having the voyces of al the Tribunes on their parts. But the *Olive* especially refused the scepter, as greater in itself, then the flash and luster of Purple and Diadem could make it. It is the true *Agathocles*, contented with his sallets in an earthen dish. It is even the meek and innocent Dove of trees, as the Dove is the *Olive* of birds, having such sympathie

The Impresa.

pathie and faire correspondencies with them. It was once the gladsome mirth and joyful solace of *Noe's* hart; was then, and is stil the Ensigne of peace and mercie. It is the Herald of Armes, that passeth freely to and fro, amid the holbards and squadrons of pikes, and cryes but out: hold your hands, and al is whist. It decks the browes of Poets, equal with lawrel, since *Apollo* and *Minerva* were as brother and sister, and deare to each other. It works the same effects, that Musick doth to revive the Spirits after a dearth, like a livelie Galyard, after a doleful and sad Paven. And for the Oyle, the bloud of the *Olive*, it is the quintessence and creame therof. It is the fat or butter of the garden, and foyls the Dayrie, as more wholsome, and agreable with our first nature. If the Vine be the Dearling of *Bacchus*, the *Olive* is so to *Minerva*, that being the Cellar of the one, and this the Apothecaries shop of the other. The Oyle is so coy and delicate, so reserved and recollected in itself, as it opens no doores to admit anie stranger into its house. It is fierie and haughtie in its nature, and wil mount and ride on the back of al his fellowes. Yet wil it slily insinuate and familiarize itself with its neighbours; for there is nothing wil encroch so much and shew so slick and smooth a brow. And finally it is the joyful smile of the husbandman, and the leaping of his hart, his barne, his cellar, and his whole Riches. It is the Wardrop to cloath his children, wherwith he payes his rent, and lives as merrie as his Landlord doth.

THE

THE MORALS.

SPECIOSA ET FRUCTIFERA.

HE Lion is a statelie and princelic creature, *The*
and held to be the King of beasts, but is *Motto.*
not fruitful; because lightly they whelp but
one at once, and that but rarely too, as
once in five yeares only; while the Wren
wil bring forth a 16. or 20. yong in a neast, that besides
a litle skin and bone is litle more then a tuft of feathers.
The *Sicamour* is a goodlie and beautiful tree, and hath
so faire a leaf, so smooth and delicat, as a reasonable
Taylour might wel have made therof a gowne and
cloke for *Adam* and *Eve*. And yet this galland tree is
wholy barren; wheras the Slowe, though she beare a
world of fruit, they are but sowre, and she no more
then a thorn. *Sara*, the wife of *Abraham*, was so faire
and beautiful, as *Abraham* himself had some litle jealousies of her; and *Pharao* was so passionatly enamoured with
her; as to snatch her away from him, and to carrie her
to his Court. But yet she was not fruitful, while she
had much ado, to bring an *Isaac* into the world. *Lia*
indeed was very fruitful, and brought her *Jacob* manie
children; but she was but bleer-eyed and ilfavoured,
and *Jacob* illuded in taking her for another. *Rachel*
indeed was gracious and extreme faire, but barren,
that with al her *Mandragoras* was hardly able, to bring
her *Jacob* a *Joseph*; and the litle *Benjamin* cost her her
life. Only the *Virgin Marie* was truly faire and fruitful
both togeather, who remayning stil a Virgin, was yet
so fruitful, as to bring forth not a *Joseph*, or a Saviour
of a few, or a *Benjamin*, Wo to his mother, but a JESUS
and a *Saviour* indeed of the world, being the true
Primogenitus

Primogenitus of an infinit ofspring of Christians, suc-
ceeding in the world; and particularly of true *Parthenians*. And therefore was truly SPECIOSA ET FRUCTIFERA.

THE ESSAY.

Y the *Olive*, is understood the tree, the
fruit, the oyle. As for the tree, if man be a
tree, turned upside downe, as some wil have
it, whose bodie is the trunck, his legs and
armes the branches, and whose head the
root, where, by the mouth, it takes its nutriment; the
Olive is that tree, since no other tree resembles him so
wel. For no other tree, is so civilized as it; no other
tree so useful and profitable to the neighbour; no
other tree, so medicinal. The first makes him a Citi-
zen, at least a free Denison amongst men; the second,
a Marchant; and the third, a Physician; and what are
these but trades, faculties, and professions of men?
Minerva was the first as the Paynim Antiquitie wil
have it, who found-out the culture and planting of
the *Olive*, and expression of the lickour thence, or pressing of the Oyle; howbeit they grant the Plant had
been ever existing, and had growne before, but altogeather unknowne to men, among the other trees.
And for a good while was not the *Olive* to be found,
but with the *Athenians*; and therefore the *Epidaurians*
contracted with them, to send them yearly *Olive*
branches for their Sacrifices. And for as much as the
lickour of the *Olive*, as the Oyle expressed, is apt for
al arts, they held *Minerva* was the Inventresse of al
arts. For surely, there is hardly anie Art, that makes
not use of this unctuous lickour, we cal *Oyle of Olives*.
There are two sorts of these Olive-trees; the one Civil
as I sayd, and fit for Citties, bred and trayned up in

Gardens,

Gardens, wel cloathed with Olive-coulour suits without, and faced or lined with ash-coulour within; the
other Wild, and fitter for the forrests, being somewhat
of a harsher and more churlish disposition; as being
ful of thorns and prickles mingled with the leaves, and
whose fruit seldome or never come to good, as having
little acquaintance or familiaritie with the Sun, that
perfects al things, by reason of the thickets of the
forrests where they dwel, which hinder it. But for the
nobler and more generous *Olive*, they are high and tal
of stature, wel branched, and with as manie armes and
hands to feed us with, as had *Briarius* to fling and hurt
with. Their flowers and blossomes cluster togeather,
like to grapes; the fruit, made Oval-wise, being long
and round, about the bignes of our damsons; whose
bones within, were they as small as the flesh is good,
the marchants needed not to venture so far as to the
Indies for gold or spices, while *Spayne* and *Italie* would
hold them trade enough. As for the Oyle, the Poets,
who are punctual and Religious in their Epithets, are
wont to adorne and mark out al other lickours with
their proper attributs, as to tearme the mild, candid;
the honie, liquid gold; the Rose, crimson; the wine,
brisk; but the Oyle of al others, they cal humid, a
qualitie common to al lickours, chiefly, for that it hath
no ariditie of anie mixture with it, as other lickours
have, even the water itself, there being nothing more
smooth, slick, and lesse porie, then it. It hath besides
very faire correspondencie with the eyes, and little
lesse then good wil between them; affording itself to
be easily gazed on, as a glasse; and though not so
transparent as other lickours, yet more reflective and
representative, then others. It is apt to burne, as being
so liquid, as I sayd; for were it ayrie, it would vanish
into smoke; if earthlie, turne to ashes; but being humid,
it spends

it spends itself, and nourishes the fire. Finally this sweet lickour, as the friend and dear companion of Nature, restores the fraile forces, comforts the languishing vigour, repayres and nourisheth the bodie in decay, clarifyes the voice, dissipates, resolves, and quite consumes the coldnes of humours, and asswages tumours; and what not?

THE DISCOURSE.

The
Survey
Judic. 9.

He Sacred Scriptures shew, that when the Trees decreed among themselves, to elect a King, the first they cast their voyces on, to have advanced to that Regal dignitie, and weild the Scepter, was the *Olive* of al other; for that, the first and principal thing they require in such a one, to govern subjects with, must needs be Pietie and Mercie, whose type indeed the *Olive* beares. No man denyes, but the Incomparable Virgin is worthily heer

Eccl. 24.

compared to the *Olive-tree*; of whom is sayd: *As it were an Olive specious in the fields.* Since then that Supreme, Soveraigne, and more then Royal dignitie of *Mother of God*, was conferred so upon *her* in *her Annunciation*, as on the mystical *Olive*, after the receaving of that Imperial title, *her* Charitie and Mercie appeared more then ever, as became a *Queen*. And as in the *Annuntiation* of the immaculate *Mother* of *God*, the Dove was a true type of *her*; so is the *Olive*-tree no lesse, wheron *she* sate a livelie and representative figure; between which two, are so great correspondencies, which *Philisophers* cal a sympathie. Cal them to mind that admirable Dove, which *Noe*, the great restorer of the world, from that vast and huge Argofrie of his, or rather unmeasurable Chest, wherin he had enclosed and shut-up the world, as under lock and key,

sent

sent forth to be his Spy and Intelligencer abroad, to
understand, how matters went with the other world
so buryed under waters. Who flying freely through
the emptie world, within the liquid ayre, prying everie
where with the pearcing cast of her litle eyes, the elder
world beginning now at length to discover some part
of its lamentable ruines, when she mought wel have
lighted either on some statelie Cedar, or victorious
Palme, upon some mountainous Cypresse, or robustuous Oak, or els on a prudent Mulberrie, the most
sweet Fig-tree, or most florishing Almond: yet she
belike as slighting them al, and al other kinds of plants
or fruits whatsoever, made choice of the *Olive* to set
her litle foot upon; and with her litle bil, as a wise and
ingenious Spy, to fasten on some proof or argument,
to bring away with her of the faire dispatch of her
negociation, which was to bring her maister certain
and infallible tidings of the discoverie and recoverie
anew of that greater world. Returning to the Arck
againe, as Scriptures testify, she brought along with
her a branch of that *Olive*-tree: the 70. reade a leaf, a
sprig of *Olive*, or, as others, a fescue (as it were) thereof,
to wit, with leaves, or the top only and most slender
twig of an upper bough, as *Delrius* expounds it; for so
might the Dove very easily twitch it off.

Wherefore we aptly marke the *Olive* in the whole
Mysterie of the *Annunciation*, as the Symbol of Mercie
and Peace. For in the same was made the first beginning of human Redemption, as also of the Divine
benignitie and liberalitie; which to the end that Patron
and lover of men the Sonne of GOD might truly shew,
it was needful, *through the bowels of mercie to visit us
rising from above*; which in this Mysterie was truly done,
when *Gabriel* taking the person of an Embassadour,
delivered his Embassage to *Marie*, whom if you conceave as

ceave as the Dove of *Noe*, bringing in his hand a sprig of green and flourishing *Olive* with him, as the ensigne of his Legation, you shal not think amisse; since the *Olive*-branch is even with the *Gentils* themselves, the Symbol of mercie, but in a singular and peculiar manner denotes to us the *Virgin* in the Theater of the *Annunciation*.

But heer may we demand with *S. Ambrose*: how came it to passe, the *Olive* should flourish so suddenly after the Deluge, and put forth a twig so soone? doubting, whether that leaf (for so he calles it) sprung before the floud, or, during it; concludes it did, and that the just *Noe* rejoyced, to see some fruit reserved of the old seed; and gathered thence a notable signe of the Divine Mercie, for that as then he had removed the deluge, shewing the fruit which the inundation could not hurt, as holding the litle branch of green *Olive* to be a signe therof, which even flourished in the midst of the waters and universal inundation of vindicative Justice, since this *Olive* of Mercie could not be drownd, swallowed, or withered wholy. Wherein truly may we worthily contemplate our blessed *Virgin Marie* expresly deciphered, as the especially and most singularly preserved plant of this mysterious *Olive*, which even flourishing before the floud, ceased not likewise to be green and prosper in the verie floud. For if the just man worthily rejoyced to behold yet some fruit to remaine of the old seed; could he choose but admire this mystical branch of our *Olive* heer, which even so great an universal floud of Sinne could no whit domage?

Heer now the *Hebrewes* would have *Mount-Olivet* not to have been covered wholy with the waters of the floud, and how that branch of *Olive* was taken from that *Mount-Olivet*. Others report it to have been

fetcht

fetcht out of Paradice. Both which I hold fictitious, if we speake of the Mount or Paradice in a literal or historical sense; and otherwise most certain, if we understand it in the mystical. For the *Mother of Christ* is mystically indeed the Mount of *Olives*, and she also the Paradice of pleasure, wherin our *Lord* hath placed the man whom he had formed. This Mount of *Olives* then, this Paradice, no floud of over-flowing sinnes hath drowned or covered.

THE

THE EMBLEME.

THE POESIE.

The
Pause.

NOT *without cause the Olive-tree is slow*
And backward in it's growth: The fruit doth show,
By th' oyle it yealdes (the type of Mercie) long
We did expect, before that tender, yong,
And fruitful tree, the Olive, from the earth,
(The blessed Virgin) *sprung, by whose blest birth,*
The oyle of Mercie, from the fruit did flow,
Which with the tree grew up, and grew up so,
As the first Olive tree, not slow in growth,
But branch'd, and leav'd, and fruitful. Mercie both
(Like oyle) the Tree and Fruit, produce: a Priest
Messias *in her Womb's annoynted* Christ.

THE

THE THEORIES.

Ontemplate first, that as the *Olive* is *The*
ever green, both in Sommer, Winter, *Contem-*
Spring, and Autumne; and what hew it *plation.*
receaves in the Spring, it stil retaines
the dead of Winter, when al other
trees besides have either no leaves, or els are changed into other colours, as tasting the common
calamitie of al Plants, some few excepted. So the incomparable Virgin *Marie* never lost the flourishing
greennes of her sanctitie, eyther in the smiling Sommer
of her abundant consolation in her joyful passages with
her deer *Sonne*; or in the sad Winter of her greatest
desolation, as when *she* lost him in the Temple, and
when *she* found him afterwards hanging on a forren
tree, so strangely altered, as he could hardly be knowne,
in his passion; nor in the Spring of her youth, while
she lived in the house of *her* Parents, and especially in
the Temple of our *Lord*, during *her* minoritie; nor yet
in the Autumne of *her* elder age, since look what fervour *she* had in youth, the same *she* stil retained in
her elder yeares.

Consider then, how the blessed *Virgin*, and *her deer
Sonne*, were both *Olives*, to wit, the fruits of *Olives*. For
as the *Olives* are first green, then red, then brown or *Isid.*
black: so was the Virgin-Mother green through the
precious and intemerate flower of her Virginitie; red,
through her burning and enflamed Charitie; and
brown or black, through humilitie. *I am black*: behold *Cant.* 1.
the brownnes of her humilitie; *but faire*: see there the
flourishing state of her Virginitie; *like to the skins of
Salomon*: where you may note the rednes of her *charitie*.
And for *her Sonne*, the yong *Olive*, He was green in his
whole

whole conversation. *If in green wood they do this, what wil be done in the dry?* He was red in his passion: *Wherefore is thy garment red, and thy vestments like to those, who stamp or tread in the presse?* And black he was, at his death : while *the Sun became black as a Sack-cloth.*

Ponder lastly, how *Christ* himself was truly the *Olive;* and the *Virgin-Mother,* but *as the Olive.* He was truly the *Olive,* because he had the total and universal Mercie with him, and was indeed the natural Mercie himself, since it was indeed *his* verie nature, and proper to him, to have mercie, and take compassion of al: while the *Virgin* was but as an *Olive;* for that *she* was so accustomed to pittie, and so readie and prompt to compassion, as *she* seemed in a sort most like unto him.

THE APOSTROPHE.

Delicious and fruitful Mother, *doe thou* shew thy self a true Mother; *and doe not reject me from thy bosome, so open to al sinners.* O Virgin Mother, O Olive truly fruitful in the house of GOD: *according to thy name, let me prove the effects therof: for thy name dilates itself like Oyle; thou healest the wounded, thou givest light to the ignorant; thy name seemes to carry a bitternes with it, and yet affords us a sweet and delicate oyle or balme of mercie and grace, more sweet then honie, or the honie-comb, and thy name, in the mouth, is ful of suavitie*

and delectation. O how faire is thy mercie, in time of tribulation! *For then dost thou powre it forth, when the necessitie is most evident,* Mother of mercie, *who presentst thyself most prompt to al, that erre and goe astray: Doe me the grace, to participate of the fruit of thy name: Give me a special devotion to praise thee, a love to love thee, and a perfect humilitie to follow thee, through the fruit of thee, the* Olive, *thy blessed Sonne* JESUS.

THE

THE XIII. SYMBOL.
THE NIGHTINGAL.
THE DEVISE.

THE CHARACTER.

THE *Nightingal* is the litle *Orpheus* of the *The* woods, and the true *Amphion* of the for- *Impresa.* rest, that hath for Lyre the litle Clarigal, or Organ of his throat; wherin he is so expert, as not contented to outstrip others, he wil never lyn, til with running his divisions, he hath put himself to a Non-plus, for want of breath: and then wil look about him, as he had done something, and some notable conquest, when it is but himself or his owne Eccho he hath so foyled, and put to silence.
He is

He is the pety Quirister of the Groves, that sings his *Anthems* and prettie *Alleluyas* in the night, giving the word to Chantecler, the obstreperous Cock, to ring the world an Alarme or peal to *Mattins*. He is so prowd of his musick, and hath so good a conceipt therof, as he wil not consort with anie other minstril besides, to fil-up his melodious Symphonies, but wil alone have al the pipes to himself. He is a true Musician indeed, that hath a litle of the fantastick with him; and wil in a humour, if he jarre but never so little with himself, of meer choler be readie to break his pipes to peeces. It is wel he sings no words or Dittyes to his *Sol-fa;* for if he did, we should doubtles loose ourselves, and be ravished and reft of our senses. And much I doubt, whether the Intelligences themselves would not quite give over their musick, to listen to his Mottets. His usual songs are certain Catches and Roundelayes he hath, much after the manner of the French Braules; you would take him verily to be a *Monsieur of Paris* streight, if you heard but his *preludiums;* for then indeed is he set on a merrie pin. Sometimes againe wil he be in a melancholie dump, and strik you such Notes, as *Dowland* himself never strock, in al his Plaints and Lachrymies. It is then perhaps, when he feels so the prickle at his breast, in the midst of his *Nocturns*. For then like a right *Michael-Angelo* with his statue framed to the life, which seemes to live and breath, wil he make his pipes to speak out plainely: *Ay me! Ah! Eheu!* They are *Hermits* al, for the most part, and keep in the wildernes; and are so contemplative, as they hate the Citties, and never come there but as Captives, sore against their wil. It is marvel, there is such store of them, and that ever they should leave the single life, and betake them to the conjugal state, but that *Chastitie* indeed is a strayne beyond their *Ela*.   THE

THE MORALS.

IN ORE MELOS, CORDE JUBILUS.

IT is a common Proverb: *Musica in luctu,* *The* *importuna narratio*: as much to say, as *Motto.* *Musick in mourning, is a harsh hearing.* And yet the Raven hath had the commendation of a good voice, and been seriously told, she had a good one; but whosoever it was, he did but to flatter her grosly to her face, and spake not as he thought indeed, but to bring her into a foole's Paradise, and to sooth her up for some politick ends of his owne. But what have we heer to doe with such *Saxtons*, as she, that rings but knells to passengers out of this world? Welfare the Swan yet, who though she sings very dolefully, yet doth it very sweetly; nor should I think the Swallow had reason of her side, to contend with her for skil in musick; for if her tune be reasonable good, she hath no varieties; and though she sing very cheerfully and hath jubiley in the hart, yet hath she no great melodie in her mouth. The *Philomel* is truly she of al wind-instruments, that carries the silver bel away. For she wil jug-it forth both cheerfully and sweetly to. She wil sing from the hart, as having an innocent soule of her owne, not an ounce of care within, nor so much as a Doit of debts to pay. A good Musician indeed can not choose but be an honest man; nor doe I see, how an honest man can be ought els, then a good Musician; since Musick is no more then a harmonie and sweet accord of divers tones into one melodie, without any jarre or discord between them. And Man is a Harp; the Powers and Faculties of the Soule, the strings; and Reason, the Harper. If Reason then playes

M   wel

wel his part, which makes the honest man, Oh what
a harmonie there is in al, and especially where the
tongue and hart agree togeather? When *David* played
on the harp, the il Spirit fled from *Saul*. And why?
because he hateth unitie and concord: Whereas had he
jarr'd but never so litle, the Spirit had stayd no doubt.
Is it so in the Harp, and not in the Organ of the voyce?
No doubt it is. As the hand striks, what the hart
dictats, so the mouth puts forth, of the abundance of
the hart. The hart then of the Incomparable *Virgin*, so
innocent and free from al engagements, how cheerful of
necessitie must it needs be? and being so ful of glee and
jubiley, how must *she* needs exhale and vent forth
melodie? and consequently, how divinely brake *she*
forth into that melodious Canticle of her *Magnificat*?
And if ever els where, was that truly verifyed in *her*:
IN ORE MELOS, CORDE JUBILUS.

THE ESSAY.

T is one of the prettiest sports of Nature,
when she is in her deepest silence, to heare
the litle *Nightingal* to warble, in telling and
recounting her delights and pleasures to
Zephirus and the forrests, tuning a 1000.
Canzonets, and sweetly cutting the ayre with repetition of a hundred thousand semi-semi-quavers, which
she lets go without cease. To take her pleasure and
recreation, she wil ballance herself upon a branch that
shakes, to dance Lavaltoes as it were at the Cadence of
her lighter songs, and to match her voyce with the
silver streames of a chrystal currant, gliding there along,
which breaking against the litle pibles, murmures and
sweetly purls, while she pearches and sets herself just
over a banck enameled al with litle flowers. This litle
Musician

Musician alone making up a song of foure Parts, and
a ful Quire of musick, you would say she held within
her throat, a thousand Quiristers, and as manie Violins,
and that the litle cornet of her beak were in steed of
al the wind-instruments. It is admirable in so smal a
bodie, so cleere, so sweet, so strong, and pleasant a
voice should be found; that in the Spring, when trees
begin to bud their leaves, whole dayes and nights perpetually she should sing without intermission at al. For
whence from so litle a bird, so bold and pertinacious a
spirit? Whence that force of containing yet the soule,
in chanting so manie diversities in the continuation of
one song? and where, I pray, are the livelie streight-
nings and remissions of the voice contained? Whence
so artificious and so perfect a knowledge of musick,
so ingenious a modulation, so gratful a tone to the
eares, which now with a continued breath is drawne
out at length, now turns againe with a strange and
admirable varietie, distinguished with a slicing voice,
and then with a wreasted, peeced togeather? There is
truly no Song so hard and abstruse, which she cannot
expresse, ful, flat, sharp, quick, long, high, meane,
base, what more? Now in these litle throats, are al
kinds of songs to be found entire and perfect; which,
with so much labour, with so much industrie, and with
so manie instruments invented, the Art of man hath
devised. But oh what sport it is, when this litle feathered
voice, this prettie harmonie in the shape of a bird, this
litle end of nothing, as it were, being vivifyed with
musick, is even readie to kil herself with singing, when
she heares the counterfet *Nightingal* (the Eccho) to mock
her, in repeating and returning her whole melodie
againe! For then she mounts up, as it were, to the
heavens, and then stoops againe to the Center of the
earth, she flyes, she followes, she sighs, she sobs, she is
angrie,

angrie, and then pleas'd againe, she mingles the sharp
with the sweet, the sharp with the B. flat; one while a
Chromatick, then a sweeter stroke, now strikes a Dia-
pente, and then a Diapason. She counterfets the Haw-
boy, Cornet, and Flute; she devids, she gargles, and
hath her Groppo, the trills, and the like, and al in that
her litle throat, but yet can varie nothing, but the
Eccho imitates and expresses; til at last, as it were, she
looseth al patience, falles into a litle chafe with herself,
in that seing nothing, she heares notwithstanding, and
so flyes into some bush to hide herself for shame, til
prickt with a thorn, at last she is pushed to sing againe;
which she doth without measure, where al is delicious
as before.

THE DISCOURSE.

The Survey.

Ut what are al these to the sweet modu-
lations of *Maries* voice, wherewith she
tuned a *Canticle* of her Divine Soule, surely
a magnifying of GOD, to be imitated of no
Nightingal els inferiour to her self, whether
we regarde the manifold varietie of her voice, or the
delectable sweetnes, or pertinacitie in the continuation
therof? The *Orpheans*, *Amphions*, *Arions*, the *Orlandos*,
and *Marenzas*, yea the *Sirens* them selves, with casting
downe their eyes would goe their wayes confounded,
and breake their harps and other instruments into
peeces, had they heard the melodie of that Divine
Cant. Voice of hers. *O let thy voice then sound in mine eares?*
for thy voice is sweet. The *Nightingals* are sayd to be
of two sorts: some conversant in the mountains, and
some in the marishes; which wil appeare by the manner
of their singing, there being no comparison between
them; since the one doth far excel the other, whether
it be

it be the litle pipes of their organs be stopt by the
vapours of those humid places, I know not, but am
sure of this, that *Julius Alexandrinus* upon the 9. booke
of *Galen*, puts a notable difference between them; for
thus he sayes: It is noted, that the *Nightingals* of the *Alex.* 9
plaine and marish places, are wont to give forth a voice *l. Galen.*
a great deale shirler, then those of the mountains,
the organ of the voice relenting no doubt through too
much moisture, as they cannot have so smart, cunning,
and tunable a voice with them, as the others have.

Behold then our *Ladie* a *Nightingal* of the mountains:
For Marie arising went into the mountains, and so became
the *Nightingal* of the mountains. *She* inhabited not the
fens or marishes of dissolute lubricitie, abode not in
the playnes of an ordinarie vertue, but left the vallies
of baser cogitations, aspired to the tops of Heroical
vertues, placed the nest in the sublimitie of Divine
contemplations, and dwelt in the top of the mount of
Perfection; whence proceeded that sweet voice, more
sweet then anie mortal harmonie besides: *My Soule
doth magnify our Lord.*

Let others with the tongue, hand, or breath charme
the delicate eares; let them wind the Cornet, with a
thousand diminutions, runne divisions on the Harpsicon or Virginals: Let them play the Violin as much
as they wil, spatter the Lute, touch the Orpharion
never so sweetly, the Cithern, Pandore, and the Harp
itself: Yet this Canticle of *Magnificat* in my mind exceeds them al, and wil stand for Organs, Flutes,
Cornets, Harps, Lutes, Citherns, Pandoras, and a thousand the like. This is the Musick indeed that pleased
GOD, and which I like best, which the syllables of the
Soule and hart doe make, while the tongue playes the
Harp. GOD magnifyed *Marie* because he made her
great; *Marie* magnified GOD, because she proclaimed
him Great.   When

When I think of our *Nightingal*, what hast she made
to goe unto the mountains, it comes into my mind,
what a certain Authour hath, writing of the nature of
things: That the *Nightingal* is wont to sing with ex-
pedition and celeritie. But what are the causes of her so
hastie and precipitous speed? The *Naturalists* wil tel
you: perhaps, because she feares, least the time of her
singing passe away; perhaps she hastens, least her tunes
otherwise would seeme harsh and ungratful to delicate
eares; perhaps, because she would charme the eares
more powerfully and politely withal. But why made
Marie such hast then? Let *Ambrose* tel us: The *Virgin*
made hast, that she might not remaine long in publick
out of her house.   Learne, you Virgins, sayth he, not
to stay in the streets, nor to hold unprofitable chats in
publick. Againe let *Ambrose* tel us: She hastned for joy,
wherewith the *Virgins* hart exulted to GOD. Let him
tel us a third time againe: The *Virgin* being ful of GOD,
whither should she goe but to the higher places, with
ful speed? The grace of the *Holie-Ghost* knowes no
delayes. Let *Origen* yet tel us: For that CHRIST, who
was in the *Virgins* womb, made hast to sanctify *John*,
and cleanse him from Original sinne. O let our *Nightingal* therefore sing apace.

But hearken awhile, you Musicians, how the *Nightingal* sings; observe her wel, and you shal note, how
she pauses not, but equally sings at length with a continual breath without anie change, stil holding out her
wind to the ful: now she sings her diminutions, and
divides *in infinitum;* now she wrigles and curles her
voice as it were, now she lengthens it againe, now she
drawes it back; one while she chants forth longer
verses, as they were Heroicks; another while, more
short and sudden, much like unto Saphicks; and sometimes againe, extreme short as Adonicks. Now she

tunes

Uliss.
Aldr.
Ornith.
l. 28.
p. 780.

tunes with a fat and grosser voice, you would verily say, it were a Sackbut at least: anon rings she forth a most shril treble, as fetched a note above *Ela* at least; cleer, to fil the eares with a silver sound; sweet, to charme the hearing with deliciousnes, running Descant as it were, upon the ground of her lower Notes; and now she goes smooth and even againe, now seeme you to heare a Tenour voice, then a Counter, and a Counter-alt following and chasing one another with certain fugues. But Oh terrene Philomel, thou art but a babler heer, with al thy trilloes, if thou standst in competencie in Musick with this Divine *Nightingal*.

Let us heare then this Celestial *Bird*: *My soule doth magnify the Lord*. What is this I heare? what is it, that filles so mine eares? What is it? what a melodie and most delicious sound it makes? which being conjoyned with unequal pauses, but yet distinct, with certain quaver-rests, and not with an artlesse voice unskilfully come off, nor with affectation ridiculously handled; nor with a swelling of the throat uncomely to see to, nor expressed with instruments il tuned, but most divinely and sweetly done, with a gratful inflection of the natural voice, which tempering the Flat with the Sharp, the rough with the sweet, the obscure with the plaine and perspicuous, the ligatures with the free, the slow with the quick, in one expresseth most different harmonies. Let us examine the musick *Magnificat &c.* which if we relish wel, and the eares of our soule be not wholy out of tune, we shal find most melodious indeed, and framed not only with admirable artificiousnes and skil, but tempered with a singular sweetnes and varietie withal. For therin is heard the height of Divinitie in the Treble, *My spirit hath exulted in* GOD *my* SAVIOUR: the vilenes of the Humanitie, and so the bottom and the Base of demission, *He hath regarded the*

lowlines

lowlines of his hand mayd: the Alt of Power, *He hath done great things for me, who is powerful:* the Tenour of Mercie, *And mercie from generation to generation to them that feare him:* the Grave or Flat of vindicative Justice, *The prowd hath he dispersed in the mind of their hart:* the Sharp of Exultation, *My spirit hath exulted in* God *my* Saviour: the Sweet of Refection and refreshment, *He hath filled the hungrie with good things:* the Chromatick or harshnes of Rebuke, *The rich hath he sent emptie away:* the fatnes or fulnes of Fidelitie, *He hath receaved his child:* the artificiousnes of Revelation, *As he hath spoken:* the consonance of both Instruments, *to Abraham and his seed for ever.*

THE

THE EMBLEME.

THE POESIE.

EVE, *like a* Nightingal, *was plac'd to sing*
In Eden, *where, with everlasting spring,*
GOD *for her solace pleasant arbours rays'd,*
Had she with lowlie straines her Maker prays'd.
But to an Alt *her mind aspir'd too high,*
Would be like GOD, *affecting Deitie.*
Therefore from Eden's *spring she was expel'd,*
Sad Philomel, *to mourne:* Til GOD *beheld*
A Nightingal *with an exulting straine,*
That magnifyed her Lord. But downe againe
She lowly stoop'd, and jug'd it, when she sayd:
He hath beheld even me a servile Mayd.

The
Pause.

THE

THE THEORIES.

Ontemplate first, that as the searchers into natural things, have delivered, al birds have their peculiar Notes, which are as their proper Dialects, in the region of their kinds, and by which, when they are not seen, they are easily distinguished one from another, save only the *Nightingal,* which hath no proper Note of its owne, but rather alone is a Quire of al the Musical birds in the world. So is it right with our heavenlie and divine *Nightingal;* for as al other creatures chant forth the prayses of their *Creatour* with Notes each one in their several kinds, our *Nightingal* warbles them, with the diversitie of al voices, with the voice of the Angels, of men, and of things that want both reason and sense.

Consider then, that, as *Plinie* sayth, the *Nightingal* sings not so artificiously by nature so much as by art, while the yong are taught to warble of the elder. The yonger (sayth he) do meditate and receave their verses from the elder to practise, to imitate: the scholars attentively listen, and prove their Notes, and by turnes hold their peace. You may note a correction in the learner, and a kind of reprehension in the teacher. Where behold, how *S. John* was a yong *Nightingal;* and if you doubt it, aske of him, if he be so or no: he wil tel you: *He is the voice of the desert;* Which is nothing els but a *Nightingal.* For if you pul but the feathers of his titles from him, you wil find but a voice, and nothing els, and what is that but a *Nightingal,* that sings as it is taught by an elder one? when being in his Mothers womb, and hearing this our *Nightingal,* to lead him a verse of *her Canticle* of *Magnificat,* he proving to follow and sing likewise, as then could no more, but skip and dance.

Ponder

Ponder lastly, that as the *Nightingal*, though often *she* be jovial and ful of glee, and out of jolitie of hart doth often sing in the publick groaves among a thousand of other quiristers besides, vying and inviting them al to sing to the prayse of their common *Creatour*: Yet wil she sometimes by herself alone be singing in private also in a bush, where having a thorn at her breast, it is incredible, the varieties she wil put forth, that were even able to ravish the Intelligences themselves, could they heare her at leasure, and were not occupyed already with their owne Musick. So our blessed *Virgin*, the *Nightingal* of Heaven, though she would often sing in the companie of Angels, as likely was she rarely without their companie, with whom she would chant *Alleluyas* more audible and melodiously; yet sometimes againe she would retire herself, and the thorns of her deerest beloved through a livelie memorie sticking at her breast, and pricking the hart, it can not be imagined, how dolefully, and yet how sweetly, she would sing.

THE APOSTROPHE.

Ehold, great Chorist *and* Rectrice *of the Angelical Quire, we poore petty-Quiristers beneath, have our eyes cast upon thy al-commanding Rod, to moderate our Time, that with due proportion heer on earth, we may answer in some manner to that upper Quire in heaven, chanting the prayses of our common* Lord *and great* Creatour. *Oh* Marie, *Oh Divine* Nightingal; *thy Quire beneath is held in the whole Church: but thy private schoole is kept in the Conclave of the Hart, where thou art wont to teach thy Devotes, to sing aright, how with the Voice, the Hart should jump withal, and the hand and foot be keeping a just Time, that is, with our hart, voice, example, and good works,*
that

The Colloquie.

that we keep an even time with thee, in correspondencie of that great Magnificat of thine. Come then, great Chantresse of heaven, and erect thy schoole within my hart, and teach it to sing forth his praises without cease. Lo heer, *I say*, let thy voice sound in mine eares; for thy voice is sweet.

THE

THE XIV. SYMBOL.
THE PALME.
THE DEVISE.

THE CHARACTER.

THE *Palme* is the invincible Champion *The* among trees, whose chiefest point of *Impresa.* valour consists in bearing injuries and oppressions, without shrinking. It is even a verie *Atlas*, for the breadth and sturdines of its shoulders; which the more you loade, the stoutlyer it stands to it. It is for name and qualities a Phenix right; and therefore as they sympathize much, the Phenix wil lightly take up his Inne no where·els. And verily I think, if the Phenix were to be a tree, it would be no be no other; and I doubt much whether if the *Palme* could metamorphize itself, it would wish to be anie other, then it is. It is a whole provision for the use of man: so as a new marryed couple might wel go to howse with such a stock. They are even as Turtles among trees, and constant Lovers to each other. They are so amourous one of another, as they wil hardly live without the societie of each other; and yet so chast, as they breed and bring forth without contaction. As the Turtle-widowes sit mourning on a withered branch, or die of greef; so wil the *Palme* in loosing his mate become a withered tree, and pine away. If divers sexes they have with them (as some think) they are the constant *Ulisses*, and chast *Penelope*; if not, a *Damon* and *Pithias*. Of al trees, the *Palme* comes neerest to a reasonable soule, if Loyaltie and friendship be according to reason, who are so passionatly carryed towards each other. No marvel then the *Palme* alone, is so taken up to heaven, as Scepter of the *Martyrs*, where nought but reasonable things can have admittance. The Male, that beares no fruit himself, in a manner is endles and everlasting, because Dateles, as without dates; and the femal though fruitful and ful of dates, yet bearing pulles her not downe, but is for al her dates as durable every whit as the other. They are the Hermit's Kitchin and Refectorie at once; whose dates they eate no otherwise then as they come already cooked and dressed on the tree. They shew a far off like Tropheys hangd with Fauchions or Turkie Scimiters; but neerer hand, as loaden and adorned with strange leaves, instead of armes or branches without boughes. By reason wherof no bird can hansomely pearch upon them: which priviledge is only reserved to the Phenix, where she willingly and deliciously plants her cradle, her couch, her Temple of the Sun, her Aultar of holocausts, and finally her tomb at one.   **THE**

THE MORALS.

Depressa resurgens.

The Motto.

THE Vertues of Fortitude and Patience may seeme as two, but are easily reduced to one, that is, to a stout Patience, or patient Fortitude. If you devide them, Fortitude attempts without temeritie; and having once begun, without al feare goes through with it. Patience hath large shoulders, and fit to beare a burden of injuries, which it suffers not of pusillanimitie or basenes, as not daring to revenge itself, but out of a true and Christian magnanimitie, because he may not. Fortitude seekes not dangers, but meeting with them, beares them bravely indeed with courage and good successe. Patience is so subject to it self, as injuries cannot subdue it, as holding this Maxim, that the whole victorie consists in yealding. Fortitude is sole Mistris of itself, submitting passions to Reason's lore, through which interiour victorie it works its owne peace. Patience walkes above Nature, so long as it is beneath it self. Fortitude is troubled at nothing, but for displeasing the Soveraigne Good, and feares nothing but Sinne. Patience makes use of Lawes for its onlie protection, not for revenge, and its owne forces, to eschew indignities and not to offer them. If Fortitude have a quarel in hand, it regards not the arme, but the cause, not how stout it is, but how innocent; and where it hath equitie for warrant, wel may it be maistered, but not vanquished. The contrarie events, do only exercise, but not affright it; and whensoever it is pressed with affliction, it acknowledgeth the invisible hand to be over it, that layes very sensible scourges upon it,

against

against which it dares not rebel or murmur a whit. This stout *Patience* then, or patient *Fortitude*, this Heroical constancie (I say) the glorious *Virgin* had, through the whole course of her blessed life, but especially in bearing the dolours of her *Sonne's* passion, so equal, and persevering so long at the foot of the Crosse, and not fainting the while, but remaining firme on her feet, so victorious a *Palme* of *Cades*, as wel might she say indeed: DEPRESSA RESURGENS.

THE ESSAY.

The Review.

HE *Palme*, of trees is it, that beares away the palme. It is even the Tower of Plants, both for height and strength at once; for if the Pine be higher, it is the weaker; if the Oak be stronger, it is nothing neer so high; and therefore with Antiquitie it was the Symbol of constancie and victorie. It is (as I may say) the Phenix of trees, with which it hath such simpathies, as what with the Etimologie of the name, being the same in Greek, and the faire correspondencies they have with each other, in Authours they are much confounded. And for the Phenix, she wil neast herself in none other. The *Palmes* are likewise the Turtles among trees; for they are Male and Female, as they; they match and payre togeather as they, and are as loyal as they, and ful as chast as they. For in the absence of each other, they produce no fruit, and yet (wherin they much exceed the Turtles) they bring them forth without contaction of branch or root, but it is enough that they enjoy each others companie; and so great a sympathie they have withal, that if they be transplanted from each other, they mourne and languish likewise, if not dye. The *Palme* is even the Magazin of al provisions, for the use and sustentation of man.

of man. The *Indians* have need of manie things, and lo
the *Palme* supplyes them al; so as if anie one be industrious among them, or anie thing be very profitable,
they wil say immediatly: *Behold the Palme.* It affords
them oyle, wine, and bread, as they handle it; with the
leaves they cover their houses, as we with tiles; they
write theron, instead of paper; if they put themselves
to sea, the *Palmes* doe furnish them with al things
necessarie thereto; and not only with victuals, but even
the very vessel in itself is nothing els but *Palme.* The
trunck and branches yeald them masts and boards;
the leaves being woven, make up their sayles; with
the bark, they frame their tacklings and cordage. So
as not without some miracle, as it were, may you say,
when you see a Man-of-warre of theirs, or a marchant's
ship, behold a *Palme,* how it rides upon the seas.

THE DISCOURSE.

Ehold heer the true triumphant *Palme* indeed, the *Queen of Heaven,* who not withstanding al her combats and bitter ago-
nies in the passion of her *Sonne,* yet stil she
triumphed over al, especially in her glo-
rious *Assumption: I am exalted as a Palme in Cades,* that
is, *in my Assumption,* since *Cades* is interpreted: *Translation;* for who sees not the *Assumption* of the *Mother of*
GOD, to be nothing els, but a certain translation of her
from this Militant to the Triumphant Church? A *Palme*
being oppressed with a heavie weight, was put up in
the Obsequies of *Marguerit* of *Austria,* with this Devise:
Subacta mole resurgo; representing therin, how the Just
shal arise at the last Resurrection, like the *Palme,* more
faire and beautiful then before; though formerly oppressed, by the burden of death and of human necessitie.

N   And

*The
Survey.*

And so was it with our incomparable *Ladie* in an eminent degree, especially (I say) at her glorious *Assumption*.

Among the *Palmes*, there are Male and Female; and the Female never brings forth fruits, but standing opposit by her Male: and hence it is, that two *Palmes*, being planted by two banck-sides of a river, are the Hieroglifick of Nuptials, with *Valerius*: and especially, say I, of the Spiritual Nuptials between the *Spouse*, and his *Spouse*, between *Christ* and his blessed *Mother*. Among these *Palmes* likewise, is noted this difference; that the Male growes and flourishes sooner then the Femal; and so fares it heer with our two *Palmes*, our *Saviour Christ*, and his deare *Mother*. Where, of the first sayth the Prophet: *The just shall flourish like the Palme;* And the latter sayth of herself: *I am exalted like a Palme in Cades;* with this difference, that *Christ* much sooner then his *Mother* arising to immortal life, seemed to flourish sooner: as he testifyes of himself: *And my flesh hath flourished.* But the blessed *Virgin* dying some yeares afterwards, and gloriously resuscitated, did flourish indeed, but so as after him.

It is sayd moreover, that though the *Palme* grow higher then manie trees, yet never arrives it to the height of the Cedar. So likewise, though our mystical *Palme*, our admirable *Ladie*, were raysed and exalted so high, as she far transcended the glorie of al men and Angels, yet to the height of the glorie of *Christ*, very aptly signified by the Cedar, was she never assumpted, as wel for sublimitie as innated incorruptibilitie; because our *Lord Christ* as wel in the Triumphant as Militant Church is the Head of the mystical Bodie, whereof his *Mother* was a member only, though the noblest part of al, as being *the neck.* Heerto may be added that prettie Devise of *Mark Anthonie*, being this:

a Pillar

Psal. 31.
Eccl. 24.

Psal. 27.

a Pillar wreathed and composed about with two
branches, the one of *Palme,* the other of *Cypresse,* with
this Motto: *Erit altera merces;* signifying thereby, the
recompence of a generous man, was either a noble
Victorie, or an honourable Death; for that the *Palme*
representing victorie, the Cypresse of the other side is
a Symbol of death, being ordinarily used in the Funerals
and Sepulchers of the dead. So was al the life of the
blessed Virgin a perpetual standing pillar or Trophey,
as is were, of incredible Mysteries, especially in the
palme of her glorious *Assumption,* yet by the meanes of
the Cypresse of her death, since that was to be the way
and the next step to her highest advancement, and the
greatest victorie of al.

The *Palme,* is sharp and rough beneath, but smooth
and handsome above; wherein *S. Gregorie* sayth in his
Morals, the life of the just man is aptly represented,
being bitter and rough in the exteriour shew and in
the sensitive part, but yet sweet and delightful through
contentments which the soule receaves the while: So
was the whole life of the Mother of GOD nothing els
but a life of paynes and doulours, especially at the
passion of her deerest *Sonne,* which through compassion she made her owne, but yet sweet for the end,
to wit, of a life of rest and repose afterwards in the
kingdome of Heaven, and of the ineffable joyes of her
glorious *Assumption* by the way, as riding in Triumph.
Which *Saint* besides, makes yet another note, which is
this; that the *Palme* heerin is differing from other trees,
in that the other are grosse beneath, and grow slenderer
upwards; while the *Palme* of the contrarie, is slender
beneath, and bigger and grosser, the higher it goes:
So were the thoughts of the blessed *Virgin,* the true
Palme indeed, as poore and slender downe to the earth-
wards, but substantial and solid up to the Heavens,
whose

whose conversation doubtles, as *S. Paul* sayth, *was wholy in Heaven.*

Strange things are reported of the *Palmes,* to live mutually, and dye togeather. A singular type surely of the Sympathie between our two *Palmes,* our *Christ* and his blessed *Mother,* affording one life, and as it were one self-same death between them both. For *Christ* dying, she languished as dead; and he arising from his Sepulcher after his death, she revived againe as it were from death. And so that same Epitaph more fitly might be applyed to these Divine *Lovers,* our amourous *Palmes,* which a certain Poet of ours had framed for a payre of profane Lovers, dying both with one and the self-same sword:

> *His being was in her alone,*
> *And he not being, she was none.*
> *They joy'd one joy; one grief they griev'd;*
> *One love they lov'd; one life they liv'd.*
> *The hand was one, one was the Sword,*
> *That did his death, her death afford.*

THE

THE EMBLEME.

Quasi φοινιξ Palma exal tata sum. Ecli. 42.

THE POESIE.

PHænix (*in Greek a* Palme) *doth aptly sute*
With that rare bird the Phænix, *here the fruit;*
Which, when bright Phoebus *scorching beames*
  displayes, The
  Pause.
A neast of Spices (*to renew his dayes,*
By a second birth) *upon this tree he makes:*
Where burnt to ashes so himself forsakes,
Made yong, that he retaines what he had byn.
Thus th' only Sonne *of God, t'abolish sinne,*
Midst burning flames revest with mortal plume,
Revives man's nature, which he doth assume;
*The Virgin-*Phænix *is the fruitful tree,*
Where God in flames of Love, *new-borne would be.*

THE

THE THEORIES.

 Ontemplate first, in the *Palme*, what a gratful shade it affords to wearie travellers on the way, preserving them from the scorching rayes of the Sun, and yealding them Dates to expel hunger, and not so only, but is a notable delicacie besides. The Monks and Fathers of *Ægypt*, *Thebaida*, and *Arabia*, would make a goodlie living with a *Palme*-tree only by a chrystal river side, subministring them al things needful, for meat, drink, and cloath, to satisfy nature. O rare and admirable tree! But then consider the *Palme* of Paradise; I say, the admirable *Virgin Palme*, under whose shadow and protection, we are saved from the outrageous heats of concupiscence, fed with the delicious examples of her life, and cloathed with the habits of her vertues, and especially refreshed with the sweet consideration of the limpid streames of her purest chastitie, no lesse then Nectar in the tast.

Consider then, how as the *Palme* is rough without, narrow beneath, and broad on the top, wheron the Phenix takes delight to build his neast: So was our blessed *Ladie* in exteriour shew but coorse in the eyes of her Nazarean neighbours, being held for no more, then a Carpenter's wife; while she was truly indeed the *Palme* of *Cades*. Beneath she was narrow, that is, in the love of terrene things, wheron she touched as it were, but in a point only of the human nature, not acquainted with the impurities and miseries therof: but broad on the top, that is, in Divine contemplation, and love of celestial things, *where she alwayes dwelt in the highest;* and where the glorious *Phenix*, the eternal *Word*, had taken up his neast for so many moneths, to

issue

issue thence a human *Phenix*, her true and natural Sonne indeed.

Ponder lastly, that as the *Palme* ever flourisheth and never withers, so our Incomparable *Mother* of GOD, had alwayes fresh and flourishing thoughts, being holie and chast; and green intentions, because most pure and neat; and green and flourishing affections, because very livelie and active in the service of the Highest, whose lowlie handmayd, notwithstanding her maternitie, she would be; nor decayd or withered ever, because ever entire and never once subject to corruption; not in *Eccl.* 24. bodie, because embalmed with the Deitie: *As Cinamon and balme aromatizing I have sent forth an odour;* not in soule, because being united with the Soule, of her *Sonne,* they were made in a manner both as one, as by this is insinuated: *A sword shal pierce through thy verie soule:* that is, thy soule, which is his; or his, which is thyne: nor in Spirit, because through love she was truly converted into GOD; and *S. Hierom* sayth: *The grace of the Holie-Ghost had fully replenished her, and Divine Love had made her wholy white.*

THE

THE APOSTROPHE.

Statelie *and victorious* Palme *of Paradice, most triumphant Queen of heaven, Cittie of refuge, Temple of Safeguard, House of the Living* GOD, *faire Couch of the mystical Salomon, and his* Throne *of Ivorie*! *Oh Sanctuarie of* GOD, *the Arck of peace, Seat of Wisedome, the Rest and repose of the most high* GOD, *the glorious Cabinet of a thousand and a thousand guifts of the most blessed* Holie-Ghost, *the precious Reliquarie of al infused graces*! *O sacred Pavilion, where* GOD *sets himself in the shadow of the rayes of his great glorie; most delicious* Ladie, *most pure and gracious, in the midst of those Celestial pleasures, and Divine delectations of thine: Grant, I beseech thee, that I alwayes rest under the shade of thy branches, within the folds of thy protection and sweet mercie, in this life; and when I shal finish the course of my pilgrimage, in this vale of miseries, it would please his Omnipotencie, to unite my hart and spirit, with his more then holie Spirit, by the sacred linck of his most faire and transforming love. This doe I beg at the feet of thee, most soveraigne* Palme *of the heavenlie Paradise.*

THE XV. SYMBOL.
THE HOUSE.
THE DEVISE.

THE CHARACTER.

HE *House* is an artificious Plasme, framed   *The* by the hand of man, for his use and *Impresa.* habitation. It is a creature made in spite of Nature, to vye with her: That forasmuch as Man only is borne naked, and without a house to put his head in, afforded him by Nature, Art taking compassion on him, abundantly supplyes the defect. There is nothing comes so suddenly to so great a growth, as it; for wheras an Elephant being

being one of the greatest among beasts, and yet by
manie degrees not so big as manie *Houses* are, he is
twentie yeares ere he comes to his ful growth: a goodlie
house wil be reared, and brought to perfection in lesse
then a yeare. Plants wil not grow without rayne, or
waters cast upon them, where this plantation hath no
need of waters, but rather al industries are used to keep
them out. The Tortoyes in this respect, is better housed,
not charged with reparations as long as his Lease lasts,
for terme of his life: but yet having none els to trust,
to looke unto it, he is faine to carrie it about him. The
Cockle hath his *house*, tiled with slate; which having
no lock and key too, he is forced to keep at home for
feare of theeves. And not so much as the poore Snayle
but hath a *house* of his owne, which in his pace, like a
Pedler with his pack, wil he carrie about him through-
out the world, and do that with time, which the Sunne
can no more then do, with al his swiftnes. Nay you
eate not an Oyster, but you *un-house* him and put him
out of his tenement. The Sun is the *house* of light, that
needs no windowes, being nothing els but light. And
for the 12. principal *houses* and Pallaces in the Heavens,
they are but weakely built without foundation, more
then the Astronomers working braines. The Moone
is the *house* of the Flux and Reflux of the Seas, who
thence go in and out by turnes at their pleasures. The
Almond is a *house* of the kernels within, which never
comes forth til the roof comes fluttering downe about
her eares, that costs her life. The Hive, is a *house* and
Colledge of Bees, where they live Collegially togeather; the Combs are their Refectorie. The Birds,
for proper *houses*, have their neasts; whose children are
the yong ones, and she the good huswif that keeps at
home.

THE

THE MORALS.

Sedes Sapientiae.

The Motto.

Looke where the Prince is, there is the Court; and where the Court, there his Seate. Wisedome is the Prince of the whole Microcosme of man: His Court then, and seate must needs be in the Power of the Understanding, where he chiefly resides, and not where soever his dominion stretcheth; for so should he be in everie place in person, which stands not with the Majestie of so great a Prince. Wel may his Ministers, like Pursevants and Heralds, performe and execute the Royal commands: as the hands, to make provisions to maintaine the State; the feet, to travel for that purpose; the eyes, to keep Centenel in the turrets of his pallace, and that neer to his person, against forren invasions, and the like: but yet the Prince himself in his Royal person departs not a whit from his proper Chamber of presence, the Intellect. And GOD himself, the Monarck of the whole Univers, is seen to be everie where within his Dominions, through his essence, power, and presence, but not in that particular manner, as he is in heaven, in his proper seat; or as he was in earth, in his humanitie, or in the Sacrament itself most mysteriously and Divinely. For to speake in general, his seat is everie where: The Heavens, are the roof; the Starres, the Seelings; the earth al diaperd and diversifyed with infinit coulours, his footstool and pavements; and the marvels of Nature, his shop of wonders, but his proper and peculiar seat, where he resides in, as in his Court, is either in the Empyreal Heaven (as I sayd) or is

or is Christ's excellent Humanitie, or in the most
Venerable and dreadful Sacrament of the Aultar; nor
hath he made choice of any other seats to dwel in, as
not worthie or able to comprehend him. Where then
had Wisedome properly set up his seat, but in that
pallace he had built for himself, founded in so great
an humilitie, and so wel sustained with the seaven-fold
pillars of the *Holie-Ghost*, I meane, in the Virgin-
Womb of the Incomparable Ladie? who receaving,
and so long entertaining the *Wisedome* Increated, in her
virginal Lap, as the true *Salomon* indeed, reposing
sweetly in his Ivorie Throne, may wel be stiled:
Sedes Sapientiae.

THE ESSAY.

*The
Review.*

House being a meer artificial, and no
natural thing, hath its first subsistence
in the Idea of Man's brayne; according
to whose model, good or il, the *house*
so built, proves good or il. We recurre
then to the Architect, for direction in
al. This Architecture is a soveraigne Mistris of building,
which gives the addresses, for disposing of al the parts
of a *house*, with relations in themselves, in comlines,
proportion, ornaments, situation, distances, elevations,
and a thousand of the like; of al which yealds it a
pertinent and satisfactorie reason to the curious exam-
iners, why everie thing is so done, this and not that.
Some are Architects by hand only, and no more, who
frame their buildings by roat, taking forth copyes heer
and there, but can afford no reason at al for what they
do, nor invent ought that is worth a rush; and for a
final reason say nothing but, such is the custome so to
do. Others are Architects by booke only, and by dis-
courses

courses which they have read; but they have no hands
to put in practise, and know but the Theorie only; such
as they are good for nothing, but to build a *house* for
Plato, of Ideas, al suspending in the ayre. The good
Architect should linck his spirit with his hand, and the
compas with his reason, setting his hand to work, as
wel as the brayne. The first do frame but bodies without a soule, the second, soules without a bodie, the
third do build the whole, and are men of note and
reputation indeed. The perfect Architect indeed should
be ignorant in no Science; otherwise, if he do wel, it
is by chance, or els by nature, as beasts do, which do
manie goodlie things, and know not why, nor wherefore. He had need be a Painter, to make his plaines,
elevations, designes, and to copie-out a thousand rarities
to please the phantasie withal; a Geometrian, to handle
the compas, for the use of Circles, rulers, squares,
plummets, and the like; To have the Perspective, to
let-in lights into his *house*, to steale-in the day in
certain corners, to content the eye with divers aspects;
and if not directly to introduce the Sunnie rayes, at
least obliquikly through reflexions; The Arithmetick,
to cast up and calculate the charges he is at, to number
the materials and degrees that belong thereto; The
Historie: for al the enrichments of buildings, Armes,
statues, and other ornaments, are nothing els but Historie, true and fayned, which if he knowes not, he shal
commit a thousand errours; To have Philosophie, to
know the nature of beasts, the seas, the elements,
flowers, fruits, and al whatsoever in nature; Astrologie
and Phisick, in planting his *house* in a holsome and
sound climat, in choosing the best Sun, a good wind,
the purest ayre, holesome waters, a faire and free
prospect, a good situation for pleasure and profit. This
is certain, that al art is then in truest perfection, when
it may

it may be reduced to some natural Principle or other. For what are the most judicious Artizans, but the Mimiks of Nature? This same in our *House* is seen, comparing it with the fabrick of our natural bodies, wherin the high *Architect* of the world hath displayd such skil as even stupifyes the human reason to enter into it: Where the Hart, as the Fountain of life, is placed in the midle, for the more equal communication of the vital spirits; the Eyes seated aloft, to comprehend the greater circuit in their view; the armes, projected on each side for the use and commoditie of reaching; Briefly, the place of everie part, is determined by the use. Wherefore, the principal chambers of delight (as Studies and Libraries) should be towards the East: for the Morning is a friend to the Muses; Al offices requiring heat, as Kitchins, Stilhouses, stoves, and roomes for baking, brewing, washing, or the like, would be Meridional; Al that needs a coole and fresh temper, as Cellars, Pantries, Butteries, granaryes, to the North; and so likewise al Galleryes appointed for gentle motion, especially in warme climes, to the West.

THE

THE DISCOURSE.

THe chiefest grace, splendour, and glorie of a *house*, is, that the Maister therof, who dwelles therin, be markable and illustrious for singular and eminent vertues; since the chiefest ornament of a *house* is, the vertue of the Lord therof. Now then the blessed *Virgin*, being eternally ordayned to be a *House* and habitation of the Divine *Word* Incarnate, and wherin the *Holie* of *holies* for nine months, and the endles Fountaine of al sanctitie was corporally to inhabite, this sacred *House* must borrow needs so great a splendour and dignitie, as no other, nor the Empyreal heaven itself, might anie wayes compare with it. What more? Howbeit the glorie of that ancient *house* and Temple of *Salomon* were great, yet can none deny this defect in it, for being incapable to hold the greatnes of GOD in its ample galleries and spaces, even by the genuin confession of *Salomon* himself: *If the Heaven and the Heaven of heavens can not containe thee, how much lesse this house which I have built?* But the golden *house* of the *blessed Virgin*, more capacious then the heavens themselves, did close in and encompas the greatnes of GOD on everie side, as *Jeremie* sayth: *A woman shal encompas a man.* And the holie Catholick *Church* itself sings: *Whom the Heavens can not containe, hast thou held in thy Lap.*

Besides that, which highly advanceth and sets forth the glorie of a *house*, this same prerogative is of no smal moment, to have been deciphered, delineated, plotted, and contrived, and even raysed and built from the first foundation by a skilful and exquisit Architect. Behold GOD himself, the Supreme Architect, not only designed this *House*, but even finished it himself, and brought the same to that eminent perfection, it is of:

I have

The Survey.

3. Reg. 8.

Jer. 31.
Eccl.

Prov. 86.
Psal. 86.

I have been eternally ordayned. Behold the plotting, contriving, and designing of our *House; The Highest himself hath founded her,* where note the foundation.

I know, how *Ovid* in his *Metamorphosis* describes the *house* of the Sun very elegantly in this manner:

The Pallace of the Sun, on pillars highly placed,
With burnisht gold did shine, and Pyrops stone,
And seeling roofs with purest Iv'rie graced.

But who sees not, how this *House* heer, wherin the *Sun* of *Justice* dwelt, did farre exceed the same, whose ornaments surpasseth those, by infinit degrees? for whose golden pillars, were the Guifts of the Holie-Ghost erected in her; for whose Pyropus or Carbuncle, which even glowes like a burning cole, her most ardent Charitie abundantly supplyed; and for the white and purest ivourie, her inviolable and immaculate Virginitie. Whence, while the most blessed *Virgin Marie* more plentifully abounded with the guifts of the *Holie-Ghost,* she burned more ardently with Charitie; and in virginal puritie was more neat, then the heavenlie Spirits themselves; surely more strong and statelie Pillars sustained this *house,* more precious Carbuncles enriched it, and purer Ivourie adorned it, then those others did the *Ovidian* Pallace of the Sun.

3. Reg. 9.

I have sanctifyed this House, which thou hast built, to put my name eternally therin, sayd GOD to *Salomon,* not being yet (as I suppose) affected so to that material *house,* as he pretended thereby rather to shew the love he bare to his spiritual *house,* and yet corporal both, of his Incomparable *Mother,* whom he hath so sanctifyed with his eternal predestination before, and enriched so with his personal presence, to put his name eternally in her. For that saying can not so wel be verified of the *house*
built

built by *Salomon*, which was afterwards demolished
and razed; but rather of *Marie* heer, who shal be sayd
and preached for ever, the *Temple* of GOD, the *holie
House*, where al glorie hath entred in, as to a chast
Bower, and which hath never been ruined like that of
Salomon; for that her foundations have been planted in
the holie mountaines, as *David* sayth, that is to say, by
the Divine Persons of the *Holie Trinitie;* while the
power of the *Father* hath confirmed her in goodnes,
the *Sonne* hath illustrated her with Wisedome, and the
Holie-Ghost preserved and established her in his grace.

Material *houses*, which are built but of frayle matter
and transitorie stuff, diversly fal to rubbage, and are
soone demolished quite, as *Job* sayth: *Who dwel in clay* Job. 4.
houses, have a terrene foundation. But the bodie of *Marie*,
howbeit otherwise framed of a frayle matter, is never-
theles so consolidated and confirmed through the fire
of the *Holie-Ghost*, as she is subject to no demolishment
or dissolution at al; and as she sayd in the *Canticles*, that
leaning or resting on her wel-beloved, *she was strong as
the mountaine of Sion*, having such confidence in him.
So as truly the prophecy of *Aggeus* was fully accom- *Cant.* 2.
plished in *her: That the glorie of the latter house should be* *Agg.* 2.
greater then that of the former. For as in the building of
the first, was heard no noyse or the least stroke of anie
hammer: so heer in this *House* of *Marie*, could not be
heard so much as the least sound or touch of Original
Sinne, so built by the Divine Wisedome, who was a
more expert *Architect* by far, then *Salomon* was, of
whom is verifyed that which *David* so long before had
prophecyed and foretold: *That glorie and riches should* Ps. 111.
*be in the house of the Divine Wisedome, and its justice shal
be perpetual.*

O   THE

THE EMBLEME.

THE POESIE.

The
Pause.

HAu, Who dwels heer? A Virgin. What are you?
A Paranymph sent far, am come to sue
For one that pilgrime-like would lodge this night
Under your roof, and be a mortal wight,
Comes as a Bride-groome. Heer's no harbouring seat
But h' is a Monarch. Then for me too great.
H' is GOD. He now, and ever lodg'd with me.
Would be a child, your Sonne. How can this be?
By th' Holie-Ghost you shal be shadow'd ore;
You let him in by keeping closd your doore.
Then be it donne. One Fiat banisht night,
And now an other brings from heaven the Light.

THE

THE THEORIES.

Ontemplate first, that as in everie *House* wel built, and orderly disposed, there is a Dining-roome at least; and a handsome chamber for some principal guest to lodge in; so this *golden House*, the *Mother* of GOD, which he had so eternally prepared for himself, was not contrived without them both. And first for the Dining-roome, King *Salomon* made him a Throne of the wood of *Libanus;* which wooden Throne was the blessed *Virgin*, because the heavenlie Prince and bride-groome sate and lay sweetly reposed in her armes and wombe delightful unto him, while he took flesh of her. She was a Bride-chamber, because *a golden couch.* For as gold is beautiful, incorruptible, and refulgent: So was her vertue *golden*, because beautiful for sinceritie of manners; *incorruptible*, through priviledge of Virginitie; and *refulgent*, for her luster of Vertues. *O how beautiful!* behold the beautie of her manners; *Chast generation:* see the priviledge of Virginitie; *With clarity:* note the luster of Vertues. *Sap.* 4.

Consider then, that as a *House* hath also Galleries for recreation and delight, so had our Mystical *House* heer, delicious galleries to walke in, and, for varietie, three: to wit, the lower, the middle, and the upper gallerie. The lower was sustained with silver pillars; and therefore is it sayd, that *wisedome erected silver pillars.* The middle was paved with precious stones, according to that: *The middle was strewed with charitie.* The highest was hangd with silks and purples; and therefore is added *a purple ascent.* The lower gallerie of this virginal *house*, was the precious bodie of the *Virgin;* the middle, her purest soule, and the highest, her sublime and Angelical spirit. Her bodie was the lower gallerie, because

because her sensualitie was never prone to evil, but alwayes conformable to reason. Her soule, the second; because strewed with precious stones, that is, Divine vertues. Her Spirit was the upper gallerie, and adorned with purple hangings, for being so enflamed with charitie, or wounded with the sorrow of her *Sonne's* passion, or sprinckled with his bloud.

Ponder lastly, as a *house*, especially the Pallace of Kings, requires to be spacious and ample; so was this *House*, our *Ladie*, being the *House* of GOD, most spacious and wide; according to that which the *Church* sings of her: *Whom the heavens can not containe, hast thou held in thy lap.* Secondly, wide and ample in compassion, while she receaves al, and refuseth none, into the bowels of her mercie; receaving the tempted, in protecting them from the snares of the Divel; Sinners, in obtaining mercie and grace for them; the Just, in conserving them in grace obtained; and lastly the Dying, in receaving their soules into her protection: and therefore sayd to be *Mother of grace, and mother of mercie.*

THE APOSTROPHE.

The Colloquie.

O Sacred House, *Temple of the Divinitie, and Divine Tabernacle of the living* GOD! *A work surely much greater then the workmanship of the world besides! O sacred Pallace framed by the Divine hand, with admirable art, and most exquisit and choice matter; a peece of workmanship without peer, erected by the Divine Wisedome, imputrible Arck, incorruptible vessel, Celestial Temple, Cittie of God.* Oh what glorious things are sayd of thee! *Thou wast ordained eternally, before the earth was made.* The Lord hath possessed thee from the beginning of his wayes, and thou wast before his works. Thou wast begot, when as yet there was no abysses seen; thou wast formed

Psal. 86.
Eccl. 24.
Prov. 8.

med before mountaines were yet placed. When he prepared the heavens, was thou present. *By al these faire
prerogatives we beseech thee, Incomparable peece of his
handiework, so long designed and premeditated before hand,
and so exactly framed at last to his owne Idea and designe,
that in us likewise his eternal designe of predestination
through our defaults may not utterly perish.*

THE

THE XVI. SYMBOL.
THE HEN.
THE DEVISE.

THE CHARACTER.

The Impresa.

THe *Hen* is that gentle Hart, that contents herself with the common Apellative of her sex; and as others ambitiously usurp strange titles, as in Hawkes, for males or females (as the manner is) to be called Ladie, Mistris, and the like, she wil go no higher then the stile of plaine Goodwif, and be called the *Hen*, and wil take it amisse, to be termed otherwise. Yet is she the dear consort of the generous Chantecler, and his deerest beloved partner, and most individual companion.

panion. She is very familiar and domestical, and that so truly as she wil never goe from home so much as a flights shot. But is so kind-harted to al, especially to her owne children, as she hath not a dish, which she shares not among them. It is a sport to see, how she knocks to her dresser, to have them come quickly, if she have but a bit worth the eating, and then to see what strife there wil be amongst the litie fry of them, for a single graine of corn, as the ambitious of the world for a Crowne and scepter, or as *Cæsar* and *Pompey* for the Empire and Dictatourship of *Rome* itself; while the *Hen* falles a delving and digging afresh for more. She wil be as fierce as a Tigre or Nemean Lionesse against the assassinats, who are so bold as to seaze on her familie, when she wil bristle herself and fly in the faces of the cruelest Bandites that are of the land, or Pirats of the ayre, on behalf of her brood; and triumph as fast, if she come but handsomly off with her owne. And then must al the world take notice of her conquests, and she be recounting the same to her deer consort, who wil swel therat and bristle as fast; and even menace the skyes in his greatest choler. She is no great Arithmetician, and hath but a shallow memorie; for she never knowes, how manie yong she hath; and so she have anie at al, she is pleased alike. She loves not her children so much, as the name of Mother; which holds in one, as wel as a 100. She is not a Castle, or Bulwark, which keep their stands attending the assailants; but as a Pinck at sea, wel man'd, wil meet and encounter the Adversaries themselves, and defye them to their teeth, and with the sayles of her wings wil seeme to fetch the wind of them, to fly the fuller into their faces. But if she be let alone, and not provoked, there is noe Dove more meek and gentle then she.

THE

THE MORALS

TUTELA FIDISSIMA.

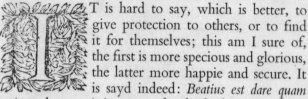

T is hard to say, which is better, to give protection to others, or to find it for themselves; this am I sure of, the first is more specious and glorious, the latter more happie and secure. It is sayd indeed: *Beatius est dare quam accipere*, because it is supposed, who hath to give, hath otherwise no need to crave, wherin the beatitude consists; wheras who finds protection now, was of late in distresse, or feare of danger; so as though he hath the happines now, to dry up his waterie eyes, yet not the priviledge, to have them never to dry. To give protection, involves a power to be able to afford it; to take the same, implyes a necessitie to recurre unto it: the first hath a kind of obligation with it, if not of justice, of charitie at least, to yeald his succours: in which estate he ever stands, and consequently in a state of servitude, because obliged. But the second discovers his impotencie only, and present il condition; but yet with a hope of enfranchiʒment, and a kind of title unto it; yea manie times an absolute freedome and quite discharge of further cares. The truth is, howsoever the first, as it is more honourable, so is it more happie, and as approaching neerer to the soveraigne excellencie of GOD himself, is acquit from anie imperfection of servile obligation; but al what is, is meerly a goodnes in him, that seemes to put the obligation upon him, which is no more indeed, then a kind of vertue in him, that makes him so prompt and readie to help the miserable in al necessities. This excellencie and singular priviledge the glorious *Virgin* hath, of

power,

power, to protect; and of benevolence, to have the wil
to protect; with the happines besides of an infallible
efficacie in al whatsoever she undertakes. And therefore
is she implored of al, and held to be the common
Sanctuarie of the necessitous that fly unto her, and
especial Patronesse and sure Protectrice of her Devotes,
and by consequence rightly and deservedly called:
TUTELA FIDISSIMA.

THE ESSAY.

HE Cock is very glorious, when he hath
al his attires and accoutrements about
him; for then he wil strout it, as a souldier
right; he buckles himself against his
enemies, and with his wing making a
target or buckler, defends, covers, and shroudes the
chickens from the assaults of the Raven; and falles a
quarrelling with everie one, either friend or fo, that
approches or but looks upon them. And for the *Hen*
herself, before she layes her egs, as others doe, she begins
to provide and take care for her lying downe. For
she chooses her a quiet place to breed in, and builds a
neast or couch to sit in, and makes it very soft, as
knowing wel her egs would bruise and destroy one
an other, if they be not commodiously and handsomly
layd. Her yong are no sooner hatched, but she presently
clucks them with her wings, least the cold or sharper
ayre should hurt them; and is so tender of them, as that
if a Kite or Wesel come in sight of her, receaving them
under the shaddow of her wings, she opposes herself
as a stout champion against them, with a great clamour
and outcry, to strike a terrour into them, defending
them herself with spurre, bill, and wings, with might
and mayne, so as she wil rather even dye in the place in
defence

The Review.

defence of her brood, then by flying away leave them in anie danger. To some she wil present her wings to cluck beneath, to others yeald her back to mount upon, nor hath she anie part about her, which she is not willing to afford them what she may, to cherish and conserve them; nor that truly without joy and alacritie, as appeares by their kackle and tone they have at such times. When she is alone, and hath no more to care for then herself, she trembles at the Hawke and buzard, and wil fly away from them; but if she have yong, and espy anie danger neer, she comes forth like a Lion against them in their defence, and fights oftentimes far beyond her forces.

THE DISCOURSE.

The Survey.

 Ow is this *Hen* truly a gallant Symbol of the fruitful *Mother* of GOD, as wel for the plentie of egs she layes (for they wil lay, some two, and some three a day) as also for breeding so each moneth of the yeare, whereof though *Aristotle* and *Plinie* except the two winter-moneths, yet experience shewes and some Authours affirme, they wil lay also in those moneths, and some there are, that wil lay two a day even in those moneths likewise; which surely is a great fecunditie, not lightly found in anie fowle besides. For lo, the blessed *Virgin* hath a double fecunditie with her, one natural, and the other mystical: the natural, in bringing forth CHRIST, whose natural *Mother* she was; and being his *Mother*, she was *Mother* in a sorte to as manie, as are called and are truly *Christians;* whilst of this one her seed became multiplied beyond the Starres in heaven, and above the

the sands, that lye on the Sea-shores. But what shal I say of her mystical fruitfulnes, which even filles and embraceth the whole world, that invocates and calles upon the name of MARIE, as their common *Mother*? Behold al the kingdomes therof, and al the ample Provinces, and you shal find them ful of her Devotes and Children. Nor is *Hungarie* only her proper familie, which title she hath taken, and yet holds from the donation of *S. Stephen* King of that Nation, who freely and devoutly once consecrated the same to the *Mother* of GOD; but even our *England* is knowne also by the name and title of our *Ladies Dowrie*. Yea *France*, *Spayne*, *Italie*, and *Germanie*, and the rest of the Kingdomes and Provinces of the world, whose affection and devotion is no lesse to this common *Parent*, our Incomparable *Ladie*, the *Mother* of GOD. But nothing demonstrates her spiritual fecunditie so much as the innumerable multitude of Families of the *Sodalitie of her Immaculate Conception*, the true *Parthenian Children of our sacred Parthenes*. For in how short a time, throughout al *Europe* first, and then through *America*, the new world, the *Indies* as wel the *East* as *West*, have *Sodalities* of al sorts and conditions whatsoever either Secular or Ecclesiastical been instituted, under the soveraigne and most blessed name of MARIE? which with al observance and due worship serve her as the *Mother* of GOD, and their common Parent: while they doubt not by her meanes to be led and conduced to a better life, and to obtaine Eternal salvation, if they serve her truly indeed, and but observe the Rules of her said *Sodalities*.

Besides the propertie, the *Hen* hath to defend her chickens, during life, this is singular in her, that even after death, she is soveraigne and medicinal for infinit diseases, and her bodie the choycest diet for the sick and infirme. And therefore is the Cock consecrated to *Esculapius* the Inventor of Physick. And

And for our *Ladie*, what need I say more then that versicle of her Litanies: *Salus Infirmorum*? because she procures health both of bodie and soule. For is there a disease in anie part of the bodie of man, even running through the whole Catalogue of maladies, whereto present remedie hath not been begd and obtained of our mysterious *Hen*, the soveraigne *Mother* of God? O what a thing it were to reckon up the Temples and Chapels, and therin the Votes, tables, and waxen images set up as testimonies of her infinit cures! Nor helps she the bodie more then the soule. For Pride she heales no lesse, then the head-ach; *Vanitie* no lesse, then the *vertigo* or turning of the head; *Wrath* no seldomer then the frenzie; *Slouth*, then the Lethargie: Ignorance as easily, as the Pin and web in the eye; *Lust*, as the disease belonging to it: *Gluttonie*, as the Consumption: and *Avarice*, as the dropsie.

Arist. l.
9. c. 49.

There is yet another thing which I note in the *Hen*, not so much out of *Aristotle*, as by experience, though *Aristotle* hath it likewise: that the *Hen* is a great scraper in the dust, which especially they do for three causes: as wel by busking therin to satisfy the itching they have in themselves, and to mend their plumes and feathers, as also to shake off the vermin about them. Our *Hen* likewise most willingly busked and rould her-self in her dust and ashes also. Dust is the beginning of human generation, and the origin of our vile extract-ion; and Ashes the verie Epilogue therof: whence both are the symbol of our birth and end; and thence

Ec. 19.
Ecc. 10.

Humilitie. *Al men are earth and ashes. Why art thou proud, thou earth and ashes?* In these cogitations and the like, as in a heap of dust, the most Blessed *Virgin* con-tinually volved herself, revolving nothing so much in mind, as her dust and proper extraction. Whence that: *Behold the handmayd of our Lord. God hath regarded the lowlines of his handmayd.* But

But how then, O mysterious *Hen*, lovest thou dust so wel, hating al fowlnes and sordities so much? Feltst thou the itching of Vanitie a whit, that thou shouldst scrape in that sort? No, not the least itching of vaine ostentation infested *thee*, the immaculate *Virgin*. Or wouldst thou have pranckt thy quils and plumage of supernal affects? It was not needful, since they were without anie lets to hinder them at al. Or was thy intention, to shake off at least any evil cogitations? Not so likewise; no such thing had ever accesse or ingresse into that purest mind. No temptation of arrogancie, ostentation, or pride could ever find admittance there. But truly, this it was; thou lovedst Humilitie, which thou knewest to be gratful and acceptable to thy *Sonne*, which could no where more appeare, then in the dust of human nullitie, then in the ashes of mortalitie, and thy proper annihilation. An other reason may be also, why *thou* diggest so in the dust of thy Nothing: to find, as *Hens* are wont in the dust, some food more acceptable to them; for this is a maine cause likewise of their so frequent scraping in the dust; and who knowes perhaps, whether they may not light on a gemme or no? for so it hath been knowne. The most humble *Virgin Marie* indeed even nourished herself with humilitie, as a most savourie food unto her; this she supposed to lye in the dust of her proper abjection; and therefore with clawes of consideration, never left she digging and scraping it forth; nor was she anie whit deceaved; the earth of her abstraction, gave her abundantly to feed most deliciously. And which is more, she found, in so doing, the precious *gemme* indeed, which was so enamoured with her humilitie, as he even stoopt into the dust, to be there found by this mysterious and blessed *Hen*.

THE

THE EMBLEME.

THE POESIE.

The
Pause. NO mother, like the Hen, preserves her yong,
Protects, and shelters with her wings; her tongue
Is clucking with a sad and doleful note;
Call's back her chickens, when they are remote;
And if they come not, chides sharp, shril, and lowd;
With beck and tallions fights for them. Thus shrow'd,
O Virgin Mother, while the Puttock flies,
(The Prince of darknes) who with watchful eyes
Seekes for my Soule, his prey. The Hen is knowne,
Careful of al. Yet if she hath but one,
Her care's as great. So's thine of one, or other.
Then to me Sinner, shew thy self a mother.

THE

THE THEORIES.

Ontemplate first, the great magnanimitie *The*
of the *Hen*, in defence of her chickens, as *Contem-*
above sayd. And then reflect upon the *plation.*
courage and fortitude of our victorious
Patronesse, the glorious *Virgin*, especially
in the protection likewise of her Children; for to her
enemies is *she terrible as a battail wel arrayed*. As an armie *Cant.* 6.
wel marshalled, is a terrour to the enemies, and makes
them fly at the sight thereof, before they enter into
fight: so are the Divels danted at the presence of this
invincible *Champion*, standing in defence of her Clients
and Children.

Consider then, the great compassion of the *Hen*
towards her yong; which appeares in this, that with
the sick and infirme, she wil be infirme; she is so sollicitous in feeding them, as she finds not a graine, but
she calles them to her, to participate therof: And for
her care of preserving them from danger, she clucks
them under her wings, from the rapin of the kites, and
the like ravenous fowle. And then weigh withal the
tender compassion the *Virgin-Mother* hath ever shewen
towards us her Children and Servants, in being so sollicitous to feed us, while she was on earth, with the food
of her doctrine: *She hath opened her mouth in wisedome,* *Pro.* 31.
and the law of clemencie in her toung; and for custodie,
how she hides us under her wings, and protects us from
the snares of the Divel. For this is she, *to whom* was sayd,
that two great wings were given her: The one, the wing *Ap.* 12.
of Mercie, to which Sinners do fly to be reconciled to
GOD; according to the Prophet: *Protect me under the
shadow of thy wings;* The other, that of Grace, under
which the Just remaine, to be conserved in grace, and
may say with him likewise: *She hath shadowed us with
her shoulders.*

Ponder

Ponder lastly, how the *Hen* not only sits upon her owne egs, but sometimes strangers likewise, as the egs of Ducks and pea-hens, put into her nest, which being hatched, the Ducks according to kind wil betake themselves to the waters, and there dive and plunge themselves over head and eares; and the young pea-hens enamoured with their owne beautie wil forsake their tender nurse that bred them up. And then weigh withal, how manie strange and ungrateful children our mysterious *Hen*, the admirable *Virgin*, cherishes and nurses with her daylie protection, who requite her il for al her care in trayning them up.

THE APOSTROPHE.

The
Colloquie.

Queen of Angels, saluted by the Archangel, adored by the Powers of Heaven, Mistrisse of Vertues, Dutchesse of Principalities, Ladie of Dominations, Princesse of Thrones, more highly advanced then the Cherubins themselves, more enflamed with ardour of Divine love, then al the Seraphins; The first next to God, the second in the Role or Register of the Predestinate: Thou most terrible to thy foes, as an Host wel arrayed; and yet infirme with the infirme, as a Hen amid her chickens, most tender of them, and a most sure bulwark for them, against al incursions and assaults of forren and domestick enemies, either visible or invisible. O thou, who through thy Sonne, and thy matchles humilitie, hast crushed the Serpent's head: through thy holie prayer and intercession, I beseech thee, let Sathan be trampled likewise, under thy Servants feet. O grant this same, mysterious and Indulgent Bird of Paradice.

THE

THE XVII. SYMBOL.
THE PEARL.
THE DEVISE.

THE CHARACTER.

THE *Pearl*, or *Margaret*, the Lillie among Jewels, *The* is the peerlesse Gemme of Nature, so much *Impresa.* happier then the rest, as nobler descended then they: this being bred in the womb of the sea, and they in the bowels of the earth. If they be stillicides from Heaven (as some think) they are the milkie drops distilled from *Juno's* breast, which *Sol* parcheth into seeds; which seeds empearle in those litle Ovens lying on the beach. The Diamant that sparcles so, though rich indeed, arrives not to that wealth without trade, and

P exercise

exercise of the Jeweller, in passing the file and chizel, wheras the *Pearl* needs none of those to raise its fortunes by, but is truly borne a Prince. They are the ordinarie companions of the greatest Ladies, and so chast as they wil be dandling in their necks, without sensualitie in themselves, or those they dallie with, without jealousie of anie. They are true Subsidie-men, and such Sureties indeed, as their credit wil be taken for as much as they are worth. If you would epitomize an ample estate, and put the same into a litle *Compendium*, with *Bias* to carrie your wealth about you, sel what you have, and put it into *Pearl*. If you have anie suit in Court, it wil purchase greater friends, and procure you better preferments, then the best deserts. Like a pin and web, it wil put out the eyes of *Linceus* himself, not to see what he should. It is the key, that wil set open the Jayle to the worst conditions; and the bolt to shut upon the best deservings. What civil warres could never effect, the *Pearl* or *Union* hath infallibly brought to passe, to wit, the ruine of that great Triumvirat, being disunited or dissolved: what would it then have done, if united? It is called *Oriental*, as much to say, as it makes al men to arise unto it, to do it homage: and wil make you more place in a throng of people, of meer respect, then a rufling Whifler shal do with torch in hand. In fine, it is a rich Treasurie of rarities enclosed in a box of *Pearl*.

THE

THE MORALS.

Preciosa et caelestis.

Are things are likely precious, and prec- *The Motto.* ious rare: not that scarcitie alone should set the price, or price and valew make them rare; but that the ordinance of God is such, to have them so, that things which are excellent in themselves, should be rare and scarce to be found, that *pearls* (for worth) might not be cast to swine, or trampled under foot. Monsters are rare indeed, and yet most hateful, and prodigious. It is the worth then that gives the price to things. The Sybils Books were valued lesse being nine, then when they were but three; not for the plentie of the nine, or scarcitie of the three; but to let *Tarquinius* see, the true estimate and value of each one; and had he not perhaps taken her at last at her word, as he did, he had payd as much for one alone, as for the nine, or gone without it. Yea gold itself, were it as common happely as manie other things are of litle worth, would yet be in as great esteeme as now it is, through a certain excellence it hath in itself above others. And therefore *S. John* did very wel, to dresse up God al in gold, and pave the Paradice of joyes with the same: for otherwise, do I feare, that manie an one, would never have had anie great thirst after it; who perhaps would better have liked the horns of *Lucifer*, tipt with gold, then those of the Moon with silver, or the burning cristal of the Sun. Who would thinke, that a peece of earth, taken, as it were, with the disease of the yelow Jaundise, being no more indeed then a yelow earth, a glittering Stone, a kind of froth boyling from Hel, should have such a

power

power upon reasonable men? So as wel it may seeme,
to be the Golden Age, since al is set upon gold; they
wish but gold, they speake or thinke of nothing els but
gold, when lo, the Gold of gold, the precious Margarit
of *Pearls*, is truly valuable indeed, the Incomparable
Virgin-Mother, I meane, who is either the *Pearl* itself,
or *Mother* of the true *Oriental Pearl*, which descended
from heaven, and therefore is worthily called: PRE-
CIOSA ET CAELESTIS.

THE ESSAY.

HE true *Pearl* hath a luster of silver with
it, which wil not soyle a whit, nor wax yellow; its skin feares no nipping of the frosts,
nor the tooth of Time. It is bred in the Sea,
and seemes to disdayne the fare of its Hostesse, the
Scallop, wherin it is a prisoner, while it takes its food
from the heavens, and hath its whole alliance with
them. They use to counterfeit the same in a thousand
manners with glasse, and above al, with the *Mother-
Pearl*, in beating it to powder, and making a past therof,
and then causing pigeons to let it downe, which with
their natural heat do boile and polish it in the manner
it is, and then put it forth againe. The *Mother-pearl*
engenders from the heavens, and lives but of celestial
Nectar, to bring forth her *Pearl* withal, either silver,
pale, or yelowish, according as the Sun makes it, or the
ayre, whence it feeds, be more or lesse pure. Receaving
then the deaw of Heaven into the gaping shel, it formes
litle graines or seeds within it, which cleave to its sides,
then grow hard, and geale, as it were: and so Nature
by litle and litle polishes them through favour of the
Sunnie beames, and at last they become the *Oriental
Pearls;* and as the Deaw is greater or lesse, the *Pearls*
                                                    become

become the bigger and fayrer. The *Pearl* in powder, is good in a manner for al maladies. It growes not only in the flesh of the fish, but in the mother itself, or shel without the fish. It is tender within the mother, but growes hard as soone as taken out of the water. The greatest gallantrie of Ladies, is to have them dangling at their eares by half dozens, whence are they called Cymbals; they wil say likewise: a faire *Pearl* in the eare, is as good as an Usher to make them way in a presse. *Cleopatra* wore two of them, which were worth a million and a half; wherof one she swallowed downe, being first dissolved by vinagre.

THE DISCOURSE.

F you look now into the mysteries of al natural Secrets, you shal find none to symbolize better with the *Virgin Marie*, this *Margarit* of ours, then this same *Pearl* or precious *Margarit* of the Sea: if especially we regard but the names only, wherewith they are stiled, the one of *Marie*, the other of *Margarit*, and both having so great alliances with the Seas: the one being, *amarum mare*, a bitter sea: and the other, as wholy borne and bred in the seas; the one importunatly begd and obtayned of GOD, by *Anna* her Mother: and the other, as greedily gaped-after from the Heavens, and especially from the Sun, by the Mother of *Pearl*, so properly called by like, for her motherlie and maternal appetite to engender and bring forth; and we al know, what *Pearls* of sanctitie are lightly brought into the world, with so great import-unities. But if we looke into the other congruities between them, we shal find them to sympathize so, as we may wel tearme our *Virgin-Mother*, a *Pearl* or

The Review.

Margarit

Margarit of the Heavens, as the other of the Seas.

The *Margarit*, as I sayd, is bred in the Sea; which *Isidor* affirmes, and that in this manner. At certain times of the yeare, to wit, in the Spring and Autumne, the cockles, oysters, or scollops, or cal them what you wil, approach to the Sea-shore, and lye there gaping, and opening themselves, and receave the celestial deaw into their bowels; from the coagulation wherof, as abovesayd, are the *Margarits* engendred. Now this Shelfish, oyster, or *Mother-Pearl* (for the Mother, or issue *Pearl*, are al of a substance, as mothers and embrions use to be) is the *Virgin-Mother-Pearl* it self, which opened her Virginal soule, at her mysterious *Annunciation*, in the Spring of the yeare, by the quiet shore of her tacit and silent contemplation, to receive the heavenlie Deaw, the new *Margarit:* that is, to conceave that precious *Pearl, Christ Jesus,* in her womb. For she opened her consent, to the great Angel, her singular Paranimph, to obey GOD in al things, saying: *Behold the handmayd of our Lord, &c.* and her soule likewise to the *Holie-Ghost,* to overshadow her: and after the opening thus of her free consent, and her Angelical soule, the Celestial deaw of the *Holie-Ghost* descended into her, and so this infant-*Pearl* was divinely begot in the virginal womb of the Virgin-mother-*Pearl.* Of which deawing of the *Holie-Ghost,* and opening of the *Blessed Virgin* thereunto, it is prophetically sayd: *Deaw* *Isay.* 45. *you heavens therupon, and let the clouds rayne downe the Just; let the earth open and bring forth the Saviour.*

These *Pearls* besides, if they be right *Margarits* indeed, are faire, white, and cleer; for such as are so, are truly of the best, and a great deale better then those which are dimmer, and of a yellow and duskish coulour: For those which are faire, white, and cleer, are bred of the morning-deaw; and the others, of that which falles in

the

the evenings. And our Incomparable *Margarit*, was predestinate so from the morning of the eternal Decree in Heaven, so created, as it were, *ab initio et ante secula*, while the other *pearls* of lesse regard were only produced in the evening, after that sinne was brought into the world.

This *Margarit* therefore so faire, so white, and cleer, signifyes our heavenlie *Margarit* and glorious *Virgin*, who was beautiful and faire in mind through a more then Angelical puritie of hers consisting in the mind; most snowie and white in bodie, through an immaculate chastitie and virginitie; and cleer and sincere in works, through a simple sanctitie, and Saintlie simplicitie in al her actions, in the whole course of her blessed and incomparable life, which she led on earth.

I sayd above, that *Pearls* being stampt and beat to powder are holesom, soveraigne, and medicinal for manie maladies; wherof I find the *Naturalists* chiefly to reckon three: *First*, they are purgative, because they purge and evacuate the bodie of al noxious and superfluous humours; secondly, restrictive, staying the flux of bloud or venter; and thirdly, they comfort and corroborate the hart, being readie to faynt or swoune through debilitie of the spirits, or the vital parts. To these infirmities, the applications of these pownded *Pearls* so beat to powder, are of singular avayle. In this manner the Blessed *Virgin*, being seriously pressed with importunitie of prayers, and often urged and called upon with incessant vowes, relenting and mollifyed at last, as fallen into powder, applyes herself, first through a purgative power to purge us of our sinnes, by procuring us the grace of Contrition, and the holesome Sacrament of Pennance, to bewayle and purge our sinnes past; secondly, with her restrictive vertue, to restraine the soule from flowing and falling againe
into

into future sinnes; and thirdly, with her restorative, comfortative, and corroborative power, to strengthen and fortify the hart, in present occasions of sinnes.

THE EMBLEME.

THE POESIE.

The
Pause.

 Rare and precious Pearl *is hardly found,*
That's Great, *and* Heavie, *Smooth*, pure-white
and Round.
    The Sonne *of* God *came from his heavenlie*
  Throne,
Factour for Pearles, *at last found such an one.*
Great, *to containe* himself; *and* Heavie, *ful of grace.*
And therefore sunck unto a Handmayds place.
Smooth *without knob of Sinne.* Virgin *pure-white.*
Round *in perfection, more then mortal wight.*
This pleas'd his eye; a long time having sought,
Gave al that ere he had, and this he bought.
Union's *a* Pearle *(no twinnes) it-self, but one;*
Such was the Virgin-Mother *Paragon.*   THE

THE THEORIES.

Ontemplate first, how this *Pearl* or *Mar-garit* is usually called, as we sayd, by the name of *Union;* whether it be for the great union and sympathie there is be-tween the Mother and the *Pearl*, I know not; for you can not mention the Mothers name, but needs must you bring-in the *Pearl* withal: or for the union of the Celestial deaw, with the Conchal nature, to make up a *Pearl*, in the lap of the fish, I wil not say: this I am sure of, that our blessed *Pearl* heer is called *Deipara*, as much to say, as the *Mother* of GOD; nor can she be so called a *Mother*, as she is, but GOD must needs be united to her, to make up her name.

Consider then, that as the *Mother-pearl*, being other-wise only a meer shel-fish of its owne nature, and of no greater a ranck then a playne oyster of the Sea: yet through the appetite she had to suck, and draw in the heavenlie deaw into her bowels, obtained the especial priviledge and prerogative, to become indeed the *Mother* of the true oriental *Pearl*. So the *virgin-mother*, though she were, as she sayd herself, the sillie handmayd of our Lord, and of our human nature, subject to the natural frayleties therof; yet through a singular immunitie with the puritie of her intention, integritie of bodie, and Angelical candour of mind, dis-posing herself most affectuously and ardently indeed, to receave the Celestial deawes from heaven, that is, the grace of perfect Union with GOD, in her pure soule, she deserved to become the *Mother* of the *Pearl* of *Pearles*, sweet JESUS.

Ponder lastly, that if a meer *Pearl*, being so basely bred in an oyster-shel, whose extract at the best is but meer Deawes let fal from the nether Region of the

Ayre,

Ayre, and those but drops of fresh water, as it were impearled in the fish, through benefit of the Sun should come to be so highly prized as we have sayd, being no more then a meer seed of *Pearl* somwhat fairer then the rest of that kind; how are we to prize and magnify, trow you, our heavenlie *Pearl* heer, whether you meane the *Pearl*, or *Mother* herself? the *Pearl* himself, for being such a *Pearl* so truly descending from heaven; and her, for being the *Mother* of such a *Pearl*.

THE APOSTROPHE.

The Colloquie.

 OST *sweet, most debonnaire* Virgin-Mother, *the Immaculate through emphasis, the Mother of fayre dilection, Mother of* Jesus, *regard me poore wretched soule, and obtaine, that my hart and affection be pure and clean, at least like the seed* pearl, *according to the proportion of my litlenes, and my bodie wholy free, from the duskish blemishes of the least sinnes, and that by day and night my thoughts being repurged from al immundicities and uncleane objects, the flourishing bed of my Fancie, may never be soyled more, to offend thine eyes, and those of the Immaculat Pearl of thy womb, the. Spouse of my soule,* CHRIST JESUS.

THE

THE XVIII. SYMBOL.
THE DOVE.
THE DEVISE.

THE CHARACTER.

THE *Dove* is the true and perfect type of Love; let them but change caps with each other, and the *Dove* shal be Love, and Love a *Dove*. If *Venus* betake her to her Chariot, she is drawne with the teame of foure of them, as Poets say. This are we sure of, the Holie-Ghost, the essential Divine love, hath been seen to appeare, as carried with Charitie, in the forme and figure of a *Dove*. The *Doves* are never in their proper element more, nor better pleased, then in digging them

The Impresa.

them holes in the rock, and planting their litle pavill-
lions there. And the Eyes (the Agents of Love) like a
payre of twin-like *Doves* have set up their rests, and
built their nests, as it were, in the hollow concaves of
the browes, in service of Love. The *Dove* is the trustie
messenger, or winged Post of the Ayre, that carries
letters to and fro, in matters of the greatest importance;
which she fayles not to deliver with the hazard of her
life, nor ever misseth, but it costs her the best bloud of
her bodie. She is even an arrow, and verily as swift as
it, but without a steelie head to hurt withal, as having
no gaule within her, or curstnes in the bil. She is a very
sociable creature, and apt for Citties; witnes their
Dovecots, where they live in great peace and neigh-
bourhood togeather; and not of feare, as some, do
they flock togeather in great troupes, but meerly of
love and charitie one to another. She is very abstemious
and religious in her dyet, and wil not feed on those
flesh-pots of Egipt, that first came-in with that Patriark
and second Parent of our kind; contenting herself with
bread alone, allowed even from *Adam's* time, who
tilled and ploughed the first of anie. She is hot by
nature, and yet of condition a *Moyses* for meeknes, and
even the verie Lamb of birds; if not so able to cloath
our nakednes with her wool as he, yet surely she would,
if she could; yet ever readie and prompt to lodge us in
her downes. And when she can not stead us otherwise,
she wil afford her bodie, to be sacrificed by us, as an
entire holocaust of her good nature.

THE

THE MORALS.

IN FORAMINIBUS PETRAE.

W HO *wil give me the wings of a Dove* (the Prophet sayth) *and I wil fly and rest?* The Dove would fly, and then rest: fly in the exercise of al vertues, and then rest in the contemplation of the Divine attributes; or fly in the meditation of our *Saviour's* life, and then rest in the deep contemplation of his bitter passion; fly in reading the Divine Scriptures, that point us the Rock; and rest in digging in the holes of the said Rock, the blessed stigmats of his venerable and sacred wounds. For Reading indeed, though it much avayle to lead us to the Rock, yet dives not so deep into the Rock, as serious Meditation doth; and Meditation though it dig into the Rock, yet dwels not so quietly there, nor rests so sweetly in the Rock, as a deep Contemplation doth; while Reading regards but the shel only, that is, brings to the Rock; Meditation, the kernel, that is, digs into the Rock; but Contemplation swallowes and relisheth the kernel, that is, dwels and sets up its rest in the Rock. Reading looks but superficially therinto; Meditation bores and enters into it; but Contemplation dives and sounds into the depth. Reading exhibits the breasts of the Mother-Church, in opening the books of the Old and New Testament; but Meditation, and more Contemplation, wrings them, to fetch out the milk to nourish withal. Reading crops off the eares of corne; and Meditation and Contemplation, as with the fingar and thumb, wrings out the grayne; then grinds it to meal, til it comes to be bread and food of men. And this the tender and compassionate *Mother* did, who

flying,

The Motto.

flying, like to the *Dove*, al the time of her life, never rested herself, til finding her *Sonne*, become a Rock of scandal and reproch, and piteously bored on everie side, she enters into them, and dwelles within them; and if you ask her, where she is, might very wel answer: IN FORAMINIBUS PETRAE.

THE ESSAY.

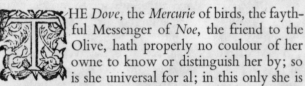

The Review.

HE *Dove*, the *Mercurie* of birds, the faythful Messenger of *Noe*, the friend to the Olive, hath properly no coulour of her owne to know or distinguish her by; so is she universal for al; in this only she is singular above the rest, that being of what coulour soever, her neck being opposed to the Sun wil diversify into a thousand coulours, more various then the Iris it-self, or that Bird of *Juno* in al her pride; as scarlet, cerulean, flame-coulour, and yealding a flash like the Carbuncle, with vermilion, ash-coulour, and manie others besides, which have no name, but as you borrow them from other things. And though she be never so chast, innocent, and loyal to her mate, yet can she not avoyd his jealousie. Which you may see, and it is a pleasant contemplation to note the while, when the Cock returns to his Dovecot, how, discovering his jealousies, his litle breast wil swel up to the bignes of his bodie; then with the voice to break forth into a hoarse and angrie note; by and by to walke in state, as it were, and encompas his mate about; and with the shew of a wrothful *Nemesis*, rake the ground, with the swift trayling and strotting of his trayne, and that you may not doubt but he is angrie indeed, with the pecking of his bil, and strokes of his wings, he persecutes the poore wretch, deserving it not. Yet she abides very

patient

patient to al, nor is troubled a whit at his causeles indignation, proceeding out of vehemence of love; she flyes not away to shun him, and withdraw herself, but rather approaches neerer and closer to him; she returns not blow for blow againe, but meekly endures and suffers al; until the diuturnitie of sufferance and her meeknesse do vanquish and mollify the choler and fiercenes of the furious thing. And so at last the Cock forgetting his suspicion, is quite tamed; and laying the enemie aside, puts on the Lover, returns to reconciliation of friendship againe; and the joyning of their bils togeather, with more ardent affection, renewes the same, as the flame is encreased with the sprinckling of frigid drops theron. She is a meek creature, and hath no gaule; she feeds on no living thing; she brings up others yong, she makes choice of the purest grayne, she builds in the rocks, she hath groanes for singing notes, and sits very willingly by the waters side, that she may suddenly shun the hawke foreseen by his shadow therin; and a thousand other qualities besides.

THE

THE DISCOURSE.

The Survey.

Ow then, as the *Dove* builds her nest not in trees nor on the earth, but in the holes and concavities of the Rock, not so curious as some birds be, to plaister and trim up their nests, or to seeke for the softest downes to prepare their beds with, against the hatching of their yong: So our *Ladie*, the mystical *Dove* we treat of, built not a whit, nor placed her hart, in the baser earth of terrene desires, nor in the higher thrones of princelie Maiesties, but even in the wounds and passions of her dearest *Sonne*. *Arise, my friend, make hast, my Dove; I say, make hast, and come into the holes of the rock,* where our *Dove* is sayd to inhabit. In the holes of the rock, I say, because in her thoughts and remembrance was she stil conversant and lodged, as it were, in the wounds of *Christ*. Or we may say, and not unaptly to, that *Christ* had sundrie nests, to wit, the Crib, the Crosse, and his Sepulcher or monument. In these nests now of *Christ*, our *Dove* would often inhabit, because she would often visit these places with incredible ardour and devotions. Of which opinion is doubtles *S. Hierom*, though he say, perhaps: Perhaps, sayth he, through excesse of love she is sayd to have dwelt in the place, where her Sonne was buryed. For one hardly would beleeve, how much internal love and affection is fed with looks.

Cant. 2.

S. Hier.

The *Dove* againe feeds not on the flesh of other fowles and birds, as some do, but of the graynes of corne, and that the select and most choice of al. Nor was our *Dove*, the blessed *Virgin*, affected or given to terrene and worldlie things, but to Celestial and eternal; she fed

fed not on the flesh-pots of *Egipt*, nor yet of Manna, being but only the bread of Angels, but rather fed of the Bread of life, the thing represented by that Manna, she fed on the sweet thoughts of the Divine Word it self Incarnate in her womb, and fed of that grayne of corne, wherof it is sayd: *Unles the grayne of corne* Joan. 10. *falling into the earth be mortifyed and dy &c.* This grayne of corne refreshes and satiats; and therin may signify our Saviour *Christ*, according to the Psalmist: *He satiats thee with the fat of corne;* and hath rednes without, Isay. 63. in regard wherof may it signify the flesh of *Christ;* agreable to that: *How red is thy garment &c:* and besides is white within, and expresseth the soule, which is fulgent and bright with the candour and splendour of Sap. 7. puritie; For indeed it is *the candour of light.* And there-fore in the *Canticles* the *Virgin* sayth: *My beloved is white and red, and chosen of a thousand;* White, for his blessed and divinifyed soule; red, for his precious flesh, em- Cant. 3. brued with his bloud; and the choice of a thousand, for his soveraigne and supreme Divinitie. This *Dove* then fed of such a grayne, because she was wholy and fully delighted with the Divinitie and the Humanitie of *Christ*.

And for her groanes, the ordinarie musick of the Lyre of her hart, they were the lamentable and sad accents, which the Passion of her deer *Sonne* had caused in her. For lo, this *Dove* with the rest of that desolate and mourning flight of *Maries*, her fellow-doves, did nothing els, but sigh and groane, in beholding the onlie Pearl of doves, her deerest Sonne, in so piteous a plight, so hampered and entangled in the fowler's nets. *Like Doves that meditate, they groned sore*, as the Prophet sayth, especially this *Dove* above the rest, the incom-parable *Virgin-Dove*, being the natural Dam and parent of the poore distressed one, most sadly powring forth

Q   a floud

a floud of teares without measure. Whence *S. Anselm* sayth in a certain place: My most merciful *Ladie*, what fountains may I say brake forth of thy purest eyes, when thou sawest thy onlie innocent Sonne to be scourged, bound, and so cruelly entreated before thee, and the flesh of thy flesh so mangled in thy sight? What groanes shal I imagin thy breast sent forth the while, when thou heardst him say: *Woman, behold thy Sonne;* and agayne: *Behold thy mother?* For she could not see her Sonne to be so crucifyed, without groanes, and motherlie laments for her dying Sonne, the joy of her hart, and hart of al her joyes, so pierced with a souldiers speare, that even transfixed withal the mothers breast, a verie *Niobe* of teares, or rather *Noome* of bitter groanes.

Now for the wing, which so eternizeth the *Doves*, and makes them most illustrious among fowles of the highest pitch, this I note, they love not much to fly alone, but to assemble themselves in flights. The blessed *Virgin*, is that Woman cloathed with the sunne, of whome it is sayd in the *Apocalyps, that two wings were given her to fly with, in the desert;* Which two wings are the wings of *Love* and *Hope*, wherewith she flyes into Heaven. *Who wil afford me wings as the Dove?* But yet she would not fly alone, but draw others also to fly along with her, to wit, the Apostles, during her life, and through her example afterwards al other Saints.

They were accustomed of old, the better to attract strange pigeons to their houses, to use this industrie or flight, to annoynt some one tame and domestical *Dove* with an oyntment, which they knew most grateful unto them, and so annoynted to let it fly at large; when she so flying in the ayre, through the fragrance of the odours about her, would draw to her a number of them; and so she, who first flew alone, would returne

turne back againe in triumphing manner. The *Virgin* of herself alone at first was the onlie lover of vowed Chastitie, who professed, she knew not, nor ever would know man. This *Dove* then the heavenlie Fowler had sent forth into the ayre of the world, as annoynted with the perfume of al graces, and especially of Chastitie; but now she flyes with an innumerable number of Virgins, led by her example, singing altogeather with one consent that verse: We *wil runne after the odour of thine oyntments; the yong virgins have loved thee, O lovelie Dove.*

Lastly, for the sitting of the *Dove* by the waters side, heare what the *Holie-Ghost* in the *Canticles* sayth: *Thine eyes like Doves upon river-waters, which are washed with* Can. 5. *milk, and sit by the fullest streames.* S. *Hierom*, that great Contemplatour of Celestial Secrets upon the *Canticles*, speaking of this most holie *Virgin*, how she was assumpted to Heaven, sayth: I saw one specious as a *Dove* ascending from the waters. She was a beautiful *Dove*, as it were; because she shewed the forme and simplicitie of that *Dove*, which came upon *Christ*, coming out of the streames of waters. Now as the *Dove* is sayd to dwel upon the streames, as wel to discover the shadow of the hawke, as to refresh herself against the heats: So the blessed *Virgin* rests and abides upon the fulnes of the flouds of the *Holie-Ghost*, as wel to admonish her Devotes to beware the Diabolical snares, as to enjoy the plenitude of the waters of the same *Holie-Ghost*, to wit, the guifts therof.

THE

THE EMBLEME.

THE POESIE.

The
Pause.
★ Co-
lumbam
nigram
pingebant
Aegyp-
tii ad sig-
nificandam
viduam
castam &
constantem;
inquit
Pierius.

THE Holie-Ghost, *that nestles like a* Dove,
Betwixt the Father *and the* Sonne *above,*
Is flowne from Heaven *to seek a mate below,*
A Virgin, *chast,* pure Dove, *as white as snow*
Fethred; *a like consort; she without gal,*
Simple *and mild; he* Love *essential.*
Thus they accord, as they in colour sute,
And to the flower correspond's the fruit.
The Virgin's *shadowd, yet remaines pure white;*
(Shadowes expeld) the substance brings to light.
But while her Sonne *is shadowd on the* Crosse,
The mourning★ Dove *in blackes laments her losse.*

THE

THE THEORIES.

Ontemplate first, how the *Dove*, being *The* a most pure creature, feares to be defiled, *Contem-* and abhorres whatsoever is foule and *plation.* sordid, as appeares by that which hapned in *Noë's* Floud. *Noe* sent forth a *Dove* after fourtie dayes, to discerne whether the waters were fallen and ceased upon the face of the earth or no, who not finding wheron to rest her foot, returned into the Ark againe; and the reason was, as *S. Augustin* thinks, *Gen 88.* that though the tops of hills appeared bare, yet they remained moist and slymie, and therefore the *Dove* being a nice and delicate bird, and extremly amourous of puritie and cleannes, would by no meanes put her foot theron. And heer reflect upon the *Virgin* pure, in whome no spot appreared of Original Sinne at al, in that great inundation and deluge therof in *Adam*, but remayning in the Ark of her Innocencie Immaculate, because the mother of the Immaculate Lamb.

Consider then the singular providence of the *Dove*, which is a part indeed of the prudence of this creature, in that to shun the hawke, she shrouds herself in the secret holes of the Rock, and there securely reposeth in great peace. And then consider, how this *Dove of Doves*, this same most prudent *Virgin*, being higher then the rest, and more profound, had placed her nest or chamber in *Christ* her Rock; where being alwayes safe and kept inviolable, the flights of the Divels and the subtleties of Hereticks could doe nothing against her; but what they did, was against the Rock itself, rebounding back upon the impious themselves, like the waves against the cliffes, the ships against the shelfs, the rusling of the winds against the towers, the fomie froth against the beach, the edge of the sword against the

the Adamant, the reed against a target, drifts of snow against a helmet, fire against gold, and lastly a slender cloud against the Sun.

Ponder lastly the great similitude and resemblance, which is between the salvation of mens lives in *Noês Ark*, and that of Soules in the Church, whose foundation was layd in the *Virgin*-mothers womb, our true *Dove* indeed, at the *Annunciation* of the *Angel Gabriel*, when that stupendious miracle of grace was wrought within her. But as then that *Dove* of the Ark carryed only the message of salvation, the figure of that embassage heer brought by *Gabriel*, whom when you behold so painted with a branch of Olive in his hand, as a token of peace and mercie, what see you els, but *Noe's Dove*, bearing a bough of olive, in the feet?

THE APOSTROPHE.

The Colloquie. Most innocent Dove, *Lady of meeknes!* O *would you please to remember me for my good, most sober and demure* Virgin, *and amourous* Mother *of my deerest Spouse. Oh pray the eternal Love for me; reject me not poore wretch, most wretched Sinner, so wholly immorti-fyed in al my senses, who heer present myself before your goodnes in the demand and pursuit of mansuetude of mind. Oh grant, most precious* Virgin-Mother, *that I perish not for ever, and be lost. O admirable* Ladie, Ladie, *I say, of heaven and earth next* GOD *your deerest* Sonne, *placed above al the Hierarchies of Heaven: Let me not quite perish, Queen of the heavenlie Empire; for alas, what profit wil there be in my utter ruine? Alas, Alas, let me not fal, a caytif and unworthie worme as I am, to nothing, or worse then nothing, so wholy drowned in Sinne and vice.*

THE

THE XIX. SYMBOL.
THE FOUNTAIN.
THE DEVISE.

THE CHARACTER.

THE *Fountain* is the liquid Glasse or Mir- *The* rour of the *Naiades*, where they haunt to *Impresa.* contemplate their beauties in; or rather is the Nimph herself, who gazing on her proper beautie, through a strange Meta- morphosis of self-love had lost herself in her owne Glasse. Hence it is, she runnes the Hay, as it were, in the meadowes, to seeke herself in the waters which she is herself, got forth to take the ayre, in the fields abroad; and as it runnes, it playes on the Harpsicon

the

the while, whose jacks are the pible stones, checking
the litle waves as strings, that so with purling frames
the harmonie it makes. The feathered Nimphs there,
are much taken with it, especially the Swan, that wil
be tuning her Descant to that ground. Al the care she
takes, is but to haste to pay her rents, which she doth
to the Brooks and Rivers, as Baylifes to that great
Exactour, who takes them grumbling, as never satisfyed. She is the breast of Nature, and Nature the Nurse
that suckles al things with her milke, and is so good a
Nurse and so prodigal of her sugred lickours, as where
she can not els communicate herself, of her owne
accord wil she break out into Springs: Springs so called
indeed, because they leap and spring forth of the earth.
For so shal you see the litle lambs and kids prickt with
this milk of Nature, wel concoct with youthful heat,
to spring, to jump, and frisk; whence doubtles the
season of the Spring tooke first the name. For what is
the blossomes, trow you, to spring and bud forth, but
for Nature to breake out as into Springs? The Rose
springs forth, while Nature breaks a veyne as it were,
that springs into a Rose. The Lillie springs, while
Nature spilles her crystal milk, that sprouts into a Lillie.
The Springs and *Fountains* therefore, are the life of
Nature, if the life, as some maintaine, abide in the
veynes, which may wel be. They are the verie ticklings
of Natures hart, that make her sprug up herself in the
season of the Spring, to court the world with, in her
best array. For then she crownes herself with a garland
of al flowers, puts on the mantle of her goodlie meadowes diapred al over, and tricks and decks up her hayre,
the fruitful trees, with gemmes of blossomes of infinit
varieties, to feast and entertaine the new-borne world.

THE

THE MORALS.

PERENNIS ET INDEFICIENS.

L things that are, have their certain *The* tearmes; and ther is a stint and period *Motto.* to be seen, in al things. Be they treasures of immense riches how vast soever, they may be summed with good Arithmetick, to a last farthing. The Cataracts of waters, in *Noe's* time, that powred downe so fast, at last were exhausted quite, and gave leasure to the Earth, to swallow and digest so huge a draught. They were neither perpetual, for they lasted but a time; nor yet without measure, for it may be supposed the Springs were dryed, or that the hand of GOD had put a sluce to the torrents. *Elias* called for rayne, and it powred downe so fast, as manie were affrayd of a second deluge; but the glut and tempest ceased in a certain time, and al was wel. To leave these, and to come to Man, whose pride makes him oft-times to pretend to a kind of eternitie of felicitie; Let him lift up his crest never so loftily, his pride wil soon have a fal. *Alexander* how great soever, when he saw he could not eternize himself, and become dreadful enough otherwise, used a stratagem, which was to be drawne by *Apelles* in sundrie manners, now mounting on his Steed, that brave *Bucephalus*, in the action of making the earth to tremble with his looks; and then to be admired in the habit and equipage of a GOD, calling himself the Sonne of *Jupiter Amon;* but the truth is, his looks made not the earth to quake, but only in his picture; nor was he adored, but in his pourtrait, and he no more then a mortal man, whose *Aurora* and cursorie day, had a speedie sun-set.

Nero

Nero caused a coyne of gold to be stampt, where his owne *effigies* was engraven of the one side, and of the other *Fortune* enchained at the foot of a Rock, with this word: *Nec scopulos metuo*. But he shortly found the contrarie, when killing himself, he suffered ship-wrack in the sea of his owne bloud. *Otho* represented himself in such peeces of gold, with his hand armed with thunder, with this: *Aliis non utor armis*. But soone the spring of his life and Raigne, was the winter of his death; and what death but a death which his life deserved? There is nothing sure and perpetual in this world; but al things slide away like running streames from the spring-head, which leave not so much behind them, as the memorie of their passage. The Spring only is it, which stil remaynes, whose waters after they have runne an endles time, shal then but seeme to begin to runne, as being an Abysse of waters sprung from an endles source. Looke then what the Spring is of elemental liquids, the same is the *Mother* of GOD, an endles *fountain* of spiritual graces and perfections, and is truly the FONS PERENNIS ET INDEFICIENS of al Graces.

THE ESSAY.

The Review. O speake of the *Fountain* truly, as the thing deserves, one had need of a *fountain* of wit and brayne about him, to decipher it aright. For who can draw a picture of one that can not sit, but is ever jogging up and downe? For lo, the *fountain-water* never stands, but hath the palsey in the veynes, that wil not rest. It is sometimes taken for the Fabrick itself, as built of stone; which if we should, the difficultie would en-crease. For so were we obliged to expresse as manie formes wel nigh, as there are fancies in the Brayne.

For

For some shal you see of one fashion, some of another, as everie one abounds in his sense. Witnes that so artificially wrought by the famous *Michael Angelo de Bonaroti* in figure of a Woman washing and winding of linnen clothes in her hands; in which act of hers, she straynes forth the Fountain-waters. Another have I seen of an Elephant spouting the waters from his *Proboscides* or trunk, to the pleasures of the Spectatours; another of a Whale, that spouted the waters so high, as even did diselement the same into a dust of powder of waters. Another so cunningly set and contrived, as what with the waters so disposed, and the Sunnie rayes togeather, it would make a perfect Iris in the eyes of al men; and a thousand other, while Art in nothing more wil vye with Nature, then with her workmanships of this kind. The *Fountain* therfore is properly neither the manufacture alone so wrought, nor the water of itself, as it creeps in the veynes of the Earth. For so the one were a livelesse Statue of Man or beast, and the other a Spring only, and no *Fountain;* The one would be but a dead or sensles Carkas, and the other only in the Concha, as the bloud abiding in a boule; so as to have a *Fountain* indeed it must be alive, and have the silver bloud, as in the veynes, that spouts, streames, or trickles from it: Such as *Niobe* herself was transformed into a *Living Fountain*, as it were, when she wept out her eyes; such, I say, as *Magdalen* was at her *Maister's* feet, or as that great *Porter* of Heaven and the Keeper of the keyes therof, when he so bitterly wept at the Cock-crow. I can not tel, whether there can be a braver sight, then such as these, curiously represented in marble, with the azure veynes appearing in the bodie, and the rest of the lineaments lively set forth; and then to behold the trickling streames to fal from the eyes, either as pearls by drops, or as open Cataracts burst forth.   THE

THE DISCOURSE.

Ehold we now the Incomparable *Fountain* itself of living waters of Grace, that flow from thence: to wit, the Signed *Fountain*, the most pure *Virgin Mother* of GOD, according to that of the *Canticles: The fountain of gardens, the well of living waters which flow with violence from Libanus;* and againe: *My Sister is a signed or sealed Fountain.* She is a *Fountain* placed by or neer GOD; she is a *Fountain* turned into a River; She is a *perpetual Fountain;* and lastly a sweet and pleasant *Fountain.* She was a *signed fountain,* because she was likewise an *enclosed Garden.* She was a *Garden,* because *Her* understanding was ful of fayth, and knowledge of GOD, with infinite varietie of flowers of al kinds; and *closed* it was, because no errour or ignorance might enter therinto. She was a *Garden,* because her affect was ful of love to GOD and her Neighbour; and *closed,* because no terrene love or base desire of the flesh or world, could find accesse to her hart. She was a *signed Fountain,* because her Virginal womb was ful of the water of Celestial grace; and *signed,* because *sealed* with the irrevocable Vow of perpetual and immaculate *Virginitie.* She was a *Fountain* placed neer to GOD, *Because with thee is the Fountain of life; A Fountain,* in that she refrigerates from the heat of concupiscence; and a *Fountain* of grace, for that she vivifyes from the death of mortal sinne; and because she is very neer to GOD, she plentifully and aboundantly powreth forth herself to al.

    This litle Fountain encreased to a huge River, and flowed into very manie waters. Fo lo she was a litle *fountain* in her humilitie and conversation; but then grew into an immense River, in her *Annunciation* and *Conception*
of the

of the *Sonne* of GOD; and flowed into manie Waters
in her glorious *Assumption*, when she flowes so abundantly, as al participate of her fulnes; as wel they
without (as yet in banishment) as those also in the
streets of the Celestial Hierusalem; according to that
of *Salomon* in his Proverbs: *Thy fountains are derived* Prov. 5.
abroad, and thou dividest thy waters in the streets. She is a
perpetual Fountain, because (as *Esay* sayth) *a Fountain of*
waters, whose waters never fayle. Other *Fountains* wil Esay. 1.
soone dry up, but this never. For the love of the world 6.
is no endles or perpetual Spring, but slides away, goes,
and comes, and oft comes to nought; but is a Cestern
rather, that wil in time be exhausted, and that ere very
long. *They have left me the Fountain of living Water,* Hier. 2.
and framed to themselves broken Cesterns, that leake and
can hold no water. Lastly, this *Fountain* of Ours, is sweet
and pleasant. For as Springs and *Fountains* of waters,
arising from the Sea, and passing through veynes, as
it were, and subterranean places, become very savourie
and sweet; and that by certain degrees, having first of
al a kind of bitternes with them, and then a more gratful, and lastly a pleasant and delicious tast. So the blessed
Virgin like a *Fountain* springing from the source and
origin of the bitter and harsh people of the *Jewes*, was
through a singular and especial prerogative preserved
from the least tack of those brackish waters, whence
she came; and being divinely sanctifyed by the *Holie-*
Ghost, became a most delicious *Fountain* of al graces;
according to that of *Judith: The bitter fountains are made* Jud. 5.
sweet to drink. From whence, as from a publick Conduit of a Cittie, the universal *Church* derives infinit
streames of graces and favours. And, as in great Citties
there is wont to be some Conduit or Concha, or most
ample and spacious Channels erected in the open mar-
ket-place, from whence may al at their pleasure fetch
waters

waters without limit or restraint, for al their uses;
besides some special pipes conveighed into some mens
houses, as a singular favour: So the blessed *Virgin*, like
a copious and endles Conduit, abundantly affords the
waters of her graces to al that have their recourse to her
for them; and more particularly and familiarly to those,
that are her special Devotes, as being of her families
and holie Sodalities.

Let us now see then, what waters she affords; for
surely her waters are ful of Vertues. And first, they
coole and refrigerate, and are therefore most welcome
to the thirstie soule. And as *Fountain-water* in Sommer
is more cold, and hotter in Winter: so the Incomparable *Virgin*, in the sommer of prosperitie gives fresh
and coole waters, to wit, a cooling and refrigerating
grace, that the mind be not too much enflamed with
terrene affects; but in the winter of Adversitie yealds
her waters hot, that is, inflaming, least the mind with
adversities being too much depressed, might coole, and
at last grow utterly cold in the love and service of God.
As these waters coole, so do they quicken and vivify
withal; and are therefore called living or the waters of
Num. 13. life. *Heare the clamour of this people, and open them the*
treasure, the fountain of living water.

These *Fountain*-waters have an humective and vege-
tative vertue with them, to water and to make things
Gen. 2. prosper and grow up. *A fountain ascended from the earth,*
watering the universal superficies. So *Genesis*. And for
Esa. 55. growing, *Esay* sayth: *The shower falles and snow from*
heaven, and returns no more; but inebriates the earth, powers
upon it, and makes it to spring and grow up. For the earth
indeed is sayd, first to put forth the blade of the wheat,
then the green eare, and lastly it becomes a ripe and
ful-grayned eare of corne. And this heavenlie *Fountain*
of ours, first makes the earth of our soule, to put forth
the

the green hearb of the feare of God, which is the beginning of a new life; then the green eare of Pennance,
which is bitter and sharp; lastly a ful perfect fruit in the
ripe eare, which is Charitie: since *Dilection is the fulnes
of the Law.*

And to conclude, the vertues of these waters have *Rom.* 13.
the power to ascend and mount up, according to that:
The water which I shall give you, shal be (in her) *a
Fountain of water arising and springing to eternal life.* And
as the nature and propertie of the water is especially *Jo.* 4.
in pipes to arise the higher, the lower it falles: so the
Virgin stooping to the center of her Nothing, is advanced so high, above the Cherubins and Seraphins
themselves; and so consequently the waters of grace,
that flow to us from her, rayse us the higher in Heaven,
while by her example we stoop downe and abase our
selves, and especially despise these base and terrene
things.

THE

THE EMBLEME.

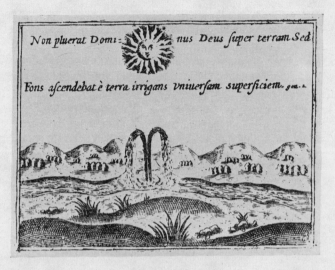

Non pluerat Domi- nus Deus super terram Sed

Fons ascendebat è terra irrigans vniuersam superficiem. gen. 2.

THE POESIE.

*The
Pause.*

I T had not rayn'd, and so the earth was dry,
No showres of Grace were falling from the sky.
An universal drought possest the Land
With dearth and famine; God's revengeful hand
On Eve, pass'd to her progenie. For sinne,
Man's soule, like earth dried up had ever byn,
But that there did a cristal Spring arise,
To drench the barren soile, and fertilize:
For Naamans (Jordan-like) it made a floud,
That flowd with Grace. *'Twas Troubled (not with mud,
While She's cal'd ful of grace) But sinner I
Am troubled, 'cause I want. Fountain, supply.

★ Tur-
bata est
in ser-
mone
eius.

THE

THE THEORIES.

Ontemplate first, that as an Aqueduct hath length and breadth with it: so our glorious *Virgin*, the *Fountain*, I mentioned above, of living waters, as an Aqueduct hath so great a length, as she reaches even from heaven to the earth; according to that mellifluous *Doctour*: *Marie* is an Aqueduct, whose top like *Jacob's* ladder, reaches to Heaven. And the breadth of this Aqueduct is such, as she was able to containe the Divine *Fountain* itself, as the same *S. Bernard* affirmes: A *Fountain* is borne to us, because that Celestial veyne hath descended by the Aqueduct, though not affording us the whole plentie of the *fountain*, yet powring out certain stillicides of grace, into our dry and arid harts.

The Contemplation.

S. Ber.

Idem.

Consider then, that as we can not derive the waters of the Heavens into our Conduits on earth, without some conveyance or other: so can we not expect the waters of Grace to come from thence without some Aqueduct of Grace, which is the blessed *Virgin*, the Incomparable *Fountain* therof; for that, as *S. Bernard* sayth, the flouds of graces were wanting so long to human kind, for that as yet no Aqueduct had made intercession for it. Seeke we therefore grace through the invocation of *Marie*, Mother of Grace, and whatsoever we offer to GOD, commend we to *Marie*, that grace may returne back by the same channel, by which it flowed.

Ponder lastly the manner how this Aqueduct or *Fountain* of ours communicates its waters; for to some she communicates in manner of a Well, to some againe in manner of a Spring, and thirdly to others in manner of River-waters. The Well hath its waters hid in the bottom of the pit, and not to be drawne without some

R   difficultie:

difficultie: in which manner she communicates herself
to sinners only, to whom the waters of grace are hidden, but yet to be fetcht and had with the labour of
contrition and pennance, but the water of the Spring
is drawne without labour at al, and flowes continually:
and in this manner she communicates herself to pious
Soules and her Devotes, because continually she affords
them graces with much facilitie; and lastly, as touching
the River, that flowes so with great abundance, she
communicates and powres forth herself to the Blessed
Soules, with ineffable graces, which are not communi-
cable to mortal wights.

THE APOSTROPHE.

The
Colloquie.

O *Virgin* Marie, Fountain *of grace,* Fountain, *I say,*
of the Paradise of pleasure. Thou cristal Well *of*
the living waters, which flowe with impetuositie
from Libanus. O *signed and sealed* Fountain, *such as the*
Wise-man *so points forth, that beganst to rise from the earth*
of a barren soile, to fructify the world with thy Merits, and
to water it with thy Graces. Thou litle Fountain *as then,*
now growne to a great and ample River, who in thy birth
appearing as a litle Spring by humilitie, and then a Fountain
of more note, and so encreasing stil with sanctitie in conver-
sation becamest at last to be a swelling River, when so thou
conceavedst in thy Womb, the source of al graces, that precious
Oyle CHRIST JESUS; *so as now from the plentitude of this*
Fountain, *through al places of the* Church, *have balsomed*
liquours been derived to us. Obtayne, ô *incomparable*
Virgin, *inexhaustible* Fountain *of Graces, of that deare*
Sonne *of thine, that the waters of his Celestial graces may*
so water my soule, that through spiritual ariditie it be not
enforced to languish utterly. This I beseech thee, thou
Fountain *of living waters.*

THE

THE XX. SYMBOL.
THE MOUNT.
THE DEVISE.

THE CHARACTER.

THE *Mount* or *Mountains* are of the noblest and best extraction of the earth, and therefore aptest to take fire, witnes *Ætna* or *Mongibel*. They are as great Barons in England, and Grandes in *Spaine*, for their eminencie above the rest of Hils, in the Upper-house, and the other as Knights and Bourgeses of the Lower; the Vallyes being no more then the Commons of the Land, who choose them out to stand for the people. They are the Cedars of the earth, and *Cesars* in the

The Impresa.

Senate

Senate of the highest towers, as topping them al and keeping them under. They are the Piramides of mould, more ancient and more lasting then those of *Egipt;* and the true Mausoleums of the Monuments of Nature; the statelie Collosses of earth, erected as Gog Magogs among the lesser people of the Hils or Hillocks. They are as *Sauls,* far higher then their brethren by head and shoulders: and the rest as litle *Davids,* more fit to keep sheep in the lower playnes. Had not *Mount Arrarat* stood so a tipt-toe as it were, the Ark had been forced to have made a longer navigation, and Natures shop had not been opened so soone, to expose her Specieses of living things to the new world, nor yet the doores and windowes therof so soon had been unbolted within. The *Mountains* then, are as *Atlas* shoulders; to sustaine and bear up the Welkin with. If the earthlie Paradise be yet on earth, it must be surely on some *Mountain* top, or els as hanging in the ayre, and so no earthlie Paradise. They are the Rocks of the Ayre, against the which the racking clowds, like *Argoseyes,* dash and breake themselves, and suffer shipwrack. They have the honour of the first salutes of the glorious Sun, in the Aurora of his first appearing; and have his last kisses, ere he goe to bed. They have their intelligences with the Intelligences themselves; and were they not so pursie and unweildie, might even dance to their musicks, howsoever they may listen to them as they stand.

THE

THE MORALS.

IN VERTICE MONTIUM.

Here is nothing honourable, that is not *The* good; nothing good, that is not equit- *Motto.* able; and nothing equitable, that is not wholy opposit to al deordinations. True honour consists in fearing GOD; and to spare neither life nor ought that is deerest, in augmentation of one's glorie. It stands not upon its Ancesters, in seeking so much to borrow luster from them, as to earne it of itself. So as if it can not arrive to their vertue, who have left it anie Title by inheritance, it blushes more for its owne infirmitie therin, then vaunts of the blazon of its House, whose greatnes makes it not haughtie or imperious, but rather, as the fixed starres, the higher it is, the lesse it desires to appeare; nor regards it so much an outward pomp, or swelling ostentation, as the solid veritie of a Soule truly noble. Courtesie and sweetnes can no more be severed from it, then the bodie from the soule, to remayne true honour; nor doth it of anie base facilitie to insinuate with, but out of a natural courtesie coming from a true esteeme of its self. None more enclined to compassion towards the afflicted, or more disposed to succour them, then it; and then most, when they have least help otherwise, and lesse possibilitie to requite. It is more careful to yeald true honour to the Creatour, then to receave it from anie one. In a word, it so behaves itself, as it holds the Bodie of true honour, to consist not in the bloud or dignitie only, but the Soule in the eminence of vertue above others. This true Nobilitie and honour the glorious *Virgin* had in high measure, who being lineally descended from the race of Kings,

of Kings, and, which is more, exalted to the soveraigne
degree of the *Mother* of GOD, and consequently raysed
above al the hils of the blessed Spirits in Heaven, yea
the Cherubins and Seraphins themselves; stiled herself,
the *handmayd of our Lord*, being arrived, I say, to sit
IN VERTICE MONTIUM.

THE ESSAY.

*The
Review.*

MOUNTAINS are one of the gallantst
things in Nature, especially if we
regard the prospect they afford, to
deliciat the eyes with; when taking
a stand upon some good advantage,
you behold from thence a goodlie
river underneath; which in token of homage, as it
were, runnes kissing the foot therof, along as it goes.
But then most delicious it is, when you see on the other
side, a vast playne suspended before you, and diversifyed with litle risings, hils, and mountains, heer and
there, which bounding not the view too short, suffers
the eyes with freedome to extend themselves into the
immensitie of Heaven, while the River, creeping along
the meadowes with *Meander*-windings encloses the Hil
about, in forme of an Iland, whence manie vessels of
al sorts riding there at ancker, may be discryed, the
neerest questionles very easily discerned, and the rest
farther off through interposition of bancks between,
not perceaved, the tops of the masts only appearing,
like a Grove or wood in winter without leaves; the
litle closes or fields thereabout, with the hedge-rowes
environing the same, seeming as Garden-plots hedged
in with prim, and the lanes and high wayes as dressed
into allyes. The verdures give forth themselves delicious
to behold, like a Landskap in a table, with al the greenes
to be found

to be found in the neck of a mallard, heer a bright, there a dark, and then a bright and a dark againe, and al by reason of the levels, with the risings, and fallings togeather, with the lights and reflections caused through the dawning of the day in the morning or twylight of the evening, the rayes of the sunne being an open enemie to such neer prospects, offending the view with too much simplicitie and sinceritie of dealing. It is a great curiositie in Nature, to enquire how these *Mountains* first came up, so to surmount the lesser *Hils* and lower vallyes; or whether Nature intended them first, or no. If so; how came she partial? if not, how came they to be so? and a thousand other divels they rayse besides, which no ordinarie Conjurer can lay. But such would I have to aske the Vallyes, how they came to be so beneath the *Hils* or higher *Mountains*? which if they satisfye, I undertake, the *Mountains* shal as much. But the truth is, he that puts generositie in some above the rest, and made not al of the same evennes and tenour of mind: and so in other things he made a Cedar and a shrub, a Pine and a bramble, an *Alexander* and a *Diogenes*, a *Caesar* and an *Irus*, a Giant and a dwarf: so made he *Mounts* of *Pelion* and *Ossa*, and the vales of *Mambre* and *Josaphat*. These, from the first, were so created *mountains* and vallyes; unles perhaps, as with the Angels, al were once as *mountains*, til *Lucifer* and his Complices aspiring higher then they should, were throwne headlong, and made the vales of Hellish feinds: So such as wil aspire to be so wise, to search into the secrets of *God's* hidden Architecture, shal beranckt in the number of the sillie vales, in punishment of their daring follie to presume so much.

THE

THE DISCOURSE.

BUT then to speake of the *Mount* of *Mountains*, placed in the Garden of the Empyreal Heavens, where al are *Mounts*, and this the *Mount* paramount above them al; is a work of a higher nature, the Incomparable *Virgin* MARIA, I meane, that admirable and mysterious *Mount*, so like in name and qualitie to that of *Mount-Moria*, a certain hil in the Cittie of *Jerusalem*. For as on that *Mount-Moria*, *Salomon* first founded his Temple, the house of GOD: so in this our *Montain Maria*, was the heavenlie and Celestial Temple of the true *Salomon* raysed indeed, which he sayd within three dayes should be re-edifyed againe, in case it were ruined, to wit, the Temple itself of the humanitie of JESUS CHRIST. *Moria* signifyeth the land of vision; and what land more worthie to be seen then *Marie*, the Mother of GOD? *Moria* is sayd to be a high and statelie land, and next to GOD: and there is nothing so high and sublime as *Marie* is, no not the Angels nor Archangels, nor yet the Cherubins or Seraphins themselves. *Moria* is interpreted *shining* or *illuminating:* and *Marie* being clothed with the Sun, illumines Mortals, and truly shines, as being truly the Starre of the Sea. *Moria* as some Authours say, is derived of the Hebrew *Mori*, which signifyes *my mirrh*, and *Jah*, which is GOD, as much to say as GOD *is my mirrh*. And was he not truly her mirrh indeed, when she stuck him so in her as he lay in her lap, being taken from the Crosse, bosome, according to that: *my beloved to me is in a bundle of mirrh?* and she herself no lesse then mirrh, if we look into her name, which is *Marie, quasi amarum mare*, a Sea as bitter as mirrh itself; of whom is sayd: *As a choice mirrh have I yealded a sweetnes of odour: Maria* is derived also,

also, as some wil have it, from the Hebrew *moreh*, which is teaching, and *jah*, GOD; teaching; who taught indeed, when being seated as *Salomon* in his Throne, or rather *Wisdome* it-self in its Scholastical Chaire, in the Womb of the Virgin-Mother, for so manie months, he read to the world such a Lecture of humilitie, patience, charitie, and al vertues particularly in his *Incarnation;* but especially in the Crib, and armes of his Mother, when teaching both *Jew* and *Gentil*, in the Shepheards and Magi, at his Birth and Manifestation, he so taught them the Ghospel. It is finally interpreted the Rayne of GOD, where you may judge what a showre of grace by this our *Marie* was powred into the world, when *Anna*, as a dry and barren clowd, for manie yeares before, was at last delivered of her; and *she* powred into the world, as a showre of rayne, after a tedious famine, to fertilize and fructify the earth.

Nor is *Marie* our *Mount* restrayned to *Moria* only, but *Sinai* also seemes to represent her, no lesse in regard that Hil is accompted the *Mount* of mercie and promise, as wel as she. This *Sinai* is scituated in the province of *Madian*, wherof *Oreb* is a part, and where our *Lord* appearing to *Moyses* in a bush, and taking compassion on the affliction of his people, promised to free them, from the bondage of the *Egyptians*, through the power of this mightie hand, as we have it in *Exodus*. And so *Exod.* was the Blessed Virgin *Marie*, as the Queen of mercie, promised and prefigured in the same Bush, wherin our *Lord* appeared to *Moyses;* and for the rest, were the promises likewise performed in her, of the Redemption and deliverance of the Human kind, from the thral-dome and slavourie of the Divel, while the Sonne of GOD tooke flesh of her for our ransome and deliverie. *Our Lord descended on mount Sinai &c.* That mount was likewise as the Rendevous and haunt of our *Lord*; for there

there the Angel appeared often on behalf of our *Lord*, and spake familiarly to *Moyses;* and therefore it is said

Act. 7.

of him in the Acts: *He appeared to him in the desert of mount Sinai, in the flame of a fierie bush.* And so was the Blessed *Virgin* saluted, and as frequently visited by the Angel, and instructed no lesse of the Word of life. *Sinai* was a *Mount* of rayne, and Deaw: and so was the Blessed *Virgin*, in conceaving the *Sonne* of GOD; accord-

Psal. 71.

ing to that: *He shal descend as rayne on a fleece. Sinai* was the *Mount* of the Divine habitation; for so, according to *Josephus* was the common opinion in those dayes. And the Blessed *Virgin* was truly the habitation and

Ps. 110.

dwelling of GOD. *She was the mount in whom* GOD *took much delight. Sinai* was the *Mount* of wisdome and learning; for therin was the Law delivered to the people by the hand of *Moyses*: so likewise the Blessed *Virgin-Mother* brought him forth to the world, who is the Word and Wisdome of the Father, who is our Captain and Law-giver, through whom do Kings raigne, and the givers of the Lawes decree just things. She was a *Mount* distilling the oyle of mercie; a *Mount* of peace and alliance; a *Mount* of pastures to feed on; a *Mount*,

Psal. 75.
67. 41.
Isai. 2.

where it pleased GOD to inhabit, as *David* sayd, the *Mount* of GOD, the fat *Mount*, the holie and litle *Mount*, which *Esay* fortold of, which should be prepared, and to which al the world should resort for pleasure, and repayre for sweet consolation; the *Mount* familiar to the Angels, in their frequent visits.

THE

THE EMBLEME.

THE POESIE.

The Pause.

Gaine is rays'd (while Mortals feigne, and erre)
   The Statue of Nabucodonozer.
   Heresie on feet of Clay *and* Iron *stands,*
   Which have no Union. Lo, cut without hands
A stone falles from a Mountaine. *Sh' had a Sonne,*
Who (having vow'd) sayd: How can this be donne;
I know no man. *'Twas then the work alone*
Of th' Holie-Ghost: Thus without hands the Stone
Fel from the Mountain. Head, brest, armes, and al
By striking of the feet, demolisht, fal.
O, with that Stone, this Monsters feet misled,
May she breake downe, that crusht the Serpent's head!

THE

THE THEORIES.

COntemplate first, that as *Libanus* is a *Mount* of indeficient waters; for that, there, according as we have it in the *Canticles, are springs of living waters, which flow with a force and violence;* and *Libanus* itself is a fountain and spring of flouds; while on the foot therof, two fountaines arise, the one *Jor,* the other *Dan;* which sliding and falling into one, do make the *Jordan* at last, as *S. Hierom* sayth. So our Incomparable *Virgin* is truly a *Libanus* likewise of endles and indeficient waters, whose graces and favours continually flow to Mortals; nor can those springs of hers be ever dry, to wit, her perpetual virginitie, and stupendious humilitie; which being so united in her *Annunciation;* produced such a *Jordan* of al graces in the person of her deerest Sonne our *Saviour Christ.*

Consider then, that as *Mount Libanus* is a *Mount* of fragancie and sweet odours; and therefore it is sayd;

Like Libanus having the odour of sweets. For there are trees that beare the incence, and many odoriferous herbs besids, do there grow. So in our sacred *Libanus,* the *Virgin Marie;* are the delicious odours of al vertues, with the Incence of sublime prayer and contemplation; the perfumes of sanctitie and holie conversation, the mirrh of mortification and memorie of death, while her life was nothing els, but a continual languor of perpetual mortification, as wel in denying herself the pleasures, contentments, and delights of the world, as in sighing and groning so much after heaven, where her whole conversation was. And therefore it is sayd in the *Canticles: Fly my beloved, resemble the goat and fawn of the deer on the Mountains of spices,* as much to say, as fly from the vanities of the world, and hygh you to *Libanus* the mount of Spices, to the Blessed *Virgin the Libanus* of al graces.   Ponder

Ponder lastly, that as *Libanus* is interpreted white, for the candour of the snow, which perpetually covers the same: so is our *Libanus* no lesse white, yea a great deale more, through the candour of perpetual Virginitie, which is a kind of whitnes of the flesh; and as *Libanus* through the abundance of the Deawes, and much quantitie of raynes, that fal upon it, abounds with principal hearbs, fat pastures, and excellent fruits: so in our *Libanus* of the Blessed *Virgin;* do flow the deawes of Divine grace, and the raynes of spiritual knowledge: and therefore abounds she so with the rich pastures of the sacred Scriptures, and Celestial understandings of high Mysteries, with plentiful hearbs of the flourishing green of al vertues, and especially loaden with the gallant fruits of soules. *Her root shal break forth,* Osee. 14. *as that of* Libanus; *her boughes shal grow out, and her glorie shal be as the Olive, and her odour as of* Libanus; *sayth the Prophet.*

THE APOSTROPHE.

O Queen *of Angels and Archangels, of Patriarks, Prophets; and Evangelists; of Apostles, Martyrs, and Confessours; of Doctours, Anchorits, and Hermits, and especially the Crowne and glorie of Virgins, Widowes, and of al holie Woemen, in the conjugal state.* o Mountain *among the lesser hils of al those Saints, that have been ever, are, or ever shal be.* O *excellent* Mountain, O *eminent* Mountain. O *Mount, whose aire is temperate and never troubled, where no Serens of inordinate concupiscences ever fal, and where no injurie of times ever works anie mischief.* Mountain *of pleasure, delicious Paradice, the* Libanus *of sanctitie, the* Sinai *of Majestie, and terrour to the reprobate, the* Calvarie *of compassion of thy Sonne's passion, the* Thabor *of Divine mysteries, the* Olivet *of joy and eternal happines: In a word,* O mount

The Colloquie.

O mount *of heaven and fayre habitation of the Heaven of Heavens,* O Virgin, *Alas, make me of thy condition, draw my soule from the servitude of sinne, from the affection of the world, and tyrannie of the flesh; and put my feet on the* Mountain *of perfection, that so approaching neerer to* thee, *I may come to inhabit with thee, above the clowds,* O *grant this same, I beseech thee, for his sake, who came downe from heaven to meet thee, in the clowds, accompanied with miriads of Saints, and blessed Spirits, at thy glorious* Assumption.

THE

THE XXI. SYMBOL.

THE SEA.

THE DEVISE.

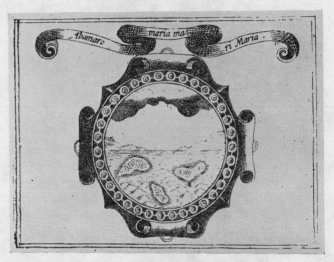

THE CHARACTER.

HE *Seas*, are the great Diet, or Parliament *The* held of Waters, at the first creation of the *Impresa.* world, when GOD himself was the onlie Speaker of the House; where they met of compulsion rather then faire accord, while everie whispering of sinister breath puts them al into combustion, when for the time, there wil be no dealing with them, so implacable they are, that the stoutest are faine to vale-bonet and stoop unto them. They are great Usurers, and likelie never let go anie pawnes they once lay hold of, which they extort ful sore against their wils who leave them in their clutches.

They

They are infinit rich with such booties, and may wel compare with their neighbour *Pluto* or *Mamon* himself. They wil sometimes notwithstanding be very calme, courteous, and seren: so as they wil invite the houshold-Nimphes and Halcions to sing and dance to the noyse of their musick, and of a sudden change the key and tune so, as none but Dolphins can brook the stage, or keep measure with their boysterous time, in the unrulie Revels they keep. As the Earth, have they also their mines of richest wealth, lying in the bowels of their Abysses, which enjoy no other light, then their owne lusters, nor ever are like to do; such covetous misers they are of their pelf. They have likewise their dales and mountains to, but those so restles, as no beasts can graze upon them, going upon foure, but such as take anie benefit of those pastures, are faine to go on their breasts. They are the humid firmament without firmnes, where al the starres are moving Planets. They are the clowdie or waterie ayre, where the birds make use of fins instead of wings. Only the Element of fire hath no friendship with them, but is at deadlie fewd with them, and therefore goes as farre from them, as possibly it can, because they never meet, but it payes wel for it, with its owne destruction. They scarcely acknowledge anie deitie above them, or homage due to anie but the Moon, to whome they are very punctual and obsequious, nor misse her a moment with their service, at her beck to go and come as hawkes in a line, or horses with the bit, that dare not go amisse. Most think, they are flegmatick, because so humid, but rather I take them, to be of a melancholie complexion, with the guift of teares only, for that their waters are ever brackish and bitter as teares are. In fine, they are another world in themselves, wherin GOD hath plunged and drencht the diversities of al earthlie creatures.

THE

THE MORALS.

AB A MARO MARE, A MARI MARIA.

He *Egiptians* for characters, had pictures; of pictures, made they books; wherin they had need to have been excellent Morallists, and consequently good Naturallists, to know the natures and properties of al creatures. I adde withal, some part of their wits also, should have layne in their fingars ends, to shape forth with cole or chisel, so manie diversities of things. *Adam* our first Parent, gave them the first ground therof, when from the beginning he so called and assembled al the new-born creatures to give them names, as a Baylif of some great Lord should goe about, to marke this Maister's sheep, with special marks, notes, or signes of whose they are. And this he did, by the pattern and example first given him by GOD in himself and his consort, the first that ever took anie name; while he was called *Adam*, as signifying, *de terra terrenus*, and she *Virago*, *a viro desumpta*. The *Patriarks* after him stil practized the same, which *Adam* did; assigning names very apt to al their children, as the present occasions put them in the head, or rather as divinely inspired by him, that best can skil, to single out and cal each thing by its proper name. Hence *Joseph*, as his type, was called a *Saviour* and *Josue* likewise, for the same reason. *S. John* the *Baptist* his Precoursour was called *Grace*, which *John* imports, to signify the coming and approach of Grace indeed, in the *Messias* at hand. Yea JESUS, which signifyes *Saviour*, came at last with that name assigned him from al eternitie, and lastly given him by the Paranymph Angel, with the surname of *Emanuel*, as much to say, as *Deus nobiscum*. And so the Incomparable *Virgin*, was Divinely

The Motto.

s   sorted

sorted with the name of MARIE, that fitted her so right.
For she was indeed a Sea of bitternes, through the
seavenfold sword of sorrow, that pierced her hart; and
therefore rightly. AB A MARO MARE, A MARI MARIA.

THE ESSAY.

The
Review.
HE richest pieces of Eloquence, and Poetry are
borrowed of the *Sea;* be it for descriptions of some
notable shipwrack, or to expresse the blustering winds,
which furrow the face of that liquid Element, raysing
up billowes, that dash and wash as it were the very
face of the Heavens, and seeme to plunge the Starres
in the surges of the wrathful *Nemesis* or *Thetys* rather;
or lastly in expressing some *Naumachias*, or sea-fights,
or that of the *Remora*, that *Caesar* of *Caesars* in captiving
so, in a floating Castle, *Caligula* the Roman Monark,
to the stupour and amazement of the world. These are
the uses Poets make therof, but Philosophers goe further yet, and tel us stranger things of this stupendious
work of Nature, of the Flux and Reflux therof, and
faire correspondences it hath with the Moon. The
fabulous Antiquitie hath reckoned ever the Sirens those
chanting Nimphs, and great enchantresses, to be the
Hostesses of the *Sea;* and even the sagest of them in
their follies, take it for a grace to their Goddesse *Venus*,
to fetch her extraction from the impure flames of the
waves. This we know by experience, the fome and
froth of the *Sea*, being dryed with the rayes of the Sun,
convert to sponges, and they againe into pomice-stones,
as light as *Venus* herself; it is ordinarily veyled with
vapours, curtened over with clowds, enwrapped with
fogs, and sometimes buryed in Cimerian darknes; then
of a sudden it changes the countenance, and becomes a
cerulean *Sea*, as various in hew, with as manie coulours,
as the

as the changeable neck of a Dove gives forth with the reflection of the Sun; when the former furrowes al of wrath in the face of this stern *Ocean* wil turne to smiles and daliances with his amorous *Tethis;* the Halcion, the joy of Marriners wil streight appeare upon the decks of ships to glad the passengers, and the Dolphins dance before them with a pleasant glee; the waterie pavements seeme as swept the while, to invite them likewise to dance lavaltoes with them; and the gentle *Eurus* and *Zephirus* in disposition to tune their pipes for the purpose. And for *Cosmographers* (whome we must beleeve, unles with measuring the world ourselves, we wil disprove them) they tel us, the *Ocean* is that universal Choas of waters, which environs the land of al sides: for looke what coasts soever they sayle unto, they alwayes find the *Seas* to waft them thither; which on the east is called the *Indian Sea:* on the West the *Atlantick:* on the North and the Regions opposit, the *Pontick* and the frozen *Sea:* and on the South, the *Red* or *Ethiopian;* beyond al which, manie striving to reach to the utmost shores, have made vast navigations, and have sooner found their victuals to fayle them, then ample spaces of immense waters undiscovered.

THE DISCOURSE.

Ehold heer a singular Symbol of our Incomparable *Virgin*, a vast and immense *Sea* of *Charitie;* for so is she pleased to go shadowed at this time, nor may it seeme to anie strange, she should do so, or we presume so to stile her, since lo the Blessed *Cyprian* tearmes her, not a Microcosme only, as we are al, but even an ample, compleat, and universal "World within herself, adorned with the *Species* of al "creatures. I reade, sayth he, and understand, that *Marie* is a

"is a certain intelligible and admirable world, whose
"land is the soliditie of humilitie; whose *Sea*, the lati-
"tude of *Charitie;* whose heaven, the height of Contem-
"plation; whose sunne, the splendour of Understanding;
"whose moone, the glorie of Puritie; whose Lucifer,
"the brightnes of Sanctitie; whose cluster of seaven
"starres, the seaven-fold Grace; and whose other starres
"are the beautiful ornaments of the rest of her admirable
"Vertues.

The Histories report, that *Helena* among the Grecian
Beauties carried the prize away; and that *Zeuxis*, a most
exquisit painter, in the Age immediatly following,
would needs draw her pourtraict, though he had never
seen her while she lived: and therefore gathered he
togeather al the fayrest damzels in those parts, and
whatsoever he found rare and excellent in anie, he
would exactly put into his peece, not leaving, til he
had finished a most admirable peece of work, delineated from them, which even ravished the eyes and
harts of al. So may we say of our blessed Ladie, Mother
of the eternal King, that she was an abstract of al the
perfections possible, dispersed not only in that sex, or
the human kind, but even likewise in the Angelical
nature itself; and therefore wel might be called a *Sea*
of al perfections; since both her name, in the Hebrew,
sounds as much as *Sea;* and as the *Sea* is nothing els,
Gen. 1. but a certain *congregation togeather of al waters*, so is she
no lesse an assemblie and congregation of al graces and
perfections to be found elswhere.

The *Sea* indeed hath three properties; It is the Spring
and origin of al fountains; it is alwayes ful; and is bitter
and brackish in tast. Our Ladie likewise is the spring
and origin of al graces, from whose virginal womb
did JESUS flow, the fountain of this Fountain, the increated Grace, from the plenitude of whose grace, we
                                        al receave

al receave grace, in what measure soever we become
capable of. And as from the sea do flow great quantities
of waters which it receaves againe, not being kept; so
do graces flow from this *Sea* of *Marie* in great plentie;
yet with flowings and ebbings, through our ingrati-
tude, and not making use therof. But if after our
neglect of her favours we returne, as we ought, to beg
them againe, though we receave no effectual benefits
by her first offers which we refused, yet doth she dayly
offer them againe; with this difference from those
flowings of the liquid seas, that they go and come to
and fro of course, and at certain times with stints; but
she is readie everie moment to communicate her
favours without limits, so we wil but open the chanels
of our harts to let them in.

As al Wels, Springs, and Fountaines derive from
the *Sea*, the *Sea* virtually containes the nature and
qualities of al Well-springs, current fountaines, and
rivers. By which waters are aptly understood the three
degrees of graces, which through our Ladie flow into
our harts; to wit, the Incipient or prevenient grace, in
the first beginnings of our conversions; the Proficient,
by which we proceed; to vertuous actions through
grace receaved; and the Perfect grace, which is the ful
consummation therof, and is indeed a constant perseverance to the end in al vertues. This Incipient or com-
mencing grace, is signifyed *by the Well* or spring *of
living waters;* because these springs have their waters
secret and hidden under ground; they suddenly arise,
and no man knowes from whence, and so prevenient
grace, is by us not merited at al, but springs, and is
powred into us, through a secret and hidden inspiration
of God, no man can tel how, or whence, but often
comes through the intercession of the Incomparable
Mother of mercie, and the *Sea* of graces, being called
the

the living Waters, for that by this grace, are sinners dead in sinnes, as vivifyed to life. The Fountain-water, is understood to be grace Proficient; wherof is sayd: the *Fountain of the Gardens;* which gardens of GOD, are the good Proficients in grace, and vertues; in whome are the hearbs and plants of al vertues, in a flourishing state; which yet could not spring at al, nor grow a whit, much lesse seeme to prosper and flourish, unles by this fountain they were watered with grace, *Gen. 2.* being a *Fountain indeed ascending from the earth, which waters the universal face therof.* By the River-water, which flowes with violence, is perfect grace to be understood, which is sayd *to flow with violence,* because such as are replenished therwith, are very earnest and sollicitous in the works of vertue, and proceed with *Esech. 1.* fervour therin. *Looke where the force of the spirit leads them, thither wil they go with a violence and impetuositie as it were.*

The *Sea* is alwayes ful, and never wasts; and so our Ladie was announced by the Angel, to be ful of grace, as truly she was a vast and immense *Sea* of al graces. Of whom the mellifluous *S. Bernard* sayth upon those *Bern.* words of, *Ave gratia plena: In the mouth truly was she ful of affabilitie; in her womb, with the grace of the Deitie; in her hart, with the grace of charitie; in her hand or work, with the grace of mercie and liberalitie.* So likewise are the waters of the *Sea* exceeding bitter; and our Virgin *Marie* was *amarum mare,* that is a bitter *Sea,* for divers respects. First for sorrow, for the losse of her Sonne in the Temple: *Behold thy Father and I have sought thee with sorrow.* Then was she bitter, meerly of compassion, in beholding the Spouses in the Nuptials to be abashed and confounded for want of wine; she had compassion of the *Jewish* nation, while she saw them to be reprobate and forsaken of GOD; She pittied the *Apostles* in seing

seing them dispersed in the passion of her Sonne; But especially was she bitterly sorie at the passion of her Sonne, when the sword of sorrow transfixed her hart; and lastly was she bitter for her tedious pilgrimage heer so long: and therefore would she say: *Alas, how my* Psal. *pilgrimage is prolonged!*

THE

THE EMBLEME.

THE POESIE.

The
Pause.

 O sooner was the infant-world disclos'd,
But that God's Spirit on the Sea repos'd:
Borne on the waters did impart a heat
By influence divine: a fertil seat
He made that vast and barren Ocean's wombe.
Twas fruitful when the Holie-Ghost was come.
The sacred Virgin was a Sea like this,
But darknes on the face of the Abysse,
Was never on her Soule, that shined bright
From her first being; for GOD sayd: Let light
Be made: the Word was in this Sea compriz'd,
When th' Holie-Ghost the waters fertiliz'd.

THE

THE THEORIES.

Ontemplate first, that when the world *The* was first created, and that the waters were *Contem-* divided, as it were, by the Firmament, *plation.* while part was put above the Firmament and part beneath, the waters beneath on the earth, were called by the name of *Maria*, or *Seas;* and the Spirit of GOD, as we have it in *Genesis*, *did incubare super aquas* cover, as we say, or overshadow the waters: Which was a work of the first Creation. So in the work of our Redemption, where the blessed Virgin, *Maria* by name, which signifyes the *Seas* also, it pleased the Eternal Word, leaving the delicious bosome of the heavenlie *Father* to descend into this *Sea*, of human miseries to take them upon him; and the *Holie-Ghost* likewise to overshadow her withal.

Consider then in the Temple of *Salomon*, that as besides other riches and ornaments there, as the Propitiatorie above; the Cherubins and Seraphins of each side therof, the golden Candlestick in the midst, the Altars of Perfumes and of Propitiation, heer and there, with the lamps, the Veyle, the Ark, and the like in their places, was planted a great vessel of Brasse, ful of water, at the entrance of the said Temple, where the Priests were to cleanse themselves, before they entred to Sacrifice; and this Vessel was called, *Mare æneum*, or the *brazen Sea*. So ought the Priests in our Churches before they enter or approach unto the dreadful Sacrifice of al Sacrifices, the *Sacrifice* of the *Masse*, to recurre to this *Mare æneum*, our Blessed *Ladie*, to procure them a puritie of soule, to assist therat, or approch therunto.

Ponder lastly, that as GOD, the soveraigne Lord of al things, communicates his offices and charges to men according to his most holie and Divine dispensation, very

very suitable and agreable to everie one: as to *Moyses* the office of a Law-giver to his people of *Israel;* to *Aaron* the office of high Priest; to *Josue*, of Captain and Leader of them into the land of promise; and consequently gave them talents accordingly to discharge the same very punctually in al things. So is it likelie, that in choosing his Mother, he used the self-same tenour in his fayre disposition therof, to wit, in appointing her so to be the *Starre* of the *Sea*, he ordeyned her no doubt to be the Ladie of the *Sea*, as her name imports. Now then as in the *Seas*, he hath drencht and plunged, as it were, an other world, since there is no living creature but hath its like in the *Sea* also: implicitively, he hath likewise appointed her to be the Ladie and Mistris of al the world. For how should she save from shipwrack, if She were not Ladie and Mistris of the waves and winds? And how should she be Ladie of the *Seas* alone, if she were not the Ladie likewise of the land? Since she who is stiled the Ladie of the *Seas*, is the true and natural Mother of him, who is Lord both of *Sea* and land, and al the world.

THE APOSTROPHE.

The Colloquie.

O Ladie of the Ocean, Starre *of the* Sea, Sea *of* graces, Fountain, *of life, Spring of living waters, that flow from the* Libanus *of the candour of glorie! Thou great Abysse of limpid waters, whose bottome, none can reach unto; whence nothing ariseth, but the purest exhalations of Paradise; light clowd whence nothing falles but deaws and showres of graces. O immense* Ocean *of* Charitie, *which bearest up al things, and where easily nothing sincks; bitter, but in the dolours and passions of thy Sonne; sweet to the creatures, that live of thee, or depend upon thee. O grant, I beseech thee, that wholy relying on thee, I perish not, and by neglecting thee and thy service, I incurre not thy disgrace, nor so running on the rocks of thy displeasure, I split not on them, nor suffer shipwrack of my soule.*   THE

THE XXI. SYMBOL.
THE SHIP.
THE DEVISE.

De longe *portans* *panem.*

THE CHARACTER.

THE *Ship* is the artificial Dolphin of the *The Impresa.* Seas, that much addicted to musick, is never set on a merrier pin, then when the winds whissel to her dancing. It is a floating Castle, that hath the gates open indeed, but trusts to her Battlements, which she hath wel planted with Canons and Sacres, wherin she more confides, then manie do in Sacred Canons; her whole salvation depending upon them. It is a litle Commonwealth, whose whole Reason of State consists in jealousies, and spyes, which she sends up to her turret-

tops,

tops, to discover, if the coasts be clear, stil standing on
her guard, against the neighbour waves, that seeke but
to swallow her up. And al her care is, to walke upright
amidst her enemies, least unawares they arrest her, and
cite her to appeare at Pluto's Court, for everie errour
or default of the least ship-boy. There is no Bride
requires so much time to dresse her on her wedding-
day, as she to be rigd, whensoever she goes to sea. If
they have their fillets to bred and wreath their haires
with, she hath her tacklings to trim her up; whose ropes
are as manie and as intricate as they; if they have their
veyles to spread upon them, she hath her sayles, to
hoyse up to go her wayes. It is the Lion of the seas,
that feares no Monsters, but is as dreadful herself, as
anie Monster, having as manie mouthes as Gun-holes,
and in everie mouth a Serpent tongue, that spits and
vomits fire, and which even spits her teeth too, in the
face of her enemies, which often sincks them under
water. It is one of the prettiest things in the world, to
see her under sayle, how like a Turkiecock she strouts
it out, as braving even the Elements themselves, both
above and beneath her, wherof the one she ploughes
with her slicing share, and braves the other with her
daring look. She is an excellent swimmer, but no good
diver at al; which she never doth, but sore against her
wil, and that with so il successe, as likely she is never
seen more. The first that ever was seen to our Anti-
podes, was thought by them to have had indeed a living
soule with her; els would the simple people say, how
could so great a bulk, so easily wind and turne itself
everie foot; and this, because they knew but the Oare
only, and not the Rudder. What would they have said
then, had they knowne the effects of her Card and
Compas? doubtles she had a reasonable soule. She
likely never goes without her Pages with her, to wit,
                                                    her

her Long-boat and her Cockboat, wherof she makes such use now and then, as without them, she might starve for ought I know. She is very civil, if a Marchantman; but when she is a Man of warre, then Marchants beware, and looke to yourselves.

THE MORALS.

DE LONGE PORTANS PANEM.

N the Temple of *Salomon*, no gold would serve his great curiositie, but that of *Ophir*. Which the Southern *Queen* of *Saba* knowing wel perhaps, thought no doubt her presents would be gratful to him, coming so from parts remote. Who is he that is not taken much with verie toyes that come from *China*, which carrie I know not how in themselves, (at least in our opinion) a kind of luster with them, greater farre then otherwise they would. The presents which the *Magi* brought unto the Crib, coming from the East were deemed by them fit presents for a King, yea for a GOD. And how were *Josue* and *Caleb* the Spyes and Intelligencers of the people of *Israel* extolled and magnifyed at their returne with those rare and admirable booties fetched from *Canaan*? And yet the gold of *Ophir* was but gold, a yellow earth; the presents made by *Saba*, such as that Countrie afforded; and those *Indian* toyes, but toyes indeed. Yea the guifts the *Magi* brought, had greater luster with them from the givers harts, then from themselves; and more respected for the place to which, then whence they came. And for those forren fruits, they came indeed from the land of promise, from *Palestin*, which was but the figure only of the Heavenlie countrie. But lo, our Incomparable *Virgin* like a Ship, most richly fraighted, hath brought us Bread from farre.

The Motto.

farre. What bread; but the true and living *bread?* How
farre? As farre as Heaven. But how bread? Bread whose
corne was harvested in the Mightie man's rich Booz-
field, framed by the hand of the Maister Baker himself
of a most pure meale or flower, to wit, of the immaculate Bloud of the holie *Virgin* herself, baked in the
Oven of an ardent Love, which She hath brought into
the world. And therefore is truly sayd: DE LONGE
PORTANS PANEM.

THE ESSAY.

The
Review.

I Can not tel, whether in the world besides,
be a more statelie sight to behold, then
an English *Ship* under sayle, riding in the
Ocean, and cutting the watrie playnes
with her sharp keel, in case she have a
gallant gentle gale in the poop; for then they feast it,
and make good chear, who are the living soules abiding
in this bulk of human art, compiled togeather in despite of Nature, to frame a living creature more then
she intended, that neither should be fish nor fowle, yet
live in the ayre and water. But if the Seas prove rough,
and al the marine Monsters rise up against her, con-
spiring with the blustering Spirits of the ayre, to sinck
her quite, it is a sport to see, how she rides and prances
on his crooked back, sporting herself the while, and
making a meer scoff at al their menaces. There is an
infinit number of several sorts of these artificial creatures in the world, each country almost having their
kinds. There are *Ships,* Pinaces, Hoyes, Barkes, Ketches,
Galleyes, Galeons, Galleasses, Frigots, Brigandines,
Carackes, Argoseyes, for the Seas; to say nothing of
Lighters, Barges, Tiltboats, Lighthorsmen, Oares,
Canoas, and Gundeloes, for the Rivers. The *Ships* do
fly

fly and swimme togeather, with the help of sayles only;
the Galleyes and their like, as Swans do sometimes fly,
and sometimes paddle with the oare. They have
maine masts, crosse sayles, top and top-gallants, they
have stern, poop, rudder, ancker, cable, decks, tacklings, gunnes, and gun-holes, where they have Canon
Demy-canon, Saker, Culvering; not to speak of the
smal shot, as muskets, harkebuses, and firelocks, and a
thousand more. And so much for the sensles bodie of
this bulk in it-self. But then to speak of the soule, or
policie, and œconomie of this admirable artificial
creature, or moving world, it is a busines no lesse, to
set them downe. For as for the Officers which are
simply necessarie either in the Admiral or Vice-
admiral of a Fleet or Royal Armado at the seas, there
is a General, a Lieutenant General, a Captain, a Pilot,
and the Pilot's mate; a Maister, and the Maister's mate;
a Marchant, and a Marchant's mate; the Maister of the
Ship-boyes, a Secretarie, a Chirurgion; a Boatswain,
a Purser, Dispensers, Cooks, Canonier, and his mate,
with undergunners, ship-boyes and marriners without
number. The Captain commands absolutely in al
things; the chief marchant hath power over the marchandize and commerce only. They double so the
principal Officers, that one may supply the others want.
The Secretarie sets downe the marchandize the Ship is
fraighted with, and takes accompt of goods unladed.
The Pilot hath no other command, but in what con-
cerns the navigation. The Maister hath command over
al the Mariners and saylers of the Ship; and of al the
provisions and victuals; he places and removes the
Officers at his pleasure. The Maisters of the boyes are
the ablest of al the marriners, and have the care of the
cordages, sayles, and tacklings, and the like, and command the yong marriners, and do only give correction
to the Ship-boyes.   THE

THE DISCOURSE.

The
Survey.

Ut now come we to our mystical *Ship*, whose wayes in the vast seas the Oraculous *Salomon* admired so much. This had for Architect and Shipwright no lesse then the Blessed *Trinitie* it-self, wherin the Divine persons bestowed their chiefest Architecture. For the Heavenlie *Father* employed his Omnipotencie therin as farre as the subject was capable of, the eternal *Word* made use of his wisedome, in preserving so entire the seale of integritie, and the *Holie-Ghost* shewed his Love, by infusing such a plenitude of grace into her. The matter she was framed of, tels us she was of herself, of wood doubtles most sacred and mys-

Eccl. 24.

terious. *As the Cedar am I exalted in Libanus, and as the Cypresse in mount Sion; as the beautiful Olive in the fields; and am exalted as the Planetree neer the waters in the streets.* This Ship then was made of the *Cedar* of virginitie, in that the *Cedar* is odoriferous and incorruptible; and therefore signifyes her virginitie, which made her grateful and odoriferous to GOD, and kept her flesh immaculate and incorrupted. It was made of *Cypresse*, which is a wood so strong and solid, as shrincks and yealds not with anie burden, being qualities most apt for shipping: nor would the charitie of the blessed *Virgin* permit her ever, to shrinck under the weight of tribu-

Cant. 8.

lations. *For Love is strong as death.* She was made of the *Olive* of pietie, which alwayes flourisheth, and looks green; in that her pietie never fayled any, either in the Spring of their youth, in the Autumne of their age, in the Winter of tribulation, or in the heat of inordinate concupiscences. She was further made of the *Plane-tree* of humilitie; for the *Plane* is a most spacious and ample tree; and humilitie made the *Virgin* most ample and illustrious;

illustrious; because thereby she receaved him into her womb, whom the Heaven of heavens was not able to containe, since *S. Bernard* sayth: *She pleased with her virginitie, but conceaved through Humilitie.*

Her stern, is her wisdome and discretion; her Oares most sacred and holie affects; the Mast, high and sublime contemplation; the Galleries, pure and chast conversation: the ropes and tacklings, the cords of love, unitie and concord; the Anckor, firme hope and confidence in GOD; the deckes and hatches, external and holie example and edification; the sayles, cleanes and puritie of bodie, joyned with the blush of shamfastnes; The Pilot or Maister of the ship, the *Holie-Ghost*, which steered, guided, and directed her in the whole navigation of her sacred life. For if they be led by the *Holie-Ghost*, who are the sonnes and children of GOD, how much rather shal she be governed by it, who is acknowledged to be not only the Daughter but likewise the natural Mother of GOD!

The forme and figure of a Ship we know to be open above, close beneath, streight in the beginning, narrow in the end, broad in the midst, and very deep. And this ship of ours the Incomparable *Virgin*, according to the superior part of the Soule, was open to receave Celestial guifts, but as for the inferiour, wholy shut up from terrene affections; and moreover so strict in the beginning of her *Conception*, as Original sinne could find no place to stayne her in; She was narrow in the end of the Passion, while for the death of her Sonne she was put to divers streights; in the midst she was most capacious or broad, because, as we sayd, *Whom the heavens could not hold, she held and contained in the lap of her womb;* Lastly she was deep through humilitie, when being raysed to the top of the highest dignitie of being the *Mother* of GOD, she calles herself his lowlie hand-

T   mayd

Luc. 1.   mayd saying: *Behold the handmayd of our Lord.* But for
the Mast indeed, and tree of this Ship, it was CHRIST
Luc. 23.   our *Lord*, the verie same, who called himself *green wood*,
saying: *If this be done in green Wood, what shal become*
Heb. 7.   *of the dry?* Erected also, as *S. Paul* sayth: *Being made*
higher then the heavens; raysed in, and born of the *Virgin*
Ex. 27.   Ship. Of which tree or mast, we have this in *Exodus:*
They took out a Cedar from Libanus to make be no other
then *Christ* erected in this *Ship* of our *Virgin* heer.

    The *Ships* are made for burden; and for as much as
Nations oftentimes stand in need of each other, they
serve for transportation of commodities to and fro;
and especially corne from the fruitful to barren countries, with the abundance of the one to supply the
necessities of the other. And therefore the blessed *Virgin*,
Pro. 31.   as we have in the Proverbs, *was made as a Marchants*
ship, bringing her bread from farre and remote parts. For
even from the fertile and most fruitful soyle of the
Celestial Paradise, brought she indeed that supersub-
stantial bread, into the barren coasts of this world;
Luc. 6.   which bread sayes of itself: *I am the living bread, who*
descend from heaven, wherewith the faythful are fed and
nourished. Whence appeares, how farre off this mysterious *ship* brought the Celestial *Bread* unto us, being
no lesse then from heaven to the earth, an immense
distance; shewing yet a greater distance of natures, in
that this *Bread* consists of the Divine and human nature,
which are infinitly distant one from the other, togeather with the distance of merits; because no merits
had ever deserved, that for our sakes GOD should become Man; Which *bread* it seemed she likewise made
herself, so signifyed by that Woman in the Ghospel,
who mingled togeather the three hand-fuls of meale,
as heer are united the soule, the bodie, and the Divinitie
itself. O glorious *Baker* of so heavenlie *bread*! O Divine
bread

bread so mysteriously made! And most rich and precious *Ship*, that conveighed the same to us from parts so remote!

Lastly, as the *Ship* useth the Winds only to sayle with, and the Galley passes not to and fro without the help of oares: So likewise between the blessed *Virgin*, and the rest of *Saints*, this difference is; that they, as Galleyes, performe the navigation of this life, with the strength of the oares, as it were, against the wind and tyde of carnal difficulties, and travel with infinit encounters of worldlie assaults, unto their heavenlie Countrie. But the blessed *Virgin* with the gentle gale of the *Holie-Ghost*, and the most sweet push therof, was conveighed thither. And as the *Ship* is driven with twelve sorts of several winds; the blessed *Virgin* like a prosperous *Ship*, with the twelve fruits of the *Holie-Ghost*, which *S. Paul* reckons up, as with so manie favourable winds, without rebellion or impugnation of sinne, or anie *Remora*, to stop her course, was sweetly wafted to the haven of the Celestial Countrie.

THE

THE EMBLEME.

THE POESIE.

The
Pause.

 Jewish Rabby sayes, the Angels fed
On Manna; But an other, better read,
Affirmes 'twas Light condens'd (and so made
   meat,
For men, (which shin'd before God's glorious seat,
As food of Angels. True; for one of three,
The Second Person of the Trinitie
Descends, and sayes, He is the living bread,
He was the light whereon the Angels fed:
Which, when the Holie-Ghost o'er cast his shade
Was first condens'd, when Flesh the Word was made
In Maries womb, wherewith our Soules are fed.
She is the Ship, that brought from farre her bread.

THE

THE THEORIES.

The
Contem-
plation.
Reg. 3. Ontemplate first, that as *Ships* of *Salomon*, as we read of in the book of Kings, brought most precious gold from *Ophir*, to adorne the Temple he had built to the Majestie of GOD; So our mystical *Ship*, brought forth our Lord, the finest gold; not from *Ophir* truly, but from the most precious Mines of Heaven; with whose merits, as the daughters of *Hierusalem*, deckt their heads in memorie of *Salomon's* yealow hayre and Crowne: So the Catholick Church is most gloriously enriched, honoured, and delighted, by our second *Salomon's* glorious merits, through whose valew and inestimable price, great summes of debts are defrayed; with whose admirable vertue, as with a most present antidote, are the sick and infirme cured, and the harts of the faythful comforted; and finally through his mervelous luster and bright splendour, the Temple of the Church incredibly shineth.

Consider then, that wheras other *Ships* are subject to infinit dangers in the Seas, being tossed with tempests and oftentimes cast away and swallowed up in the waves, or dasht against the Rocks; *for Ecclesiasticus* sayth: *Who travel on the seas, do recount their perils:* Ec. 43. either tyrannized by the winds, or falling into the hands of Pirats or running on the *Sirtes* or *Scylla*, and falling sometimes into the gulf of *Charibdis*, and lastly allured through the Sirens songs, to their owne destruction: Yet this *Ship* of our *Ladie* heer, while of the one side, the stormes of Original sinne had no power upon her, so as she felt not the least internal rebellion of the bodie or mind, against the rectitude of Reason; and of the other was invincibly through the Divine assistance preserved against the assaults of the ghostlie Enemie: So as
neither

neither the *Syrtes* or *Scylla* of riches, nor the *Charibdis* of worldlie honour, nor the Pirats of Concupiscence, nor the Sirens of eternal delights, could stopp or hinder her, in the fayre navigation, she made unto the heaven-lie Countrie.

Ponder lastly, that as heretofore in the universal Deluge and floud of *Noe*, in that general inundation of the wrath and furie of GOD, was no man saved or anie living creatures besides, except such only, as fled to the Arck of *Noe*, built in effect as a goodlie and statelie *Ship:* So no sinner escapes the indignation of GOD, but such as hye themselves and fly unto the *Virgin-Mother* for refuge, according to that of *S. Bernard*. If thou darest not approach to the Majestie of GOD, least thou melt as wax before the fire; go to the *Mother of Mercie*, and shew her thy wounds, and she for thee wil shew her breast and paps, and the *Sonne* to the Father his side and wounds. The *Father* wil not deny the *Sonne* re-questing; the *Sonne* wil not deny the Mother craving; the *Mother* wil not deny the sinner weeping. My child-ren, why feare you to go to *Marie?* she is not austere, she is not bitter, but milke and honie is under her tongue. This is the Ladder of sinners, this my great confidence, this the whole reason of my hope. And what mervel? For can the *Sonne* repel the *Mother?* or be repelled of the *Mother?* Neither one, nor other. Let not therefore humane frailtie feare to approach unto her; For she is wholy sweet, and sweetnes itself.

THE

THE APOSTROPHE.

O Thou tal and goodlie Arck, thou valiant Woman, valiant by excellence, more faire then Rachel, more gracious then Hester, more pleasing then Sara, more gentle and generous then Judith, more sweet and chast then Abiseig the Sunamite, more officious and prudent then Abigail, more magnanimous then Debora, more illumined then Marie the Sister of Moyses. Thou who hast found grace before the eyes of GOD, work with thy prayers most dear Ladie, O my most noble Princesse, that I may alwayes find grace before thy Sonne. Thou who through thy Sonne hast broken the head of the Serpent; crush likewise through thy holie prayers his head under thy Servants feet. Thou Ship of the great GOD, who from those countries so farre remote hast brought to us the bread of Paradise, true GOD in flesh: Grant, I beseech thee, I may be fed with the bread of grace, of life, and wisdome; and that receaving the sacred bread of Angels, which is the precious Bodie of sweet JESUS thy Sonne, I may even suck in the fountain itself, the most sweet pleasures, and the most pleasing sweetnesses of the Divinitie, and be wholy inebriated with the torrent of Divine consolations.

THE

THE CONCLUSION TO HIS
Proper Genius.

Ow heer, my *Genius*, shalt thou dismisse thy *Reader*, with his Ship ful fraught with the prayses of the *sacred Parthenes;* and shutting up thyself in this *Parthenian* Paradice, walk in it up and downe by thyself alone, without eye or arbiter, to witnes the secret aspirations of thy hart; while contemplating with thyself, this great rich Magazin of the treasures of Nature, enclosed in this spacious and ample GARDEN of our SACRED PARTHENES, thou enter into thyself a while, gathering the fruits and flowers, at least of good desires, from the objects them-selves. Nor be a whit dismayd, though they put thee to the blush, to be taught thy dutie so, from irrational and insensible things; but yeald and submit thy hart, to learne of each creature, how to serve the common *Creatour* of us al. And as thou walkest up and downe, taking a view of those curious knots of ever-flourishing and green hearbs, say this unto thyself: When shal I order and compose my greener and inordinat affect-ions, in so faire and goodlie a *decorum*, and so sweet proportion? Walking in the Allyes, say: Lord, conduct me by the streight and readie way; and shew me thy kingdome. Noting the neatnes of those walkes, how trim and smooth they are, say: When shal it be, I be so curious, to purge and take away the impurities from my hart? The great diversitie of flowers, wil present to thee, the great multiplicitie and wel-nigh infinitie of thy thoughts, as various as numerous, and al as trans-

itorie

itorie as they. If thou seest a swarme of Emots at thy feet, charged and loaden al with graynes of corne, and carrying them with toyle, unto their litle Grayneries, one groaning with his load, another newly discharged therof, most lightly and nimbly running for another, say unto thyself: Oh slothful wretch, looke on these people heer, how they labour to mayntaine that paltrie litle carkas of theirs, of smal continuance; and thou to mayntaine thy soule, in good estate, so created for Eternitie, art so litle laborious, and industrious. When thou beholdst the trees, ful loaden with their fruits, so faine to be shored up beneath; remember the menace of fire, the Saviour made against the barren tree. When thou seest the plants, to be watered so, against the scorching of the Sun, thinke and say inwardly in thyself: When shal we with our teares appease the avenging Wrath of the Divine Justice? The faire and beautiful Pansyes, but without al sent or odour, wil tel thee, of the unprofitable agitations of thy soule; the Tyme, the bitternes of displeasures; the Poppie, that lulles the soule a-sleep, wil admonish thee of the sweet extasies and ravishments of heavenlie Contemplation, thou neglectest so much; the Rubarb, or hearb called Patience, wil put thee in mind of that Vertue, which gives it the name; the Balme, of a good and faire reputation. Nor stay thou heer, but runne to resalute the proper and peculiar Familie likewise the genuine Symbols of the *Sacred Parthenes*, so mentioned above; and note the documents they wil yeald thee, for thine owne behoof; and then take thy leave of al. The *private Garden* wil teach thee to keep thy vertues close, if thou hast anie; and not very easily to loose their odour, through a voluntarie publishing the same to others. Saluting the *Rose*, environed with thorns, think, there is no contentment to be found, without displeasures.

Beholding

Beholding the *Lillie* among bryars, imagin Chastitie is
so conserved amid austerities. The *Violet* wil figure thee
a low and humble esteeme of thyself; which yet is a
fragrant and delicious flower. The *Heliotropion,* which
hath alwayes its look to the Sun-wards, and followes
it by day, and closes up agayne with the night, wil put
thee in conceipt of the true Sun of Justice indeed thou
oughtst to follow, and should be the whole object of
thy soule. The *Deaw,* that falles from Heaven, wil
remember thee of the heavenlie graces, that were shed
and distilled from Heaven, by the coming of the *Holie-
Ghost* in forme of fierie tongues. The busie and industrious *Bee,* which bounds and rebounds so aloft in the
ayre as she flyes, wil cal to thy mind, those words of thy
great Maister: *Work, and negotiate while time lasts.*
The *Heavens,* wil attract thy thoughts, to heavenlie
things; the *Rain-bow,* move thee to pardon injuries,
and immediatly to reconcile thee, to thine enemies. The
Moon wil tax thee of inconstancie, like to hers; the
Starre, rayse up thy thoughts to a vertuous emulation,
to become a *Starre* indeed, in the heavenlie Hierarchie,
as it is so fixed in the celestial Firmament. The *Olive*
wil warne thee, to be alwayes green in thy good purposes, and fruitful in good works. The *Nightingal,* wil
let thee heare a taste or relish, as it were, of the heavenlie Quiers, and sacred Alleluya's, sung by the Angels in
Heaven. The *Palme,* wil stirre thee to Martyrdome; at
least, to fortitude in difficult atchievements. The *House,*
wil cal the heavenlie mansions and Tabernacles into thy
thoughts, which are permanent for ever. The *Hen,* wil
cause thee to fly, to the heavenlie protection. The *Pearl*
wil invite thee to sel al thou hast, to purchase that of the
Heavenlie Kingdome. The *Dove,* wil retire thee, and
draw thee into solitude. The *Fountain,* wil allure thee,
to drinck of the waters, which the *Saviour* mentioned,
that

that spring to eternal life. The *Mount*, wil cal thee to a higher degree of perfection; the *Sea*, represent to thee an Ocean of grace, to launch forth thy Soule, as a wel-rigd *Ship*, into that Mayne, to arrive at last into the Haven of Eternal Happines; and that especially through the steering of our *Sacred Parthenes*,

> *Cui Laus & gloria in secula,*
> *Amen.*

THE

THE EPILOGUE TO THE

PARTHENIANS

Hus, *Gentle Parthenians,* you have viewed, reflected, reviewed, surveyed, paused on, and contemplated the *Mysterious* and *delicious* GARDEN of *our Sacred* PARTHENES; and after al implored and importuned your soveraigne *Ladie-Mistris,* and mine, under so manie apt and rich Symbols. So graciously she hath daigned, to condescend, for our pleasure and devotion, as it were, to deliciate with us in these irrational *Species* of things, made al but to expresse (you would think) her prayses, and al the peculiar Devotes of hers, our deare Companions, in her service. Where you must note, that these are but they only, which wayte and attend upon her, in her GARDEN; and that she hath infinit other Clients and Devotes besides, in created things, as forward al, to offer up themselves, in her service; I meane, in this Symbolical Theologie, to give forth Elogies, Encomiums, and Panegyricks, to her sacred prayse. For testimonie wherof, you might observe, the GARDEN being shut up, two noble creatures likewise, though too late, to be admitted with the rest, to come in with their Devises and Emblemes, to expresse no lesse in her honour, then the rest had done. But the GARDEN, as I sayd, was shut already, nor would our leasure afford us more, then to receave their Escuchions only, and to hang them thus on the Postern, as you see.

THE

THE PHOENIX.
THE DEVISE.

THE MORALS.

NEC SIMILIS VISA, NEC SECUNDA.

ONE *Cittie holds not two Lisanders*, the ancient Proverb sayth; nor the Heavens two Suns, say I; which never appeare in shew only without a Prodigie. *Hercules* had thought, he had set a spel to the world, when he set up his Pillar so in the then utmost Spanish *Gades*, and called it his *Non plus ultra*. But alas! Since that, hath a new whole world been discovered, far beyond it. One Painter with his art deceaved the birds, with a bunch of grapes, and he thought verily he had done a great peece of matter; when

The Motto.

when comes me another streight, and with his art like-wise, deludes the verie Painter himself in his owne art. One drawes me a line, which he held to be indivisible; comes me another with a lighter touch, and cuts that line asunder with another line. It is often seen, the Scholler goes beyond the Maister. *Plato* excelled his Maister, *Aristotle* his, and so have infinit others; the reason yealds that Reverend Father *Southwel* in his Spiritual Poems:

> *Devise of man, in working hath no end;*
> *What thought can think another thought can mend?*

GOD, when he framed the world, might as wel have built manie more, and happely a second better then the first, and so a third, and so a fourth, because al are in the compas of his Omnipotencie; but so can not man do in his works; for stil there wil be found an utmost tearme, beyond the which he can not passe; because he is finit. The Giants in their big conceipts, had framed in their imagination a Stayre-case up to Heaven, by setting *Pelion* upon *Ossa's* back; but when they had brought it to a certain pitch, they could reare their building no whit higher, but downe comes *Ossa* much sooner then he got up; and al was but a Castle in the ayre, which hangs there stil, the foundation being shrunck away. Such are the works of Mortals; and so are they limited in al they do. GOD only is he, who is boundles in al. Yet when he framed the Incomparable *Virgin Marie*, and chose her to be his *Mother*, he made her so incomparable a *Phœnix*, not only to al, that ever were, or shal be, but even to such, as he intended or was able to frame; since being not able to be greater then he is himself, he could not make her to be a greater *Mother* then she is, *making her his owne Mother; and therefore wel may be sayd: NEC SIMILIS VISA NEC SECUNDA.

THE

THE CHARACTER.

The Impresa.

HE *Phenix* is the *Cesar* of birds, and sole Dictatour amongst them, which admits no *Pompey* in his kind: and therefore Nature hath framed but one at once, to take away the cause of civil jarres. He is the miracle of Nature, and a prime maister-peece of her workmanship; wherin she seemes, contrarie to her custome, to shew some art. He is even the honour of *Arabia Felix*, or the felicitie of that Region; the offspring of the Sun, that might wel have been his father, if either two Suns had been possible, or two *Phenixes* at once. He is a Treasurer, or rather an Usurer of spices, with the interest of his life. He is the Heyre apparant to himself, and feares no other's clayme to that nature; bred of ashes, and, as we al, to ashes must returne againe; and yet immortal, while he dyes not, but renewes rather; and not as the Hawke, which mewes his feathers only, but himself. The Tomb is his cradle, the Fire his midwif, himself the Damme, the Sun his Sire. There being but one at once, they are framed without a pattern, and yet so like, as they are taken for the same. He can speake much of others Ancesters, but nothing of his owne. He is the *Alpha* and *Omega* of his kind, the first and last, because alwayes the same. Being solitarie, he is apt to scruples, but puts them over through the innocencie of his life; for though by nature he be a Prince, yet dares he not say We, because there is no more then he. If he steale, they are but spices, wherof he makes no conscience, because for his Altar of Holocausts; nor hath anie Casuist with him, to put that scruple into his head. And being so accessarie to his owne death, he makes as litle scruple of that also, as done through the inspiration of Nature, as he calles

calles it, to maintaine his House, and to rayse his seed. Were he not wel knowne otherwise to the *Arabians*, to be a bird, by manie faire demonstrations, it had been a wonder, that people had not chosen him for a GOD. But GOD, it seemes, would not permit it, as a special favour to this singular and miraculous Bird. Like the Camelion, he lives by the ayre; and no marvel, the spirit of birds should live of its proper Element, the ayre being the Element of birds, as the waters of the fish. The Fire he makes his Purgatorie in this world; and that so efficaciously, as he becomes renewed to another life, or like the Snake, which changing his coat only, is stil the same, but yet more fresh. Whereby observing the precept, *he puts off the old man, to betake himself to a new being, in newnes of life.*

Behold

Ehold, how Death aymes with his mortal dart,
And wounds a Phœnix with a twin-like hart.
These are the harts of Jesus and his Mother
So linkt in one, that one without the other
Is not entire. They (sure) each others smart
Must needs sustaine, though two, yet as one hart.
One Virgin-Mother, Phenix of her kind,
And we her Sonne without a father find.
The Sonne's and Mothers paines in one are mixt,
His side, a Launce, her soule a Sword transfixt.
Two harts in one, one Phenix love contrives:
One wound in two, and two in one revives.

U   THE

THE SWAN.

THE DEVISE.

THE MORALS.

AD VADA CONCINENS ELISII.

The Motto.

Ristotle sayth, that harmonie and Musicick, is a worthie, great, and Divine thing, whose bodie is composed of parts discordant in themselves, and yet accordant one with the other; which entring into the bodie by the eare with I know not what Divinitie as it were, ravisheth the soule. The World therefore is much obliged to the first Inventour of Musick, being the sweet charme of al the annoyes of our pittiful mortalitie. For even they, who

who are plunged in the abysse of al evils, at the least
touch of sweet Musick, do even swim, and vault like
Dolphins (as Poets say) at the feet of that Minstrel
Orion. What grief or trouble is so great, that revives
not, when a gentle Treble mounts up to heaven, and
there soaring and hovering aloft, as on the wing, comes
like a Falcon at last to seize upon the Base, as a prey,
even to the losse of breath and sense of hearing? or
when the Base after a long pursuit of the Treble, and
not able to reach it as it would, as in a rage in despite
with itself, seemes to precipitate and plunge itself even
to the Center of the earth? Who would not wonder,
to see the gentle *Orpheus* have such power upon savage
beasts, to make them to forget their prey and chase, to
feed and fatten themselves with such mincing divisions,
and by the eare feed on those Divine viands? who,
when he made his Harp to speak, and his fingers to run
so fast, marrying his Angelical voyce to the miracle of
his strings, he made even the people of the Seas to cast
themselves in sholes upon the Strond, to listen to him;
and the Sirens to come forth and dance upon the green
banck-side, al diapered with flowers; the Beares and
Lions to quit the Forrests, running in troupes to lye at
the feet of their sweet Tyrant. But away with these
fables now, and cast we our eyes and eares upon that
Divine Harp, fallen from Heaven to the earth, into the
hands of *David*, who causing his strings to speake and
chant forth his Heavenlie and Divine Psalmes, so did
exorcise and dispel the Divel from his Hold. This
Musick therefore is an essay, as it were, and tast of
Paradise itself, while in Heaven they seeme to do
nothing but sing the greatnes and marvels of GOD, in
two Quiers, of the Angels of the one side, and of the
blessed Saints of the other. But then, what musick
made the white delightful *Swan*, sitting on the Bancks,

UI   not

not of *Po, Meander*, or *Euridanus*, but on the brinck of
Death? Not of *Cocitus, Stix*, or fierie *Flegiton*, but of
the playnes of *Elizeum*, that is, by the shores of Paradice; when, like the *Swan*, feeling her purest bloud to
tickle her hart for joy of her approaching passage out
of this world, we may piously conjecture she tuned
forth her Divine *Canticle* anew for a Farwel to the
world and a last Adieu; and therefore worthily is sayd:
AD VADA CONCINENS ELIZEI.

THE CHARACTER.

*The
Impresa.*

HE sweet delightful *Swan* is that delicious
Siren of the Brook; the living Ghost, that
walks and hants those humid playnes, as if
confined to her *Eliseum* there. She is much
taken with the pleasant banck of the Continent, and
spends much time therin, but yet wil not trust it with
her houshold, nor there be brought to bed, but rather
hires some Iland for the purpose; and the rent she payes,
is some part of her children. She likes to have her walks
and gardens there, for her delights; but her mansion-
house, for more securitie, wil she have wel gyrt with
an ample and spacious Moat. It is strange to see, how
solitarie she lives; and yet otherwise, you would think
her, though she seemes highly to affect that life, made
for Citties and the Court; her cloathing al, save her
Spanish-leather buskins, from top to toe, of the richest
Minevers; her gate, statelie and Majestical; her garb
and fashion, grave, yet not affected, or sprung from an
over-weening of herself. She rather pitties the companie of men, and their good fellowships, as feastings,
bancketings, and pastimes, then hates them for it, and
so neglects them rather, with a demisse eye, then with
a brow contracted, or a look more Cinick, to appeare
Diogenes,

Diogenes, or a *Tymon*, a hater of men, rather then the deboishments of their manners. As she is solitarie and melancholie by nature, she is very Musical, as likely are al such; but chiefly doats she on the wind-instruments, and is never seen without her Howboy; wherewith, when she list, wil she enchant the verie Sirens themselves with the melodie she makes; but then especially, when feeling the chimes of her passage out of this world to sound within her, as a presage of her death to others, she wil ring forth such a peale of delicious and chromatick straines mixt togeather, as would move devotion in the hearers rather, then compassion, while they wil judge streight, she had a pure soule of her owne. She is a right Hermitesse; and hath her sallets proper to herself alone; and as she loves them wel, she wil feed of no man's picking, but her owne. Other whiles she lives in state, and keeps her kitchin, as the manner is in some places, in the Cellars, and lower roomes; which by reason of the moystnes of those places, are alwayes under waters; but she likes them never the worse for that, but rather so much the better; for so she feeds on her sallets very fresh, but new-gathered. She is further much delighted, to take her pleasure on the waters, for her meer disport and recreation; and wil have no other boat, then her owne Barge, nor other oares then her owne; and being so good a Swimmer, makes a pastime of it, to tilt her boat quite over head and eares. She is very hale, and hath a long breath, and wil keep her head under water, longer then any Moor shal doe, that hunts for pearls.

When

WHEN *milde Favonius breathes, with warbling throat*
     The milk-white Swan chants with a sweeter note;
But sweeter yet her Musick farre excels,
When death approches, which her tune fore-tels.
So th' holie Spirit breathing from above
Upon the Virgin, rays'd with wings of love,
Her heavenlie Muse unto a higher straine
In her melodious Sonnet. But againe,
When gentle death drew neare, she high aspires
To tune an Antheme with the Angels Quires.
Thy Cygnets (mother Swan) on thee relye;
O make them white, that they may singing dye.

FINIS.

THIS BOOK HAS BEEN PRINTED
FROM A COPY IN
THE PUBLISHERS
POSSESSION

APPENDIX I

The poetry of the Hon. Herbert Aston (1614-89) is to be found in H.M. 904 (Huntingdon Library); in *Tixall Poetry*, edited by Arthur Clifford (1815); while reference should also be made to *Tixall Letters*, edited by Clifford in 1813, and to Lord Aston's papers (B.M. Add. MSS. 36452). *Tixall Poetry* includes work by members of the family and friends, together with transcriptions from other sources, such as the poem, ascribed to Sir Henry Wooton, 'Quivering feares, heart-tearing cares' (*The Compleat Angler*). In date the poems vary from about 1620 to the times of the notorious 'Ephelia'. There is some interesting devotional verse, some of it by Edward Thimelby, a relative of the Aston's by marriage. It is Catholic in its incidental imagery; unlike the work of Habington (who is represented also in H.M. 904); indeed some of the poems, such as *A Sigh to St Monica's Tears* and *The Expostulation of St. Mary Magdalen*, ally themselves with the work of Crashaw, and his imitators, Joseph Beamont, Eldred Revett, etc. H.M. 904 is a common-place book of a kind peculiar to the seventeenth century. It belonged to Constantia Fowler, who married William Fowler, Esq., of St Thomas' Priory, Stafford, in 1629. Poems by Habington, King, Southwell, Katharine Thimelby, etc., are identifiable. Herbert Aston's initials appear at the end of his work, contained by an ornamental quatrefoil. The devotional poems here appear to have been written at an earlier date than those in *Tixall Poetry*. The following lines of Herbert Aston's praise the poets one might have expected: The inclusion of Fulke Greville, however, is slightly unusual. At any rate I suppose we can date the poem a little time after 1633, when Greville's posthumous Works appeared.

> By reading prophesyes long writt of you
> As that gt petrarck so divinely writt
> Titled his Laura, so admired yet,
> Drayton's Idaea, and the love-sick lines
> Of daniells delia, hee too who refines
> Our language Sidney, whilest hee Stella prayseth
> Her glory and his fame together rayseth,
> With Caelica most elegantly writ
> In emulation of brave Sidney's witt
> All these were shaddowes and meere prophesyes
> Of some true sun, that after should arise....

This is another example of Aston's poetry, present in both *Tixall Poetry* and H.M. 904:

1

> Whilst here eclipsed from those hapy beames
> I live by dreames
> Absence the certain bane of comon love
> Apt to remove
> Oft traytor-like invades with fayre pretence
> My partiall sence
> To leave this servitude in which I sterve
> And here take present pay before I serve.

2

> To sensuallists this strong temptation proves
> Butt where fath loves
> It lives and feeds upon the inward sight
> Refin'd delight

By which I view my heart thy forme my flame
Ever the same
Though shades of absence reach my Earth, those lights
Doe never know corruption nor nights.

3

By which when I compare their faces here
To thy Forme there
And waigh the sacraledge I shold comitt
Defacing it
As soone to sell my knowledge dearly bought
I may be wrought
As this False Fruite can me againe intise
To loose my inosence and paradice.

H.A.

APPENDIX II
To the ternall and æternall Vnitie

Flame of bright love and beauty, thou (whose beames
Reflected heere, have so embellished
All Creatures) finding how my fancy fed
Vpon this earthly circles glimmering gleames,
Not else reclaimable from those extreames,
Centrally drewst my heart to one faire head,
Enamelled with browne, blue, white and red;
So to allure it to those heavenly Reames.
Purify all the Passions of my Minde,
And light my vnderstanding: So may I
Reede foorth, and heed what Passions heere I find.
Kindle my will and heave it vp, for why
Even as thy love, like fire, drawes vp my love,
Right so my love, like fire, will mount above.

H.H.

A LIST OF WORKS ASCRIBED TO HENRY HAWKINS

1. A Translation of Fr John Floyd's *Synopsis Apostasiae Marci Antonii de Dominis.* St Omer 1617.
2. *Certaine Selected Epistles of S. Hierome* as also the Lives of Saint Paul the first Hermite, of Saint Hilarion the first Monke of Syria, and of Saint Malchus: Written by the same Saint. Translated into English. n.p. (Paris 1630.)
3. *Fuga Sæculi* or the Holy Hatred of the World. Conteyning the Lives of seventeen Holy Confessions of Christ, Selected out of sundry Authors. Written in Italian by the R. Fa. Iohn-Peter Maffaeus of the Society of Jesus. And translated into English by H.H. 1632.
4. *The History of S. Elizabeth,* Daughter of the King of Hungary. According to sundry Authors who have authentically written her Life. Distributed into III books. By H.A. n.p. (St Omer, 1632.)
5. *The Sweete Thoughts of Death and Eternity.* Written by Sieur de la Serre. Paris. 1632. (Preface signed H.H.)

6. *The Devout Hart* or *Royal Throne of the Pacificial Salomon.* Composed by F. St Luzvic
    s.j. Translated out of Latin into English. Enlarged with Incentives by F. St Binet of the
    same S. and now enriched with Hymnes by a new hand. Iohn Cousturier. 1634.
    (by H.A.)
7. *The Life of St Aldegunda* translated by H.H. from the French of Fr Binet. Paris. 1636.
    Nos. 2, 3, 4, 5 and 6 are in the British Museum Library; No. 1 at Emmanuel College,
Library, Cambridge; and No. 7 at The Bodleian Library, Oxford.

NOTES

These notes are necessarily curt. I have ignored references to Greek and Roman
authors and to Biblical texts, and I have not concerned myself with the sources when there
is some indication as to where they may be found. The only abbreviation is P.L. for
Migne's Latin Fathers.

THE EPISTLE.

Parthenian Sodality. The sodality of the Blessed Virgin may be called the special devotion
of the Society of Jesus.... A brief account of the origin of this practice may be found
in *Pietas Mariana Britannica* by E. Waterton. 1879. pp.99-106. The English branch of the
Sodality, originating at the English College, Rome, spread rapidly to all the Colleges
governed by the English Jesuits. In 1606 it was established at St Omer. *v.* P. Guilday.
The English Catholic Refugees on the Continent. 1914. vol. I. p. 144. R. Freeman, notes—
English Emblem Books p.181 *n.* that a sodality of the Immaculate Conception was attached
to the newly-opened College in the Savoy and its director, Fr Edward Scarisbrick,
published *Rules and Instructions for the Sodality of the Immaculate Conception flower of
Nazareth, and his sacred stem* (1703).
The flower of Nazareth blooms upon the tree of Jesse. In Mediaeval art the tree itself
lies rooted in the sleeping form of Jesse and at its apex bears Christ and the Mother of
Christ. *cf.* Isaiah xi, 1-3. (A.V.). *And there shall come forth a rod out of the stem of Jesse.*
With this connect the veneration of the rod, *virga* (de radice Issee) and *virgo* approxi-
mating to it. See A. Watson: *The Early Iconography of the Tree of Jesse.* 1934.
a slender glance of the eye. 'Slender' is a favourite word with Hawkins. 'You Queen of
Angells liued in a slender house.' *Hist. S. Elizabeth.* p. 409 and a number of other
occasions.

THE PROEME.

with Isocrates seeke a Helena. The celebrated Athenian rhetor. *ob. c.* 338 B.C. He is one of
the authors specifically mentioned in Rhetoric Class under *Ratio Studiorum* of 1599.
The point is that the Encomium upon Helen purports to be a serious work whereas
it is no more than a sophistical exercise. *v. Works.* tr. L. Van Hook. 1895. vol. iii,
p. 54ff.
wel-nigh fiftie ages.... 'Others, of those first, and purer times, not without Admiration,
observe that GOD was almost *fifty Ages* in the Meditation of the structure of this stately
Pallace.' A. Stafford: *The Femall Glory.* 1635. p. 4. Among the others was S. Germanus
whose homily forms the basis to the relevant part of the Office of the Immaculate
Conception.
intemerate — inviolate.
gloriet   — a gloriole presumably. It could be from *glorior*, to be in glory, Mediaeval
             Latin, not in use until 1200.
dotes   — a natural gift. Plural is the normal form.
patrial   — of, or belonging to, one's country.

The bashful forhead. . . . I have not traced this in Epiphanius. In *Nicephori Callisti Xanthopuli Scriptoris Vere Catholici, Ecclesticæ Historiæ,* (Paris 1652), Lib. II Caput xxiii, p. 61, the the description begins: 'Mores autem, formæque & staturæ eius modus, talis, vt inquit Epiphanius, fuit. Erat in rebus omnibus honesta et grauis, pauca admodum eaque necessaria loquens, ad audiendum facilis', etc. The Iconography of the Virgin includes all graces of the Body. v. Stafford, p. 4.

p. 6.   burse = bourse.

p. 7.   *piaculum* = a thing requiring expiation.

p. 14.   *S. Augustin* sayth. . . . I have not been able to trace this. I am informed that it is suspect as Augustine.

p. 20.   *Paranimph.* The bridesman in Pagan marriages, whose duty it was to conduct the bride to the ceremony. *cf. Paranymphus salutat virginem.* . . . Adam of S. Victor. Sequence XLVI.

p. 24.   *Heare S. Bernard.* From Bernard's Sermon on the Twelve Prerogatives of the Virgin Mary. There is a selection from Bernard's Marian writings: *Behold Your Mother* (London, 1886) which I have used.

p. 25.   *The Poesie.* 1, 6. *cf.* Stafford: 'No doubt the *Angell* no sooner pronounc'd, 'Haile Mary, *Full of Grace,* but a blush arose in her Bashful Face, and verified his Words.' p. 29.
            l. 12. *died in graine* = fast-dyed.

p. 26.   Electuaries = a medicine; a powder mixed with honey or syrup, also used figuratively.

p. 27.   dilection = choice, theologically. O.E.D. gives—1656.

p. 28.   *The Apostrophe* is the most tender and beautiful of the series. The verses which follow are from Adam of S. Victor, Sequence LXXIII, 'spina' substituted for 'spinis' and 'Christi' for 'Verbi'. Gautier's gloss: Mary is the flower who has emerged from the thorns of the Synagogue into the light of Roman day.

p. 30.   *Flamins* = direct from the Latin. Priestesses.

p. 35.   *The Poesie,* 1, 5. see note to p. 174 for the relation of 'her right intention' to the second *Fiat.*

p. 40.   specious = immediately and apparently fair. This is another favourite word with Hawkins.

p. 42.   venter = womb, paunch. cf. Cleveland, where it is used figuratively.
            With what delight her speech doth enter
            It is a kiss o' the second venter.

p. 45.   *The Poesie.* Reprinted in L. B. Marshall. *Rare Poems of the 17th Century,* 1936, where—1. 4—'thoughts' becomes 'thought'.

p. 46.   as *Plinie* sayth. . . . v. *The Historie of the World commonly called the Naturall Historie of C. Plinius Secundus;* translated by Philemon Holland. The Second Tome. London, 1601. Cap. XIX, p. 103. E.

p. 46.   *impostumes.* . . . purulent swelling or cyst in any part of the body; also figuratively, cf.:

> *But when Time*
> *M'imposthumed Members shall againe make light.*
>   George Daniel. Ode xxi.

p. 47.   Consider then. . . . *as Plinie* sayth. . . . *op. cit., loc. cit.:* 'Violet seed resisteth the poyson of Scorpions.'

p. 48.   hant = past tense of 'hent', obsolete form of 'haunt'.

p. 49.   gnomon = indicator, specially the gnomon of a dial.

p. 49.   gingeline = or gingerlinne, an obselete variant of gingerline (ginger colour).

p. 49.   *alferes* = a Spanish word meaning an ensign or standard-bearer.

p. 52.   *Sunne of Iustice.* Malachi 4, 2. The word 'justice' appears in the sense of vindication. The Jews had to be reprimanded several times for sun-worship, and the sun is the greatest of heavenly bodies—to the bare eye. 'But unto you that fear my name shall the Sun of Justice arise with healing in its wings'. (Douai.) The material sun in the eastern sky still ascends above a world in bondage to Death. The Heavenly Sun—Christ—shall arise to heal his people, and shine upon a renovated earth. (2. Peter iii, 13). There is a representative affinity with the Phœnix who has two wings suffused with spices. The phrase is in common devotional use: 'Haile by whom the most cleare Sunne of Iustice hath shined.' A New Manual of old Catholic Meditations. R. B(roughton). 1617. p. 70.

p. 54. *Plinie* wonders.... *op. cit.* The First Tome. Cap. XLI, p. 20 and Tome 2. Cap. XXI, p. 126. The *solsequium* or Marygold opening with the shining of the sun is a cliché for 17th-century poets. Drexelius' book *The Heliotropion* is built round the same analogy.

p. 55. .... and assumpted into Heaven.... The Assumption of S. Mary has (Aug. 1950) been declared a matter no longer of pious opinion, but an established article of faith. Her assumption into Heaven is construed generally as being an anticipation of the General Resurrection. Stafford has 'Some goe about to prove it by the Text, *Arise LORD into Thy rest, Thou, and The Arke of Thy Sanctification.*' p. 162. The reference is to Ps. cxxxii, 8. There is an interesting passage in *The Misticall crowne of the Most Glorious Virgin Marie*, translated by R. H. Duvay, 1638, which gives the reasons for believing the Assumption of Mary's body (pp. 135-136).

p. 60. industrious Factours for these Pearls.... a common conceit. cf. for example:
> Go, let the diving negro seek
> For gems, hid in some forlorn creek....

from the verses 'Quivering-feares, heart-tearing cares' in *The Compleat Angler*, attributed to Sir Henry Wooton. They are also, with textual variants, to be found in *Tixall Poems*.

p. 61. The Sweats of the great Monark.... cf. Stafford, p. 6. 'Such variety of sweet Odours her very pores breath'd out on all that came near her; as we reade of *Alexander's* living body....'

p. 62. seren = light tropical rain, more generally a light fall.

p. 62. Hypocras in the Vine = a cordial made of wine flavoured with spices.

p. 66. that Fleece of Gedeon.... Psalm. lxxi, 6, and Judges vi, 37-40. A hoary Patristic type for birth without loss of virginity. see Thaddeus. F. *Mary Foreshadowed; or Considerations on The Types and Figures of Our Blessed Lady in the Old Testament.* 1885, pp. 110-116. R. Freeman, *op. cit.* p. 182 and F. J. E. Raby, *A History of Latin Christian Poetry*, 1927, p. 363.

p. 71. they crock.... a dialectal verb. To put into a pot or crock. 1594.

p. 73. until the beanes begin to blowe.... *v.* Pliny. *op. cit.* First Tome. Eleventh Booke, p. 312.

p. 74. The mellifluous *Doctour S. Ambrose.* 'Rore pascitur apis, nescit concubitas mella remponit'. Pat. Lat. 16, 200. *Ambrose: De Virginibus* I, viii, 40.

p. 76. the pacifical *Salomon.* Another Type. cf. 'Hence is she that great Throne, of which is said King Solomon also made a great throne of ivory.' Psuedo-Bonaventura (Conradus of Saxonia): *The Mirror of the Blessed Virgin Mary* and Kings. i. c. 10 v. 18 (A.V.).

p. 80. vidual = of, belonging to, befitting, widowhood.

p. 80. deordination = departure from, or violation of moral order.

p. 80. so exquisita a loome of al Perfection. cf. 'the awful loom of the Incarnation wherein in ineffable manner that Garment of Union was wrought', S. Proclus. Orat. De Laudibus. S. Mariæ. Pat. Gr. Tom. 65.

p. 82.   Seraphins = Seraphin is the obsolete singular from of 'Seraphim'.

p. 83.   perlustration = the act of travelling through and surveying thoroughly.
           O.S.E.D. 1640. I was glad to find it in Peacock. 'The rose, as usual, before
           daylight that they might pursue their perlustration.' *Melincourt. Cap.*
           XXXII.

p. 85.   One Authour.... 'Septem sunt cœli, scil. aereum, æthereum, olympeum,
           igneum, etc.' Bartholomæi Angilici *De Genuinis Rerum Cœlestium Terres-
           tium et Inferorum*.... 1601. Frankfurt. Liber 8. c. 2.

p. 86.   Whom the Heavens....the anti-type is Kings, i. c.8. v. 27. (A.V.). 'If Heaven
           and the Heaven of Heavens cannot contain Thee, how much less this House,
           which I have built.'

p. 87.   *S. Epiphanius*.... this work is suppositious.

p. 88.   *S. Bonaventura*.... The citation is from *Speculum Mariæ*, now known to be the
           work of Conradus de Saxonia.

                          Such then is thy immensity, O Mary
                          Exceeding that of Heaven; in thy womb
                          Thou bearest Him whom Heaven could not contain....

p. 88.   viatour = wayfarer. This is presumably, in the Scholastic sense, one who is
           wayfarer from earth to Heaven. Scotus phrases a proposition; 'Whether
           any sure and pure truth can be known naturally by the understanding of the
           wayfarer without the special illumination of the uncreated light?' R.
           McKeon. *Selection from Medieval Philosophers*, vol. ii, 1920, p. 313. There
           is an explicit reference here and in *The Poesie* to the Beatific Vision.

p. 90.   ....the moving Angels that guide them.... These references to the cosmic
           order are typical of the age, which retains the terms of the Mediæval
           synthesis. v. E. M. W. Tillyard. *The Elizabethan World Picture* 1943, p. 38,
           and for an earlier and more detailed exposition *The Great Chain of Being*
           by Arthur O. Lovejoy, 1936. This note covers the reference to the corrup-
           tibility of the Elements, p. 91, and other incidental mention of the Intelli-
           gences, the Spheres, etc.

p. 91.   These are references to the Immaculate Conception of S. Mary. This became
           an article of faith for Western Catholics in 1854, by its proclamation in the
           'Ineffabilis Devs' of Pius IX.

p. 91.   O Great Miracle of the World.... this antithesis is an obvious reference to
           Macrocosmic and Micrcosmic order.

p. 93.   *The Iris.* v. Genesis, cap. lx. vv, 13-14. (A.V.) and Thaddeus. *op. cit.* pp. 40-47.

p. 98.   she were a bush.... Exodus, cap. 3, v. 2 (A.V.). The Office of the B.V.M. has
           'Rubum quem viderat Moyses incombustum, conservatam agnovimus
           tuam laudabilem virginitatem, Dei Genetrix.'

p. 101.   *The Poesie.* Like a *Raine-Bow* in the skie. As a type of mercy after wrath.
           W. Fraser Mitchell *English Pulpit Oratory; Andrewes to Tillotsom* 1932, p. 72
           refers to Thomas Playfere: Christ, as having 'a rainbow in his side.'

p. 103.   immortifyed—from *immortification*, ecclesiastical Latin. A condition of the soul
           where the passions are not mortified.

p. 103.   THE MOONE. In Genesis Cap. 1, allegorically, The Church is the Firmament;
           Christ the Sun, S. Mary, the Moon; and the Stars the Saints. Thaddeus.
           op. cit. refers to Richard of St Lawrence description of S. Mary as a moon
           eclipsed by the Passion and death of her Son; and to James de Voraigne
           as comparing the tides caused by the moon with the way in which Mary
           acts upon the earth. 'His Throne as the sun before me, and as the moon
           perfect forever', Psalm 88 v. 38 (Vulg.); Psalm 89 vv. 36-37. (A.V.).

p. 106.   his gracious and benigne *Hester*....

p. 110.   As *S. Augustine* sayth.... This again is suspect as Augustine, I am informed.

p. 110. and received there her double Stole. 'The Diademe with which this Queene of
         Heaven was crowned by her Sonne, at her glorious entrance into his
         kingdom, was.... graced with twelve such starrs, as adorned the head
         of the mysterious woman mentioned in the Apocalypse....' R.Falconer:
         The Mirrour of Created Perfection or The Life of the most Blessed Virgin
         Mary.... 1632. (pp. 141-142).

p. 115. *The Starre.* v. Thaddeus. pp. 242-249.

p. 120. Gemell = twins, things associated in pairs.

p. 121. if *Philo*.... A compilation giving a meaning to all the proper names in the
         Old Testament. 'Melius ut dicamus sonare eam stellam maris sive armarum
         mare'. Jerome. *Onomastica Sacra.*

p. 123. *The Poesie.* Reprinted in Marshall. *op. cit.* I adopt his emendation to the seventh
         line 'sailes' for 'saile'.

p. 128. whist = silent. *cf.* Milton:
                        The Windes with wonder whist,
                        Smoothly the waters Kist....
                                On the Morning of Christ's Nativity.

p. 129. illuded = deceived himself.

p. 133. as *Delrius.* The work referred to is presumably Martino Del Rio's *Adagialia*
         Sacra Veteris et Novi Testamenti.... 1612. But I have not been able to
         verify the citation. Hawkins appears to make some use of Del Rio's
         Canticum Canticorum Salomonis Commentarius.... 1611, where, beside the
         four interpretations, an important section is devoted to the text in relation
         to S. Mary. Mention should also be made of his *Opus Marianum Sive de*
         Lavdibus et Virtutibus Mariæ Virginis Dei paræ.... 1607.

p. 133. I mought. M.E. The imperfect of I mow (may).

p. 134. with S. *Ambrose.* v. *De Noe et Arca Liber Unus.* Cap. XIX.

p. 139. lyn = obselete past particle of lie; but here it means 'rest', I suppose.

p. 140. a strayne beyond their *Ela.* The highest note of Guido Scale. O.S.E.D. used
         figuratively in sense of 'high-flown'. *cf.* Cleveland :
                        The Hecatomb to his Mistress
                            .... were the note I sing
                        Above Heaven's Ela, should I then decline,
                        And with a deep-mouthed gamut sound the line
                        From pole to pole.... 11, 24-27.

p. 141. a Doit. Originally a small Dutch coin; in this instance meaning a very small
         part.

p. 142. The Essay. This whole passage has been compared with Crashaw's *Musicks*
         Duell by Mario Praz.

p. 145. shirler = shriller—dialectal.

p. 146. the passage quoted may be found in Ulyssis Aldrovandi *Ornithologiq* XXX
         1634. Lib. 18. p. 780.

p. 146. Let *Origen* yet tell us.... 'Jesus enim qui in utero illius erat festinabat adhuc in
         ventre matris Ioannem peritum sanctificare....' *In Lucam. Hom.* 7. G.C.S.
         p. 45.
         Let *Ambrose* tell us: 'Discite virgines, non demorari in plateis, non aliquos in
         publico miscere sermones.' *In Evang. Lucæ.* exposition 11, 20-21. C.S.E.L.
         p. 52.
         Again let *Ambrose*.... 'festina pro gaudio in montana perexit.' *Loc. cit.*

p. 150. As *Plinie* sayth.... *v. oc. cit.* Tom. 1. Cap. XXIX. p. 286.

p. 151. THE APOSTROPHE. This is very similar to a Passage from *The Devout Hart.*

p. 153. THE PALME. From the continuity of its verdure considered an emblem of
         immortality. Its significance as an emblem of Triumph and Justice is also

248 PARTHENEIA SACRA

well-known. An example of a double-Emblem of Immortality: Phœnix conjoint with Palm, from a mosaic in S. Cecilia, Rome, is given by L. Twining: *Symbols and Emblems of Early and Mediæval Christian Art.* 2nd edition 1885. p. 193.

p. 154. As the turtle-widowes sit mourning, etc. *cf.* Lodge.
> *A Turtle sate upon a leafless tree,*
> *Mourning her absent fere....* Rosalynde.

p. 157. Obsequies of Marguerite of Austria.... This is presumably found in *Relatione della Pompa funerale che si celebro in Napoli nella morte della Serenissima Reina Margherita d'Austria,* 1612. But I have not had an opportunity of consulting the work.

p. 159. S. *Gregorie* sayth in his Morals.... Morals on the Book of Job, Cap. 29, verse 18. 'I shall die in my nest, and as a palm tree shall multiply my days.' In the English translation Vol. II, p. 437. Both references on this page are from the same passage.

p. 160. His being.... Sir Philip Sidney. Arcadia. Lib. III ed. 1629, p. 288. The Epitaph or Argalus and Parthenia.

p. 161. THE POESIE. 1. 3. 'heames' in 1633. This is a dialectical word meaning 'after-birth': even allowing for the most radical, conical, desperate conceit or metaphor, this emendation still appears justifiable.

p. 163. And S. *Hierome.* This seems to be near P.L. 22. 628.

p. 172. *The Pallace of the Sun....* A translation of *Met.* ii, XX, ll, 1-13. I have not traced it anywhere. If it is only a disjointed fragment of Hawkins' own composition it seems odd that the first and third lines should rhyme.

p. 174. THE POESIE. 1. 1. *Hau.* I cannot make this out. Is it an inflected exclamation? The poem gains in intensity from its quasi-dramatic form. The whole is a close echo of Jerome *Dialogus Adversus Pelagionos* Lib. II; 'Solus enim Christus clausas portas vulvæ virginitatis aperuit, quœ tamen clausœ permanserunt. P.L. 23, 745, and other passages, no doubt. *cf.* also Jeremy Taylor: *The Golden Grove* 1654, p. 155. *On the Annunciation*
> 'A Winged harbinger from bright heav'n flown,
> Bespeaks a lodging room....* etc.
and *The Poesie of The Dove.*

> 1. 11. S. Mary's 'fiat' is considered by the Scholastics to be a perfect act. It is not so considered because of any difficulty She might have experienced in the great refusal; but because of Her own perfection. The doctrine answers the objection: how could the Blessed Virgin refuse the Incarnation since She knew no sin? If She might not refuse, then She could not merit her act. Her act of acceptance therefore, became worthless. But the perfection of an act depends upon the perfection of the agent, and not upon accidental circumstances.

p. 179. Pinck = a sailing-vessel, originally one of small size, flat-bottomed with bulging sides; later applied to warships. O.S.E.D.

p. 180. al what is—a neuter singular relative presumably. This would correspond with E.E. usage.

p. 184. volved—obsolete. She turned over in her mind.
p. 186. THE POESIE. X. 1. 7. dialectical. Its normal application is to the kite, occasionally to the buzzard.

p. 189. THE PEARL. This account is from Physiologus, 44, and Isidor of Seville 'Margarita prima candidarum gemmatum, quam inde Margaritum vocatum quod in conchulis maris hoc genus lapidum inventatur.... Ex quibus margaritis quædam uniones vocantur: aptum nomen habentes, etc.' *Isidori Hispalensis Originum Libri Viginti ex antiquitate eruti.* Basle, 1577, pp. 387-388, and for the conception of pearls. Pliny. *ed. cit.* Tom. I. Ninth Book. Cap. XXXV L. p. 254.

p. 194.   The *Margarit,* as I sayd, v. Isidor. *loc cit.* and P.L. 82. 573.

p. 196.   THE POESIE. II, 9-10. These are touching lines.

p. 198.   immundicities = impunities. Obselete after 1660 (O.S.E.D.)

p. 201.   The clefts in the rock which form the basis of this meditation are the wounds of Christ. The salient text is 'And they shall look upon him whom they have pierced.' Zach.

p. 206.   *Noome.*

p. 206.   Whence S. Anselm sayth.... This may refer to Eadmer's *Tractatus de Conceptione Sanctæ Mariæ,* which was attributed to Anselm for a long time. Edited by H. Thurston et Th. Slater, Friborg, 1904.

p. 210.   and lastly a slender cloud.... v. R. Freeman. *op. cit.* p. 197, for comment on this passage.

p. 210.   mansuetude = meekness.

p. 211.   sprug = bedeck. Sussex dialect.

p. 221.   *Marie* is an Aqueduct. These two references are to Bernard *De Aquæductu.*

p. 224.   pursie = puffed up, short-winded, puffy.

p. 227.   the neck of a mallard.... as R. Freeman points out *op. cit.* p. 190, this is a commonplace of description in 17th century. e.g. the same is often predicated of the Dove:

> Whilst I beheld the neck o' th' dove,
> I spied and read these words.
> 'This pretty dye
> Which takes your eye
> Is not at al the bird's.'.... Patrick Carey.

p. 228.   the side-note refers to Santes Pagninus.

p. 231.   THE POESIE. I, 12. Mary is identified with Eve so far as the promise contained in Genesis (A.V.) is concerned.

p. 232.   As *S. Hierom* sayth.... *cf.* Jerome. *In Genesim* XIV, 14. P.L. 23. 961.

p. 250.   What bread; but the true and living *bread?....* These sharp, rhetorical questionings are reminiscent of the method of Andrewes' Sermons.

p. 256.   THE POESIE. A Jewish Rabbi, etc. It is not easy to decide which particular two Rabbis Hawkins had in mind. 'They (the angels) feed on the rays of God's Majesty for "in the light of the King's countenance is life".' Prov. 16, v. 5 (A.V.). So runs a typical piece of rabbinic exegesis. The difference between the two views is that according to the first the Angels feed directly on Manna, according to the second they feed on light which condensed into Manna became the food of men. That the Angels eat manna is mentioned in the *Babylonian Talmud:* 'One Rabbi taught: Man did eat the bread of the mighty'. i.e. a bread which ministering angels eat. This was the interpretation of R. Akiba. This again requires further explanation. 'Bread of the mighty, may be God Himself. Such appears to be the literal rendering of Psalm 78 v. 25. 'Angels' food' or 'bread of Angels.' This liturgical interpretation has been criticised. Duncan, a nineteenth-century Scotch Calvinist, remarks of

> Ecce Panis angelorum,
> Factus cibus viatorum,
> Vere panis filiorum.'

'It is *not* angel's food. They never tasted it. "He took not on Him the nature of Angels", but our nature, and *therefore* this food is ours.' J. Duncan. *Colloquia Peripatetica,* 1870, p. 56. S. Paul sees Manna as a type of the Eucharist: 'spiritual meat'. On the other hand one of the Rabbis may well have been Solomon Bar Isaac Rashi who lived at Troyes (1040–1105). His interpretation of Manna is traditional: 'What is it?'—the question asked at its first appearance. Manna is both food and drink—: Gloss of Rabbi Solomon on Exodus 16.

p. 258.   *and shew her thy wounds.* This somewhat strong 'maternal' imagery is usual. 'Her sacred breasts, were as two Pearly-bottels, tipped with rich rubies, and filled once from heaven.... *The Misticall Crowne* p. 135, and from Stafford *op. cit.* '*You who ply your sacred Arithmeticke, and have thoughts cold, and cleare as the Christall beads you pray by....* Kneele down before the Grand White* Immaculate *Abbesse of your snowy* Nunneries....' p. 116.

p. 265.   One painter.... This is presumably Zeuxis. A favourite image in the 17th century, particularly with Cowley. *cf. Ode to the Royal Society,* etc.

p. 266.   *Father Southwel. v.* Poems. London, 1886, p. 49. ii, 11–12 of a poem beginning 'Retired thoughts enjoy their own delights.'

p. 267.   meawes = an archaic word used of hawks: to moult.

p. 272.   minevers = squirrel fur.